$PACE, INC.

$PACE, INC.

YOUR GUIDE
TO INVESTING
IN SPACE EXPLORATION
by Tom Logsdon

Crown Publishers, Inc.
New York

Grateful acknowledgment is made to the following for permission to reprint excerpts from previously published material:

Art Dula, Aerospace Counsel for Space Commercialization: Dula, Shields, and Egbert. Houston, Texas.

Peter W. Wood and Peter M. Stark, "Made in Space: Commercializing the Last Frontier," from *Outlook*. All rights reserved. Copyright © 1987 by Booz, Allen, and Hamilton.

Brian Dumaine, "Still A–OK: The Promise of Factories in Space," from *Fortune*. All rights reserved. Copyright © 1986 by Time Inc.

Dawn Stover, "The Satellite T.V. Puzzle," from *Popular Science*. All rights reserved. Copyright © 1986 by Times Mirror Magazines, Inc.

Washington Staff, "Washington Roundup," from *Aviation Week & Space Technology*. All rights reserved. Copyright © 1987 by McGraw-Hill, Inc.

John Hillkirk, "Eye in the Sky Will Keep Us from Getting Lost," from *USA Today*, March 5, 1986. Copyright © 1986 by USA Today.

Randall Rothenberg, "What They're After: Pennies from Heaven," from *Esquire*, May 1984. Copyright © 1984 by Esquire.

Representative Bob Traxler, Democrat, Michigan.

Evan Thom, "Roaming the High Frontier," from *Time*, November 26, 1984. All rights reserved. Copyright © 1984 by Time Inc.

Leonard Davis, "Commuting Into the COSMOS," from *Space World*, August 1985. Copyright © 1985 by Space World.

Copyright © 1988 by Tom Logsdon

Published by Crown Publishers, Inc., 225 Park Avenue South, New York, New York 10003 and represented in Canada by the Canadian MANDA Group

CROWN is a trademark of Crown Publishers, Inc.

Manufactured in the United States of America

Library of Congress Cataloging in Publication Data

Logsdon, Tom, 1937–
    $pace, Inc.: Your Guide to Investing in Space Exploration.
    Bibliography: p.
    Includes index.
    1. Space industrialization.   I. Title.
HD9711.75.A2L65   1988   332.6′78′0919   87-22294

ISBN: 0-517-56812-8

10 9 8 7 6 5 4 3 2 1

First Edition

Dedicated to people everywhere who believe that if God hadn't wanted us to step into outer space, he wouldn't have dangled the stars so temptingly.

Contents

ACKNOWLEDGMENTS

Dozens of people helped me write this book, including my daughter, Donna Schilder, a talented wordsmith in her own right, who researched and wrote the first draft for two of the chapters. As always, working with Donna has been pure delight.

Elda Stramel also deserves special mention. She typed all the rough drafts and the final manuscript. This time we were separated by 200 miles of burning desert, but still she managed to maintain a steady stream of flawless pages flowing from her typewriter into my mailbox. Our next project should be a bit easier, because she will be moving back to Lotus Land in the near future.

Special thanks should also go to Ed Roman, who converted my cluttered sketches into neat professional drawings. Despite the added demands of a new job, Ed handled the art in his usual even-tempered manner. He got some help from Ronnie Frye, who put together two of the figures on his trusty Macintosh computer, with its funny little mouse.

Two charmers, Cyndy Arnett and Gaynell Beale, arranged the 200 bibliography entries into a standardized format. They handled this tedious assignment on time with great skill, and, according to their own account, had fun in the process. My personal gopher, Linda Miller of the Executive Gopher Service, supplied some of the rough-draft typing and handled a number of random errands. Over the past few months, her steady contributions have allowed me to concentrate all of my attention on the final manuscript.

I would also like to thank my agent, Jane Jordan Brown, who, together with her assistant, helped me structure the first two chapters; also my editor, Jake Goldberg, and my copy editor at Crown Publishers, who skillfully guided and edited the book into its final form.

The materials and advice supplied by Jeffrey Holt of Merrill Lynch were also greatly appreciated. He tracked down several space-related investment opportunities, and he critiqued my paragraphs on fund-raising techniques.

Jim Haffner of Rockwell International, who carries more useful information in his head than most people encounter in a lifetime of disciplined study, helped me with the physics of space. His calculations on the risk of collisions with space-borne debris and natural meteoroids were especially helpful.

A number of experts allowed me to interview them in person or on the phone. The one I remember most fondly is Alan Cima of Oceanroutes, who provided me with a dramatic summary of his company's modern ship-routing techniques. Alan shares my vision of the coming era of space industrialization and he sees some of its beginnings in his own company, which routinely uses three different types of satellites—weather, communication, navigation—to find the best routes for large commercial ships on the high seas.

Another gold mine of information was Dr. B. J. Bluth, who is assigned to NASA headquarters from the sociology department of the California State University at Northridge. In addition to steady advice and council, she provided me with excellent sketches of the Mir space station and other Russian laboratories in space.

A number of other people supplied personal interviews, press releases, technical reports, and glossy photos. These cooperative individuals included:

Don Fink, James P. Samuels, and Dave Quast at *Commercial Space*; Rebecca Simmons, Kelley Robertson, and Marc Vaucher at the Center for Space Policy (Cambridge, Massachusetts); David Langstaff and Max Faget at Space Industries, Inc.; Gary Hudson at Pacific American Launch Systems; Hugo Fruehauf at the Efratom Division of Ball Aerospace; Donald D. Moyer of the Houston Economic Development Council; Edward Noneman of the TRW Space and Technology Group; Stanley K. Honey at ETAK, makers of a new kind of automotive navigation system; Jack Anderson and Tanya A. Neider from the Young Astronauts Council; Stanley Goldstein at *International Space Business Review*; John M. Cassato of Instrumentation Technology Associates; Congressman Bill Nelson, member of the Subcommittee on Space Science, U.S. House of Representatives; Peter Marsh of the *Financial Times* in London; Carol P. Nevens, Bruce Jordan, and Joseph Bellace of the Merrill Lynch Securities Division; Dr. Krafft Ehricke, Mike Martin, Chuck Gould, and Troy Miller of Rockwell International; Allen Salmasi of Omninet Corporation; Eugene Jericho of the American Bar Association; Gregg Maryniak of the Space Studies Institute; Harry Owen and James Schwinn at 3M Corporation; Steve P. Whitchen of Owens/Corning Fiberglas; Lynn M. Hansen of McDonnell Douglas (St. Louis, Missouri); Rita Capalla of the National Air and Space Museum (Smithsonian Institution); Bill Moss and Judy Katz of Lippin and Grant; Dr. Peter F. MacDoran and Dr. James H. Whitcomb of ISTAC (Pasadena, California); Richard Randolph of Microgravity Research Associates; Ron Blilie at Eagle Engineering (Houston, Texas); T. C. Swartz of Space Expeditions (Seattle, Washington); Ben Bova at the National Space Society; Beverly Johantgen of VideoNet (Woodland Hills, California); Ross N. Williams of Ocean Data Systems, Inc.; and Professor John D. Isaacs, now deceased, at the Scripps Institute of Oceanography.

Anyone whose name does not appear on this list has my apology; it is not easy to remember all the people who, during this past year, helped me so much, in so many different ways.

I would like, however, to thank one more person: Anthony Ralyea, who may never know how much inspiration he provided for this book.

Tom Logsdon
Seal Beach, California
1988

PREFACE

I write my books not for a specific audience but for a specific individual, a symbolic stand-in for the larger audience I hope to reach. Five years ago at Sunset in Cocoa Beach, Florida, I met my audience for *Space, Inc.* His name was Anthony Ralyea, a bright, intense high school student from Titusville—population 7,000. Anthony had just heard me give a talk on manufacturing in space before 250 residents of the Cape Kennedy area. When it was over, he edged his way up to the podium bristling with curiosity and enthusiasm.

For nearly three hours we talked about the High Frontier until fatigue made us nearly incoherent. I never saw him again. I don't know where he is now. But every word of this book was written for Anthony Ralyea.

Are there enough people like Anthony to justify its publication? My travels convince me there are more than enough. A few weeks after I left Anthony I had dinner with twelve of them, mostly middle-aged couples, at a Lake Arrowhead resort. We dined on succulent trout as I gradually unraveled the story of industrial facilities to be constructed in space. What would it be like to live and work out there high above the earth? they wondered. Would there be cigars and vintage wines? Concerts and picnics? Children climbing trees? Like Anthony Ralyea, they smiled when they talked and their eyes were filled with wonder and hope.

Last year I spoke to fifty more of Anthony's kinfolks in a summer seminar at Northridge University in the San Fernando Valley. Every individual there that day had given up three hours of California sunshine to come and learn about the colonization of space. And no matter how long we talked, their polite curiosity never seemed to wane. As their teacher wrote in her thank-you note: "Your talk was terrific! I think those students would have sat there and listened until you just wore out . . . they were learning physics and it didn't even hurt."

The news magazines give us further indications that our population includes a large number of Anthony Ralyeas. Consider these revealing statistics:

- The recent "Star Trek" conventions in Chicago, San Francisco, and Los Angeles were jammed to capacity. Each session drew more than 20,000 enthusiastic participants.
- The Air and Space Museum in Washington, D.C., has quietly become the most popular permanent exhibit in our country. Last year it hosted 12 million visitors.
- The *Star Wars* trilogy has smashed every box office record. According to *Newsweek*, one of the films "grossed $140 million within four months after it was released."

Clearly, Anthony is a part of a much larger group, a group that is enthralled with our future in space. But what else do we know about Anthony Ralyea? He is a curious individual with an itch to know and learn. He loves hopeful television documentaries, especially Charles Kuralt. He understands a little about computers, owns the latest pocket calculator and the latest video games. He loves challenges. He believes the future will be better than the past. He enjoys popularized scientific books. *The Double Helix, The High Frontier, The Andromeda Strain.* How will he react to *Space, Inc.*? He will find it, read it, pass the word on to his friends.

How many Anthony Ralyeas are there? Millions. We all have a little of Anthony's adventurous blood running through our veins.

$PACE, INC.

The next generation of billionaires is going to come from the business of space.
                                    Art Dula
                                    Aerospace Counsel for Space Commercialization
                                    Dula, Sheilds, and Egbert. Houston, Texas

1

THE LURE OF SPACE

Gravity. It permeates our world, influencing nearly everything we do; yet we hardly ever notice it at all.

Sit down at the breakfast table, and gravity keeps you and your cornflakes from drifting up to the ceiling. It also causes the coffee grounds to sink to the bottom of your cup, and if you cool your coffee with a cube of ice, it will make the ice float on top.

These three physical properties—weight, sedimentation, buoyancy—are virtually nonexistent in space. If an astronaut mixes oil and water, the oil will not float to the top. If he lights a match, the smoke will not drift upward. If he flips a coin, it will not fall back into his hand. Instead, it will travel in a straight line until it slams into the ceiling of his spacecraft.

In the "weightlessness" of space a shuttle astronaut is able to gulp floating shrimp from midair like a giant silver fish. This is possible because astronaut, shuttle, and shrimp are all influenced by the same gravitational force. All three experience weightless "free-fall" as they travel around the earth. The tiny g-forces felt by the astronauts are created by drag with the few whisper-thin molecules of air and the almost imperceptible radiation pressure caused by the sun shining on their spacecraft. These tiny drag forces—which amount to only about one-millionth of a g—gently slow the shuttle orbiter, but they do not affect astronaut or shrimp inside.

BENEFITING from the MICROGRAVITY of SPACE

In the next few years the weightlessness of space—so enjoyed by today's astronauts—will provide enormous economic benefits to the people living on earth. Improved pharmaceuticals, new optical lenses, and better computer chips will all result from the weightlessness of space. So will new methods of entertainment, new metal alloys, and novel construction techniques.

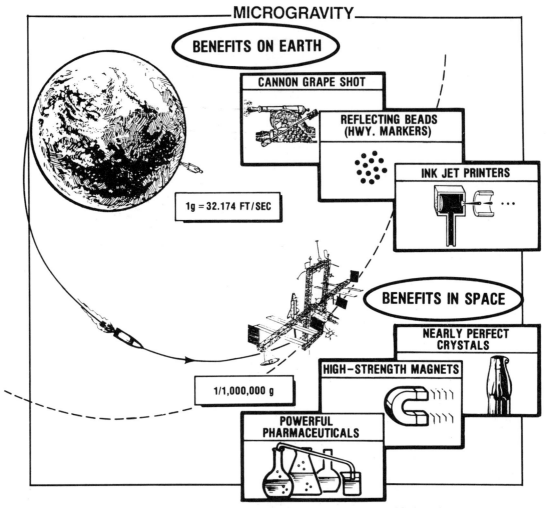

BENEFITS ON EARTH

CANNON GRAPE SHOT

REFLECTING BEADS
(HWY. MARKERS)

INK JET PRINTERS

1g = 32.174 FT/SEC

BENEFITS IN SPACE

NEARLY PERFECT
CRYSTALS

HIGH-STRENGTH MAGNETS

1/1,000,000 g

POWERFUL
PHARMACEUTICALS

The practical use of microgravity in manufacturing dates back to the 1860s, when munitions factories employed free-fall droptowers to manufacture millions of grape shots for the cannons of Union and Confederate troops. Today's manufacturers are planning to make pharmaceuticals, computer chips, new metal alloys, and unique optical glasses in the prolonged weightlessness of outer space. Even in low-altitude orbits, microgravity levels as low as a millionth of a g are relatively easy to achieve.

Metallurgists at Volkswagen plan to use the microgravity of space to produce a new lead-aluminum alloy with self-lubricating capabilities. They envision an auto engine that may last over a million miles—without major overhaul. Factories in space will allow other experts to produce an optical lens with one density at the center and a different density at the edges. This will greatly simplify the construction of the compound lenses used to correct for color separation and other distortions in today's sophisticated optical instruments.

The astronauts can also produce nearly perfect crystals in the microgravity of space. On earth, industrial-quality crystals are usually grown from a molten mix held within a special heat-resistant crucible. Unfortunately, the crucible contaminates the crystal and creates imperfections in its orderly molecular structure. In space, however, the molten material from which the crystal grows can be suspended in "midair" so that it does not touch anything. Flawless crystals grown in space can be fashioned into computer chips with switching speeds ten times faster than the ones we now make on earth.

The same weightlessness that helps the astronauts *mix* substances that will not mix on earth also helps them *separate* substances that are difficult to separate in the earth's gravity. A special technique called "continuous-flow electrophoresis" separates the components of a liquid by means of small differences in their electrical charges and their molecular weights. Electrophoresis separation has been used on earth for many years, but its efficiency is degraded by gravity, which induces sedimentation and harmful convection currents in the liquid, thus remixing the substance being separated.

Today's astronauts have already produced one valuable pharmaceutical in space using this technique. It speeds the production of red blood cells in the human body. Economists at Booz Allen & Hamilton are convinced that millions of dollars' worth of it will be sold within ten years. They also foresee at least a dozen other space-made pharmaceuticals capable of treating a variety of medical conditions including coronary problems, diabetes, dwarfism, anemia, and emphysema. According to the Center for Space Policy, space-age drugs will be a $27 billion annual business by the year 2001.

TAKING ADVANTAGE of the WIDE-ANGLE VIEW

The wide-angle view from space is also providing important economic benefits to you and your fellow earthlings. When you fly on a commercial jet at 35,000 feet, your horizon is about 200 miles away. At higher altitudes, even more of the earth comes into view. At 80 miles the astronauts can see about 7 percent of the world at any one instant. At 22,300 miles, one favorite vantage point for an orbiting platform, a satellite can observe 44 percent of the globe.

The weather maps you see on the evening news, which are transmitted from orbiting satellites, have greatly improved long-range forecasts. The Landsat earth-resources satellite, which also capitalizes on the wide-angle view from space, gives us valuable information on farmlands, mineral deposits, pollution sources. It picks up reflected light from earth with a sensitivity to color far surpassing that of the human eye. By enhancing its pictures with computers, experts can detect subtle features spread over huge areas they would fail to see even if they walked the land. Colorful clays, for instance, are associated with deposits of uranium, and certain

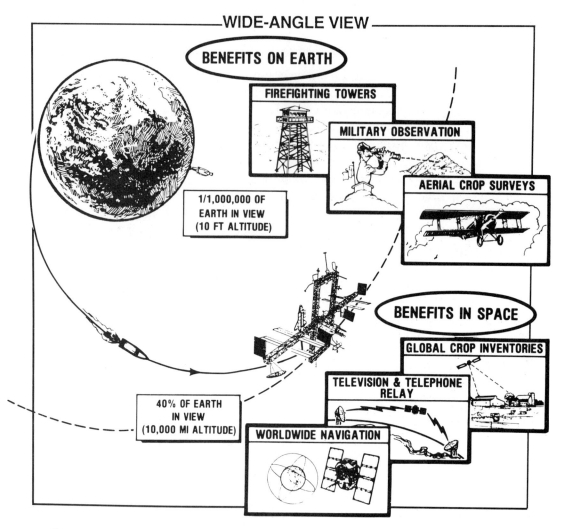

BENEFITS ON EARTH

FIREFIGHTING TOWERS

MILITARY OBSERVATION

AERIAL CROP SURVEYS

1/1,000,000 OF EARTH IN VIEW (10 FT ALTITUDE)

BENEFITS IN SPACE

GLOBAL CROP INVENTORIES

TELEVISION & TELEPHONE RELAY

40% OF EARTH IN VIEW (10,000 MI ALTITUDE)

WORLDWIDE NAVIGATION

At any given moment a low-altitude satellite is within view of about 10 percent of the surface of the earth. At the geosynchronous altitude (22,300 miles) it would be able to see about 44 percent. Three geosynchronous satellites spaced 120 degrees apart above the earth's equator could access practically all of the inhabited portions of the globe. Global communications, navigation, and earth observations all benefit from the broad coverage available to orbiting satellites.

plants are unusually healthy when they grow over hidden treasures of tin and molybdenum. The trade journals bristle with stories of minerals and other valuable deposits discovered from space, including diamonds, petroleum, copper, and geothermal steam.

Communication satellites are today's most profitable application of the broad view from space. Their revenues currently exceed $3 billion, with annual growth rates of 20 to 30 percent. Eighteen countries, including Indonesia and Brazil, own and operate their own communication satellites, and at last count 112 nations had ground antennas capable of receiving messages from space. While you are reading this paragraph, 50,000 telephone calls are passing through communication satellites. So are several dozen color television shows. Religious sermons, video conferences, computer data, stock-market quotes all depend on satellite transmissions.

Most of today's communication satellites are launched into "geosynchronous" orbits 22,300 miles above the earth. At that particular altitude a satellite's orbital motion exactly matches the earth's rotational rate. Thus, to the people living on the earth the satellite seems to hang motionless in the sky. Some modern satellites can handle as many as 12,000 telephone conversations plus several channels of high-quality color TV. Within a few years, improved versions will provide worldwide "pocket telephone" service to busy travelers and international television programs broadcast directly into our homes.

USING the HARD VACUUM of SPACE

The vacuum of space creates problems for aerospace designers, but it can also be used in economically important ways. For several decades, companies like General Electric and RCA have profited handsomely from vacuum technology. Every incandescent light bulb houses a man-made vacuum; so does the picture tube in every color television set. Hard vacuums are also necessary in refrigeration equipment, in the freeze-drying of foods, and in welding dissimilar metals such as aluminum and molybdenum.

Today's researchers have produced some remarkably efficient vacuum chambers for use on earth, but they cost millions of dollars each. Rockwell International in Seal Beach, California, for instance, recently invested $10 million in a new 40-foot vacuum chamber. Its powerful pumps must work for several hours to remove all but the last few traces of air from its vacuum chamber. However, the vacuum it can produce is not nearly as good as the one the astronauts can obtain free in space. Three hundred miles above your head, the ambient air is only one trillionth as dense as the air now filling your lungs. Open a valve to the outside of the spacecraft, and this vacuum becomes instantly available for space-based research.

The virtual absence of air in space will allow tomorrow's aerospace engineers to develop remarkably inexpensive inflatable structures. In the late 1950s, giant Echo balloons 135 feet in diameter were inflated a few hundred miles above the earth. They reflected radio messages from one ground transmitter to another. In one experiment, a crude television image was bounced from coast to coast. It originated in Boston and it read "M-I-T." Inflation of these enormous silver bubbles was possible only because of the natural vacuum of space. On the ground, working against atmospheric pressure, 800,000 pounds of gases were required to inflate an Echo balloon. But in the vacuum of space, only 30 pounds of gases were needed.

Large geodesic domes, parabolic mirrors, and other inflatable structures can be erected in space with comparable efficiencies. Unenclosed television picture

GEOSYNCHRONOUS SATELLITES

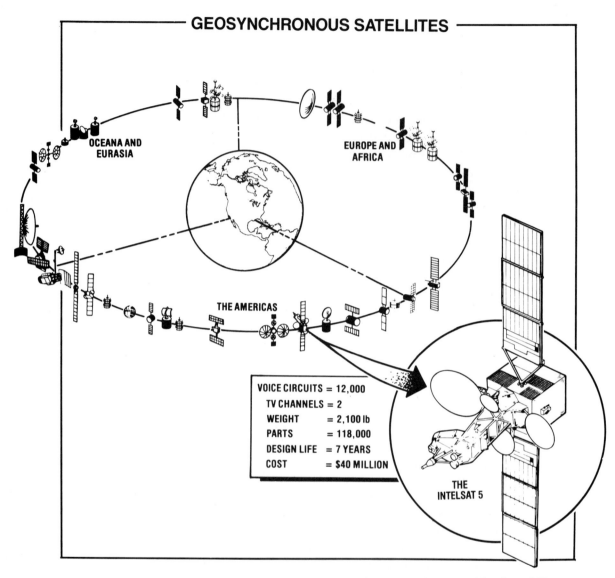

OCEANA AND
EURASIA

EUROPE AND
AFRICA

THE AMERICAS

VOICE CIRCUITS = 12,000
TV CHANNELS = 2
WEIGHT   = 2,100 lb
PARTS   = 118,000
DESIGN LIFE   = 7 YEARS
COST   = $40 MILLION

THE
INTELSAT 5

The geosynchronous altitude 22,300 miles above the earth is presently occupied by about 140 civilian and military satellites. These invaluable machines handle most of today's international telephone conversations and television transmissions. The Intelsat 5 is typical of this modern breed of communication satellites. It can handle 12,000 simultaneous telephone calls plus two channels of high-quality color TV. Intelsat 6, which is the most capable communication satellite, can handle 33,000 simultaneous conversations.

tubes and klystrons (extremely efficient microwave energy transmitters) may also be possible. In addition, scientists are investigating the practicality of processing rare metals and biological materials in the thin atmosphere of outer space.

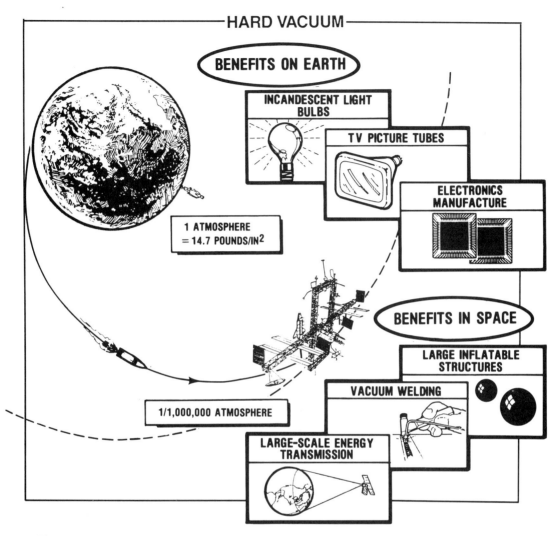

The atmosphere outside the shuttle orbiter is roughly one trillion times less dense than the atmosphere near the surface of the earth. This excellent vacuum is difficult and costly to duplicate here on earth. Promising commercial applications of the vacuum of space include biological and metal processing and unenclosed klystrons for low-cost transmission of large quantities of electrical energy.

THE PROFIT-MAKING POTENTIAL of SPACE INDUSTRIALIZATION

In 1985, researchers at the Center for Space Policy, a Cambridge, Massachusetts, "think tank," estimated that by the dawning of the twenty-first century, privately owned companies in space will be making at least $65 billion in annual sales. If these predictions turn out to be accurate, space businesses' sales will be larger than those of today's domestic agriculture and considerably larger than those of today's mining and oil production.

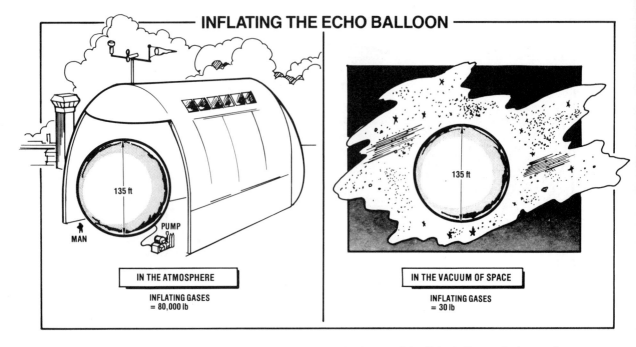

INFLATING THE ECHO BALLOON

135 ft

PUMP

MAN

IN THE ATMOSPHERE

INFLATING GASES
= 80,000 lb

135 ft

IN THE VACUUM OF SPACE

INFLATING GASES
= 30 lb

The vacuum of space helped simplify the design and inflation of the Echo balloon, which served as a passive communications satellite. In the early 1960s, when test engineers inflated the Echo balloon in an old dirigible hangar in New Jersey, they needed 800,000 pounds of gases to resist the crushing pressure of the atmosphere. But when they inflated that same balloon in space, only 30 pounds of inflating gases were required.

Solutions to many of our everyday problems with minerals, medicines, communications, and weather prediction are awaiting us on the space frontier. Most of the profits will be shared by you and your neighbors; so will most of the benefits. These practical benefits are possible because of the unique properties of outer space—microgravity, hard vacuum, wide-angle view. Communication satellites are already using these special properties to bring in $3 billion in annual revenues. Observations of the earth's crop lands, weather patterns, and mineral resources will generate additional billions in the next few years. So will factories in space.

INVESTING YOUR MONEY in SPACE

In the pages to follow, you will learn why space industrialization is becoming so profitable and how you can share in the large amounts of money to be made. In particular, you can buy stock in large corporations, furnish venture capital to high-technology firms, or develop new payloads to fly aboard the space shuttle.

NASA will carry a 60-pound "Getaway Special" into orbit for as little as $3,000. Dozens of them have already flown on a "space-available" basis. If you have an innovative idea for a new product or service that can benefit from the special environmental properties of space, do not push it out of your mind. Sketch up the plans. Submit it to NASA. Perhaps someday you will number yourself among to-morrow's space-made billionaires.

But even if you lack good ideas, you can still participate in America's exciting new adventure. Anyone, at any time, can call a stockbroker and invest in COMSAT (Communications Satellite Corporation), which manages America's international communication satellites. COMSAT stock has nearly tripled in value in the past ten years, and quarterly dividends have added another 70 percent. No one knows if this trend will continue, but many institutional investors hold COMSAT in their portfolios. Other large corporations that make substantial parts of their revenues from space include Martin Marietta (51 percent), Lockheed (37 percent), Rock-well International (28 percent), and Harris Aerospace (25 percent). All of these stocks are available to you through brokerage firms, and all fluctuate in varying degrees with the fortunes of space.

Of course, the biggest fortunes will be made from small emerging companies, companies whose names are not now household words. Eagle Engineering of Houston may be a good example. It was founded by a group of engineers from the Johnson Space Flight Center who took early retirement and funded their fledgling company out of their own pockets. When more manpower was needed, they con-tracted for the services of thirty more retired engineers on a part-time basis. When business is good, Eagle has seventy-five engineers on its payroll. They do technical analyses for other firms interested in space industrialization.

Another emerging company, Space Services, Inc., started with limited partner-ships in which investors share company profits in exchange for venture capital. This mechanism raised $6 million. When its capital requirements grew, space services retained Decuman Securities to sell a private placement for $4.2 million.

Seattle-based Spacehab, Inc., has raised $60 million from 900 venture capitalists who are convinced that a special storage and crew module can be fitted into the shuttle cargo bay to yield big profits. As we shall see in chapter 2, two useful space-made products are already on sale in the commercial marketplace. Both are made from inexpensive plastics, and both are bringing big profits to daring en-trepreneurs. Some of the other possibilities for making money in space are listed in the accompanying table, which also estimates their probable revenues and sum-marizes their current status.

Someday soon you may be striking it rich in space. But even if you choose to ignore the business opportunities along the final frontier, you will still benefit from space industrialization. Products made in orbiting factories will provide you and your family with improved health care, better medicines, and more accurate diagnostic tools. Sensors in space will give you precise information on impending hurricanes, earthquakes, and other natural disasters. More efficient computers,

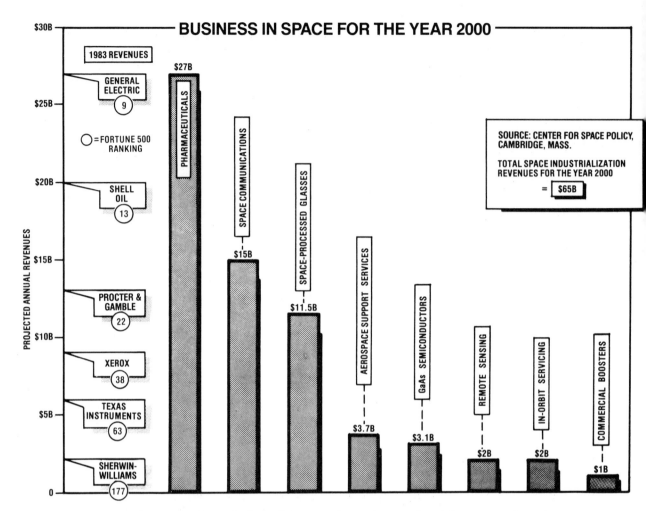

BUSINESS IN SPACE FOR THE YEAR 2000

PROJECTED ANNUAL REVENUES

$30B
$25B
$20B
$15B
$10B
$5B
0

1983 REVENUES

GENERAL ELECTRIC — 9

◯ = FORTUNE 500 RANKING

SHELL OIL — 13

PROCTER & GAMBLE — 22

XEROX — 38

TEXAS INSTRUMENTS — 63

SHERWIN-WILLIAMS — 177

PHARMACEUTICALS — $27B
SPACE COMMUNICATIONS — $15B
SPACE-PROCESSED GLASSES — $11.5B
AEROSPACE SUPPORT SERVICES — $3.7B
GaAs SEMICONDUCTORS — $3.1B
REMOTE SENSING — $2B
IN-ORBIT SERVICING — $2B
COMMERCIAL BOOSTERS — $1B

SOURCE: CENTER FOR SPACE POLICY, CAMBRIDGE, MASS.

TOTAL SPACE INDUSTRIALIZATION REVENUES FOR THE YEAR 2000 = $65B

Researchers at the Center for Space Policy near Boston have predicted that space industrialization will blossom from $4 billion per annum into a $65 billion enterprise within the next fifteen years. Pharmaceuticals, computer chips, special glasses for optical lenses, and other products made in orbiting factories will provide 60 percent of projected revenues. Direct-broadcast TV, pocket telephones, and other advanced communication technologies will also create unprecedented opportunities for tomorrow's daring aerospace entrepreneurs.

better telephone service, safer methods of travel, and more abundant food will also come with the industrialization of space. So will exciting movie adventures, television shows, and new ways to spend your weekends and your summer vacations.

Space is not just science anymore; it is business. Corporate strategists who ignore space may be doing so at great jeopardy to their company's future.

Peter W. Wood and Peter M. Stark
"Made in Space"
Booz Allen & Hamilton, *Outlook*, 1985

2

STRIKING IT RICH IN SPACE

In the past thirty years, NASA and the Department of Defense have spent more than $170 billion on space exploration. During the coming decade, federal space budgets are expected to grow 7 percent each year, but large corporations—General Motors, John Deere, AT&T—are also beginning to invest big money in space. So are hundreds of smaller companies not now included among the Fortune 500. They are attracted by industry projections indicating that within twenty years, space industrialization may produce larger sales than today's Big Three automakers combined. Space industrialization is also attracting individual investors, designers, and inventors who realize that bold new technologies have always spelled opportunity for farsighted entrepreneurs.

Today's space-based industries are grossing $4 billion per annum, and revenues are doubling every four or five years.* Whenever other industries—plastics, electronics, computers, telecommunications—have grown at a comparable rate, early investors have harvested enormous financial rewards. Some spectacular fortunes have been made with the runaway growth of the computer revolution, a revolution that has already produced four self-made billionaires. According to *Fortune* magazine, David Packard and William Hewlett (co-founders of Hewlett-Packard), Ross Perot, and Bill Gates—all of whom started with modest assets in the emerging world of computers—are now worth a total of $8.7 billion.

SALES TRENDS for SPACE INDUSTRIALIZATION

In 1985, when a team of experts at the Center for Space Policy in Cambridge, Massachusetts, studied the economic potential of space, they concluded that by century's end, privately financed space ventures will be making at least $65 billion in annual sales. Jerry Grey, publisher of *Aerospace America*, has forecast even

---

*These figures do not include the NASA budget or the military uses of space, whose combined expenditures are about $17 billion per annum.**

larger revenues ranging from $70 billion to $170 billion per annum by the dawning of the twenty-first century. If his more optimistic estimate proves correct, tomorrow's orbital enterprises would be nearly as large as today's automotive industry. In 1986 America's big-three auto companies had sales totaling $198 billion.

Pharmaceuticals will probably become the most profitable product made in space. Sales could reach $27 billion per annum for biological substances that cannot be manufactured here on earth. Diabetes, glaucoma, emphysema, and heart disease can all be treated effectively with new space-made medicines.

Communication satellites should bring in another $15 billion. Some will broadcast television programs directly into your home. Others will provide global paging services and link you with distant colleagues to reduce tiring and unnecessary business travel. Additional moneymakers will include space-made glasses, special materials for making computer chips, and remote-sensing satellites to pinpoint illegal crops, mineral deposits, and geothermal steam. Finally, private companies will provide booster rockets and launch services for other firms engaged in commercial ventures in space.

THE EFFECTS of the SPACE SHUTTLE EXPLOSION

Of course, progress has always exacted a heavy price, and, unfortunately, the conquest of space is no exception. The tragic explosion of the shuttle *Challenger* in late January 1986 shocked and saddened people everywhere. It killed seven of our country's brightest, most enthusiastic citizens a minute after their booster climbed into the stratosphere. Changes to the shuttle to make it safe will probably take about two years, thus creating a number of short-term problems for America's aerospace pioneers. A few missions, mostly scientific, will be long delayed or even canceled. Others will be shifted to expendable boosters, including the European Ariane, the Delta from McDonnell Douglas, and others from privately owned companies.

Despite the shuttle explosion, the American public is still solidly behind the space program. As *Science* magazine put it: "The outpouring of public support and confidence in the agency has been remarkable, with some 80 percent of the respondents [in one poll] saying that the shuttle flights should continue."

Large-scale endeavors are seldom stopped or even much slowed by dramatic tragedies. When the *Titanic* smashed into a North Atlantic iceberg in 1912, the world mourned for 1,400 lost souls. But cruise ships did not shut down their operations. They flourished for decades until commercial airliners took away much of their trade. When three of the first few dozen commercial jetliners, the British Comets, disintegrated in midair, jet passenger travel did not cease. Metal-fatigue problems, once they were understood by the engineers, were largely eliminated in subsequent designs. Today England's Comets have been replaced by a fleet of 6,000 sleek and efficient jet aircraft, most of them larger and faster than the Comets.

The space program itself has also experienced previous failures. Six of the first seven Vanguard rockets exploded before their payloads reached their destinations in space. Criticism was deafening, but neither the public nor the design engineers were willing to give up on space exploration. An early replacement for the Vanguards, the Thor, soon achieved a 99 percent success rate for launches into space. Even today, modified versions are ferrying payloads beyond the stratosphere.

Space commercialization is a highly profitable enterprise that takes advantage of the beneficial properties of space—hard vacuum, wide-angle view, microgravity. The shuttle tragedy will not stop (or even much delay) the industrialization of space. In fact, as chapters 8 and 11 will explain, this tragic event will actually open up new opportunities for the development of privately financed rockets and economical boosters that can carry satellites into space for one-tenth the fees currently charged by the shuttle. When the "star raker" and other similar concepts become operational, a fruitful new era of space industrialization will inevitably result.

GROWTH RATES for TODAY'S SPACE INVESTMENTS

Many people seem to have the perception that space industrialization is too risky, and the projects it involves are too big for the private capital market to handle, but Gregg R. Fawkes, principal researcher for the National Chamber Foundation, a business analysis and strategy institution affiliated with the U.S. Chamber of Commerce, has not found any evidence that this is true. In 1984 his group was commissioned to study the institutional problems associated with space industrialization. In particular, they were looking for "structural weaknesses in the private sector that could preclude commercial development of space." They found no important barriers whatsoever. In fact, there seems to be nothing special or unusual about the investment climate faced by entrepreneurs who want to invest in space.

Some of the participants had anticipated a decidedly different result. Intuition told them that many space ventures would be too big for anyone but the federal government to handle. But, in fact, according to Fawkes, "the private capital markets have tackled projects considerably larger than anything that's going to be done near-term in space." Space investors will require risk-taking initiative, distant horizons, and large amounts of patience, but according to the findings of the National Chamber Foundation, the financial returns to be expected from space can easily justify the economic risks.

Researchers at the foundation concluded that many of the most imaginative ideas will come from "nontraditional players" completely outside the aerospace industry. Promising sources of economically practical concepts will include the chemical and petrochemical companies and corporations that deal with large-scale engineering and construction. When space exploration first began thirty years ago, industry experts were the only ones who could understand its complexities; but in the meantime, we have trained a whole new generation of students during the age of space. Their youth and vitality will be an important asset in the era of space commercialization.

Despite the apparent risks, space-related investments have been growing at a surprisingly rapid rate. David W. Thompson, president of the Orbital Sciences Corporation (Vienna, Virginia), estimates that the capital flowing into new space ventures totaled only $10.5 million in 1980. In 1983 it reached $175 million, and it may soon top $1 billion as bigger, more sophisticated companies are jarred out of their complacency.

But despite this impressive growth, Booz Allen & Hamilton, New York's preeminent technology consulting firm, believes that many companies are still much too conservative in their attitudes toward space. Judicious risk-taking is proper now because NASA is offering subsidies for companies that seriously attempt space commercialization. However, those subsidies will be slashed in the near future. "Once healthy market development is assured, NASA will no longer be eager to subsidize developmental flights or provide generous incentives for commercial utilization of space."

So far none of the companies involved in materials-processing research in space have paid for shuttle transportation, but communication satellite owners, whose industry is much more mature, pay the going rate for all their shuttle launches. In today's competitive marketplace, undue caution may ensure competitive failure. As aerospace consultant Peter V. Wood puts it: "For today's space-naive executive, doing nothing may be the highest-risk strategy of all."

THE FIRST TWO SUCCESSFUL PRODUCTS MADE in SPACE

Most of today's space business comes from communication satellites and earth observations, but the shuttle astronauts have already made two commercially successful products in space. Both were constructed from inexpensive plastics, and both are valued at millions of dollars per pound.

Tiny latex microspheres one-tenth the diameter of a human hair were the first successful product made in space. On each shuttle mission the astronauts produced four ounces of the spheres with a retail value exceeding $1 million per flight. They are sold to scientific laboratories in $400 vials each containing 15 million microspheres.

Smaller latex spheres have long been used by scientists and technicians to calibrate microscopes, filters, and porous membranes. Laboratory technicians sprinkle

SPACE-MADE LATEX MICROSPHERES

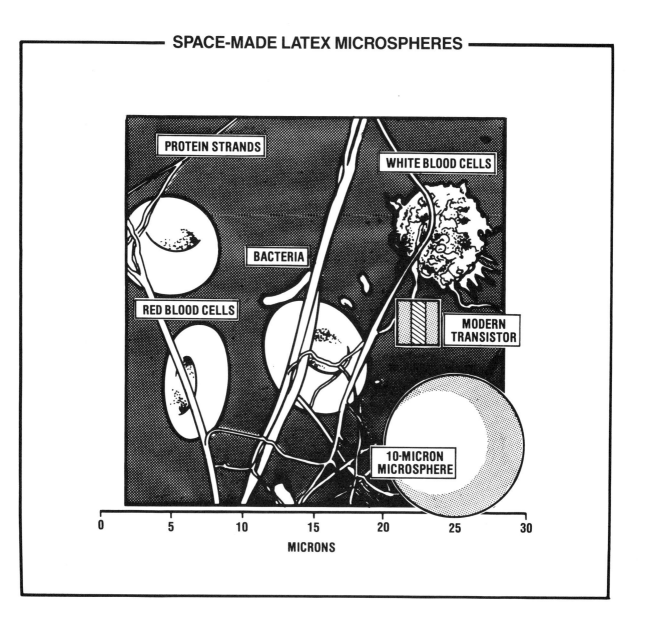

In 1985 the National Bureau of Standards began selling space-made latex microspheres for about $5 million per pound—1,000 times the value of 24-karat gold. The tiny microspheres, which are roughly the size of human blood cells, infectious bacteria, and modern transistors, help researchers calibrate microscopes, filters, and porous membranes and gauge the size of finely ground powders. They are also useful in glaucoma diagnosis and cancer research. This unique space-age product is sold in $400 vials, each containing 15 million space-made microspheres.

them into the field of view of optical microscopes to serve as tiny "yardsticks"—standards of comparison lying alongside other objects in the field of view. They help ensure uniformity in the production of paint pigments, ink granules, flour, explosives, and toner particles for copying machines. Medical practitioners use them when they are counting human blood cells and in glaucoma and cancer research.

For many years, latex spheres ranging from 1 to 3 microns in diameter (1 micron = 1/25,000 inch) have been "grown" in a bath of heated water in ground-based laboratories. Brownian motion of the water molecules buffets the small spheres to keep them in solution while they are growing to the desired size. For larger spheres, gravity causes the material to settle into a gooey cream or solidify into nonuniform sizes and shapes.

Much larger microspheres can be produced in the "weightlessness" of space because they do not settle out of solution. The National Bureau of Standards marketed them initially, but a private company, Particle Technology, Inc., is now selling the tiny spheres.

Today's microspheres are used for instrument calibration, medical experiments, and the timed release of certain drugs into the human bloodstream. Other economically important uses or product variations may be awaiting discovery by a clever entrepreneur.

The second successful space-made product is a motion picture, *The Dream Is Alive*, a thirty-seven-minute adventure filmed by the astronauts aboard the space shuttle. Tickets are sold for $4 each at forty specially equipped IMAX theaters throughout the Western world. Exhibitors are delighted with the film's money-making potential, which came as no surprise in view of the popularity of Hollywood's *Star Wars* trilogy and the millions of enthusiastic tourists that crowd into the Smithsonian's Air and Space Museum.

In the opening sequences of the film, Walter Cronkite supplies the commentary as the shuttle thunders into space. Once the astronauts reach orbit, they deploy a 105-foot solar array, capture and repair an ailing spacecraft, gulp floating shrimp directly from the air, and frolic in zero g. These sequences successfully portray the ingenuity and enthusiasm of the men and women we pay to travel into space. But the scene that sticks in the minds of viewers everywhere shows the astronauts sleeping in their space bunks. Their bodies are restrained, but their hands and arms float up toward the ceiling in eerie weightlessness.

The short documentary format of *The Dream Is Alive* packs the IMAX theaters with paying customers several times every day, but film-industry experts are convinced that a lively fiction script shot against the backdrop of space would attract much larger paying crowds. When the space station reaches orbit in the 1990s, regular news coverage and commercial TV shows will probably originate from its studios in space. Like the early arrivals in Hollywood, producers, directors, and scriptwriters who mastermind the new productions can anticipate enormous returns.

PRIVATELY OWNED COMMUNICATION SATELLITES

Worldwide communication satellites are another important source of profits in space. Their revenues currently exceed $3 billion per year. All modern communication satellites are "repeaters": they pick up faint messages from the ground, amplify them electronically, then retransmit them on a slightly different frequency. Most hover in geosynchronous orbits 22,300 miles above the equator, a special altitude where a satellite seems to hang motionless with respect to the spinning earth.

A satellite in a geosynchronous orbit is like a microwave relay station mounted on an invisible tower, a tower so tall the satellite can "see" almost an entire hemisphere of the earth. Except for two small regions near the poles, three geosynchronous satellites spaced 120 degrees apart along the equator could serve the communication needs of the entire globe. Heavy traffic loads, however, dictate a much larger number. Today 140 geosynchronous satellites—most of them handling commercial or military communications—form a thin metal "daisy chain" around the earth. They are designed and manufactured by Hughes, Ford Aerospace, and RCA. Many are owned by private companies, including IBM, Western Electric, and AT&T.

In 1965, the annual cost of the hardware needed to set up a telephone circuit through space was about $20,000 per year; with emerging technology that cost has been reduced to only $200, and a few years from now—when large spiderbeam antennas can be assembled in space—costs will likely drop by another factor of ten, or even more. As costs decline, new profit-making uses are constantly being found for our space-based transmitters. Most of today's communication satellites relay telephone conversations, computer data, and television shows. But other profitable uses, including stereo radio, direct-broadcast TV, and video conferencing, are growing in popularity.

"When I tell my friends about video conferencing, they think it's a great idea—for the future. Actually, the future is now!" The speaker is Beverly Johantgen, program director at VideoNet, of Woodland Hills, California. VideoNet has only one business: it arranges video teleconferences for other, larger companies. For instance, when a new bankruptcy law was passed by Congress, VideoNet leased time on RCA's Satcom to link thirty cities for a "live" seminar explaining the consequences of the new legislation. Four leading experts in Chicago briefed nearly 2,000 participants and answered their questions in an all-day session. The registration fee was a modest $65.

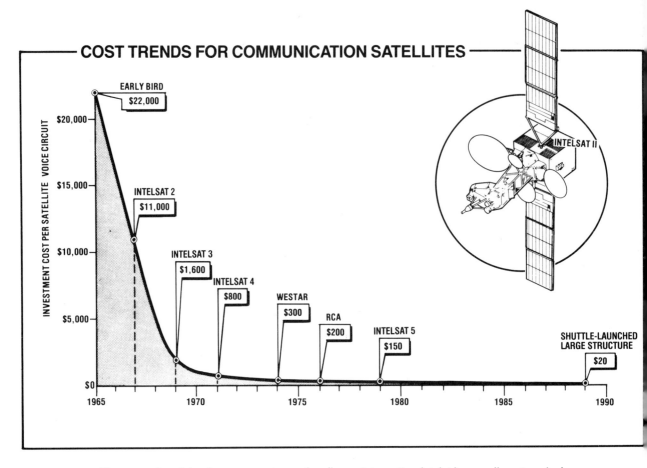

COST TRENDS FOR COMMUNICATION SATELLITES

EARLY BIRD
$22,000

INTELSAT 2
$11,000

INTELSAT 3
$1,600

INTELSAT 4
$800

WESTAR
$300

RCA
$200

INTELSAT 5
$150

SHUTTLE-LAUNCHED LARGE STRUCTURE
$20

INTELSAT II

INVESTMENT COST PER SATELLITE VOICE CIRCUIT

$20,000
$15,000
$10,000
$5,000
$0

1965   1970   1975   1980   1985   1990

The space-based hardware necessary to handle an international telephone call costs only 1 percent of what it did twenty years ago. In 1966 an Early Bird voice circuit cost more than $20,000 per year. Today the Intelsat 5 provides the same service with hardware that costs only about $150. Moreover, some experts foresee costs as low as $20 per year when large shuttle-launched antennas can be assembled in space. As costs drop, new communication services such as teleconferencing and direct-broadcast TV that would have been unthinkable twenty years ago are being marketed by private, profit-making companies.

"In some cases we lease receiving equipment from people like AT&T," she explains. "In others, we use existing on-site antennas. Holiday Inn, for instance, has 1,400 sixteen-foot dishes at hotels in forty states. They were installed to provide first-run movies to hotel guests, but we can use these same antennas for our seminars."

Video conferencing saves time, gasoline, and money—large amounts of it. VideoNet's conference on bankruptcy cost $90,000 total. Flying the participants to Chicago to attend in person would have cost $300,000 in air fares alone.

LARGE CORPORATIONS THAT ARE INVESTING in SPACE

A surprisingly large number of American corporations are involved in the industrialization of space, although in many cases space makes up only a small part of their overall business. The ones in this annotated listing are blue-chip companies traded on the major stock exchanges:

- ALUMINUM COMPANY of AMERICA (ALCOA), Pittsburgh, Pennsylvania. ALCOA wants to use laboratories in space to produce new types of aluminum and aluminum alloys that cannot be made on earth.
- BATTELLE LABORATORIES, Columbus, Ohio. Battelle's researchers plan to employ microgravity processing to grow collagen fibers that can be used in repairing and replacing human connective tissues.
- GENERAL MOTORS, Warren, Michigan. GM is studying combustion physics in the weightlessness of space. Other areas of interest to the GM research staff include the performance of engine lubricants, bonding and adhesion studies in space, and the production of new types of semiconductors.
- HEWLETT-PACKARD, Palo Alto, California. HP personnel are working on genetic engineering in space with scientists from Genentech, one of the leaders in gene splicing and other advanced bioengineering techniques.
- JOHN DEERE, Moline, Illinois. John Deere's researchers are attempting to develop stronger and lighter irons in the low-g environment of space. They are particularly interested in studying the spontaneous formation of graphite modules in commercial metal products.
- McDONNELL DOUGLAS, St. Louis, Missouri. Researchers at McDonnell Douglas are already producing commercially attractive pharmaceuticals in space. Soon they will be making larger quantities with their 5,000-pound electrophoresis unit. With American, European, and/or Japanese pharmaceutical companies they plan to market the first space-made drug as soon as the shuttle is again available to carry their hardware into space.
- 3M CORPORATION, St. Paul, Minnesota. 3M is conducting a broad-ranging experimental program in space, including the manufacture of thin films and organic crystals. Staff scientists have already launched three experimental missions, and, in 1987, they reached agreement with NASA to carry sixty-two payloads on the space shuttle in the next ten years.
- WESTINGHOUSE, Baltimore, Maryland. In connection with an ongoing research program, Westinghouse intends to produce ultrapure, bubble-free glass in space.

APPENDIX A presents more detailed information on these and other large corporations that are participating in space industrialization.

SMALL SPACE COMPANIES SEEKING VENTURE CAPITAL

Dozens of small, aggressive companies are involved in space industrialization. Most have good ideas, and many are seeking venture-capital support for their marketplace activities.

- DESTEK GROUP, INC., Falls Church, Virginia. Destek maintains its cash flow by analyzing remote-sensing data from space. It also assists clients who plan to fly remote-sensing missions aboard the space shuttle.
- GEOSTAR CORPORATION, Washington, D.C. This small company is raising money to develop a space-based navigation system using three geosynchronous satellites positioned above the equator. The satellites will also relay short "telegram" messages for an additional fee.
- MICROGRAVITY RESEARCH ASSOCIATES, Coral Gabies, Florida. Microgravity Research is working with NASA on the production of gallium-arsenide semiconductor materials aboard the space shuttle.
- MICROGRAVITY TECHNOLOGIES, INC., Solana Beach, California. This small company is designing "float zone" furnaces for producing flawless crystals in space. Exotic semiconductor materials are also a main area of interest to company officials.
- MMI (THIRD MILLENNIUM, INC.), Washington, D.C. Technicians at MMI are designing a winged orbiter vehicle (reusable space van) capable of carrying a 6,600-pound payload into earth orbit.
- SPACE AMERICA, Bethesda, Maryland. Remote-sensing satellites with stereoscopic viewing capabilities for commercial earth observations are under study at Space America. The company is also developing a software service to analyze remote-sensing data collected from this and other sources.
- SPACE SERVICES, INC., Houston, Texas. Space Services is using private funds to develop and launch the Conestoga II booster rocket to carry small payloads into space.
- WESTECH SYSTEMS, Phoenix, Arizona. Westech Systems is developing containerless space processing using magnetic and acoustical levitation. Staff engineers are also building "float-zone" furnaces to make flaw-free crystals in space.

APPENDIX B provides more detailed information on these and other small companies that are interested in space commercialization.

NINE WAYS TO RAISE MONEY
FOR A SPACE BUSINESS

INTERNAL CORPORATE RESOURCES

MONEY EITHER ON HAND OR FLOWING IN
FROM OTHER BUSINESS AREAS.

EQUITY FUNDING:
SELLING PART OWNERSHIP

PRIVATE STOCK SALES

SALE OF PART OWNERSHIP IN THE
CORPORATION ON A PRIVATE, RESTRICTED
BASIS TO SELECTED INDIVIDUALS.

PUBLIC STOCK SALES

SALE OF COMMON STOCK IN A PUBLIC,
REGULATED MARKET SUCH AS THE
NEW YORK STOCK EXCHANGE.

LIMITED PARTNERSHIPS

SALE OF A SHARED PARTNERSHIP IN WHICH THE
NEW PARTNER'S LIABILITY IS LIMITED TO THE
CAPITAL ACTUALLY CONTRIBUTED.

JOINT VENTURES

ANY CONTRACTURAL ARRANGEMENT WHEREBY
TWO OR MORE CORPORATIONS AGREE TO WORK
TOGETHER ON A PARTICULAR PROJECT.

EXTERNAL DEBT:
BORROWED FROM OUTSIDE SOURCES

PREFERRED STOCK

A PUBLICLY TRADED STOCK; THE STOCKHOLDER
RECEIVES A FIXED PREARRANGED DIVIDEND AND
PREFERENTIAL REPAYMENT.

BONDS

INTEREST-BEARING INVESTMENTS SOLD
TO THE GENERAL PUBLIC.

CONVENTIONAL LOANS

INTEREST-BEARING INVESTMENTS USUALLY
SECURED BY REAL PROPERTY YIELDING A FIXED
RATE OF INTEREST.

VENTURE CAPITAL

A HIGH-RISK EQUITY ARRANGEMENT GIVING
THE CONTRIBUTOR A MAJOR ADVISORY ROLE
IN THE CORPORATION.

There are two basic ways to raise outside money to finance a business in space: equity funding and external debt. If you use any of the four equity-funding approaches, you will have to give up a portion of the business in exchange, but you will not have to pay the money back. If you use external debt, you will maintain full ownership of the business, but you will have to repay the principal and make regular interest payments until the loan is repaid.

TOMORROW'S SPACEBORNE ENTREPRENEURS

From the very beginning, the business of America has been business. Before Virginia and Massachusetts were colonies, they were companies attempting to make profits for investors back in Europe, who put up the money to finance their existence. In their book *The Entrepreneurs,* Robert Sobel and David B. Sicilia emphasize the restlessness of today's entrepreneurs, whom they characterize as "brash, unconventional, original people, who are incapable of standing still."

Entrepreneurs have a habit of taking things apart and putting them back together again—with a clever twist. The first great theorist of entrepreneurship, Joseph Schumpeter, was convinced that "Entrepreneurs perform an important function of 'creative destruction'" in that they reexamine conventional assumptions and toss out those that no longer apply.

Clearly we will need individuals with this kind of spunk and insight on the space frontier, where seemingly "natural" conditions—air, gravity, up and down, night and day—are modified in such radical ways. "Find a need and fill it" was the classic advice given to nineteenth-century entrepreneurs struggling along a hopeful road to fabulous profits. It was solid advice then, and it is still solid advice today.

HOW to RAISE MONEY for YOUR BUSINESS in SPACE

If you have a clever way to make improved dilithium crystals in space or a better technique for handling subspace carriers, you can raise money to support your brainchild in a number of different ways. The easiest approach is to use surplus money from your own pocket or from other portions of an ongoing business you are already operating. But if you are financially embarrassed, your dilithium crystals won't necessarily have to wait, because there are still two legal ways to gain access to the money in the pockets of others: equity funding and external debt.

If you use equity funding you will give up a portion of your business in exchange for the money you need. If you use external debt you will retain full ownership, but you will have to pay periodic interest and eventually the principal from your company's profits.

Equity funding—selling part ownership in your company—can be handled in four separate ways:

1. Private stock sales
2. Public stock sales
3. Limited partnerships
4. Joint ventures

In a *private stock sale,* you retain a portion of the business, usually a controlling interest, but you sell part ownership to selected individuals, often starting with family members and friends. In exchange for operating funds, you give them a fair share of the business and a fair share of future profits.

In a *public stock sale,* you market common stock on a public, regulated market such as the New York Stock Exchange or one of the smaller exchanges. Stock sales of this type are closely regulated by the Securities and Exchange Commission. When a company sells stock on a major exchange, it is said to have "gone public." In a *limited partnership,* you sell shares of your business to willing partners whose liability is limited to the actual amount of capital they have contributed to the partnership. As the principal partner, however, your liabilities are not limited. If you go belly-up, creditors can legally claim your private assets.

In a *joint venture,* money may or may not change hands. The term is used to characterize any cooperative business arrangement, large or small, in which two or more companies agree to work together on a particular project. If another company needs your dilithium crystals badly enough, it may contribute capital, stock, free labor, or whatever else is necessary to get you to enter into the joint venture.

There are also four ways to raise money through external debt:

1. Preferred stock
2. Bonds
3. Conventional loans
4. Venture capital

If you sell *preferred stock* (once your crystal business is beginning to thrive), it will consist of publicly traded shares for which your stockholders will usually receive dividends of a fixed percentage and their payments will receive preferential treatment. For instance, if your enterprise has sold both common and preferred stock, you will have to settle accounts with your preferred stockholders each year (at the published rate of return) before your common stockholders can receive their dividends.

Bonds are interest-bearing investments sold to the general public, often for a specific project such as a dilithium-crystal factory or a ground-based relay station for subspace carriers. Some government bonds are tax exempt, so historically they have been most attractive to well-heeled investors in high tax brackets.

Conventional loans are interest-bearing investments often secured by real property such as office buildings or automated assembly lines. Usually, the loan is issued for a specific period of time at a fixed interest rate.

Venture capital is a high-risk investment with the potential for an unusually high rate of return. Unlike those who furnish the capital for other debt instruments, your venture capitalists will probably expect to have some influence on the day-to-day operation of the business. They need special reassurance because they are taking unusually big risks and because potential payoffs are so high.

We have covered the eight methods of raising money from your viewpoint as an entrepreneur. But, of course, you can also make large amounts of money by furnishing capital or expertise to promising new space businesses in any of the eight ways we have just discussed. In tomorrow's world, farsighted investors, too, will be striking it rich in space.

When you bring a successful product to market, it goes through five phases of development from the time you seriously consider the idea until its market begins to decline. The methods you use to raise operating capital depend strongly on which of these five phases of product development you are in:

1. Pre-commercial phase
2. Introduction phase
3. Growth phase
4. Maturity phase
5. Decline phase

In the *pre-commercial* and the *introduction* phases you will not be making appreciable amounts of money, because start-up costs will probably eat up any profits you manage to make. In these two phases, the best ways to raise money are usually limited partnerships and conventional loans.

In the *growth* and *maturity* phases your sales are rising and money is coming in, but you could make even more money if you had additional capital for better equipment, product improvements, and market penetration. In this phase you may want to take out conventional loans, but public and private stock sales are also a definite possibility. So are joint ventures with other companies.

The various space businesses we will be discussing in this book are at different phases on the life-cycle curve. Communication satellites are in the maturity phase, with big companies slugging it out for market share. Earth-resources and weather-observation satellites are in the growth and introduction phases. They are bringing in money and they are ripe for exploitation, but they are not yet mature industries. Manufacturing in space is in the pre-commercial phase. The industry shows promise for large profits to come, but so far, with the exception of the IMAX theaters and Particle Technology, Incorporated, nobody has yet made any money from manufacturing in space.

Are there any industries in the decline phase? Some say the companies that supply backyard dish antennas for picking up television programs from space are in a permanent decline. Others feel that signal scrambling by some of the distributors of cable TV has merely caused a temporary dip in sales. No one knows for sure, but newer, cheaper technologies seem likely to revive dish-antenna sales.

THE FIVE PHASES OF A PRODUCT'S LIFE CYCLE

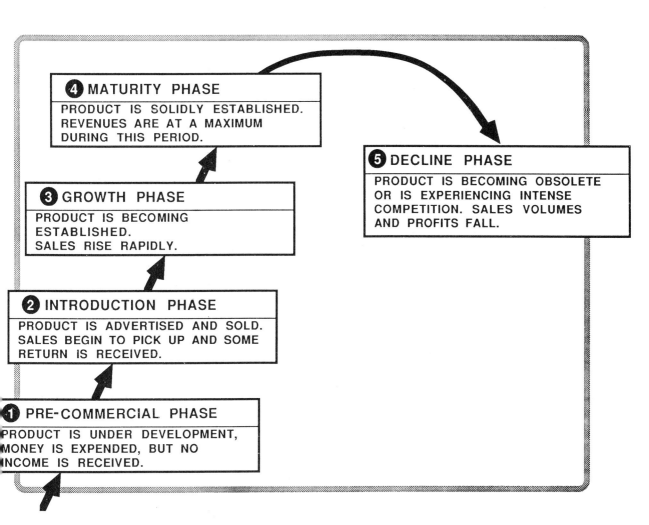

4 MATURITY PHASE

PRODUCT IS SOLIDLY ESTABLISHED. REVENUES ARE AT A MAXIMUM DURING THIS PERIOD.

5 DECLINE PHASE

PRODUCT IS BECOMING OBSOLETE OR IS EXPERIENCING INTENSE COMPETITION. SALES VOLUMES AND PROFITS FALL.

3 GROWTH PHASE

PRODUCT IS BECOMING ESTABLISHED. SALES RISE RAPIDLY.

2 INTRODUCTION PHASE

PRODUCT IS ADVERTISED AND SOLD. SALES BEGIN TO PICK UP AND SOME RETURN IS RECEIVED.

1 PRE-COMMERCIAL PHASE

PRODUCT IS UNDER DEVELOPMENT, MONEY IS EXPENDED, BUT NO INCOME IS RECEIVED.

If you develop a successful space business, it will probably go through the five phases listed in this life-cycle curve. In the pre-commercial and the introduction phases you will make little money, because high start-up costs will eat up the revenues from your initial sales. In the growth and maturity phases, money in fairly large amounts will be coming in, but you will probably be able to make even more if you can raise additional financing from outside sources to improve production efficiencies, advertise your product, or capture a larger market share. In the decline phase, obsolescence or market forces will drive profitability into a downward spiral. At this point you may try for dramatic improvements or you may choose to shift your resources into a completely different product line.

Thus we see that if you have a promising space-made product (or service), there are eight different ways for you to raise money to keep your brainchild alive. If you do pick a winner, you can expect your product to go through five phases of product development before it becomes firmly established and then begins to decline due to market saturation, evolving technology, or increased competition. At that point you will either have to come up with a fresh idea or find a way to spark new enthusiasm among your consumers.

THE FEDERAL GOVERNMENT'S DRIVE TOWARD SPACE INDUSTRIALIZATION

In July 1984, President Reagan unveiled a new national policy designed to accelerate the commercial development of space. In his speech he highlighted some of the ways space can help improve our standard of living, including the production of rare medicines and the manufacture of biological materials and "super-chips" for computers. Shortly thereafter, the Department of Transportation was assigned as the lead agency to work with private companies on new space initiatives and NASA was empowered to distribute grants, subsidies, and technical support to private companies interested in space industrialization. To date, NASA representatives have briefed more than 450 non-aerospace companies, and they have signed agreements for joint ventures with eight of them, in some cases giving their payloads free rides on the shuttle.

In keeping with his enthusiasm, the President authorized construction of the $8 billion manned space station, which will greatly enhance the profitability of space industrialization.* Larger than a football field, the space station will house at least six to eight astronauts at all times. Most space-station concepts from the 1970s called for rotating structures to induce artificial gravity, but the new version will not rotate. NASA's engineers are purposely designing it to fly at a fixed orientation to minimize g-forces. This will encourage the production of useful products in space.

Peter E. Glaser, vice-president of Arthur D. Little, Inc., shares the President's enthusiasm for space industrialization: "I believe that space in the twenty-first century will probably be what aviation, electronics, and computers were together in this century," he said recently. "It is the next evolutionary step for humanity." With generous government encouragement, space will undoubtedly contribute to the next generation of billionaires. Do nothing and your standard of living will be improved; be on the lookout for solid ideas, and someday soon you may be striking it rich in space.

*In the meantime, cost estimates have risen to $16–$26 billion.

PROMISING BUSINESS
OPPORTUNITIES IN SPACE

BUSINESS AREA	MOST PROMISING OPPORTUNITIES FOR PRIVATE ENTERPRISE	EXPENDITURE LEVELS*	COMMENTS
GOVERNMENT COMMITMENT	(See the various opportunities below)	Nasa budget = $7.2B Military budget = $7.4B Hidden military = $3.0B (est)	• $25B U.S. dollars would be required to duplicate the Soviet space effort. • 18 countries currently own & operate satellites. The Japanese foresee a $4.5B space industry by 1995.
COMMUNICATION SATELLITES	• Telephone & TV transmissions • International paging services • Electronic teleconferencing • Direct-broadcast TV	• Space communications = $3B now • Doubling every 3 years	• 64 highly profitable communication satellites now in operation. • 105 nations operate Intelsat ground terminals.
LAUNCH SERVICES	• Liquid & solid booster rockets • Upper stages for the space shuttle	Nonmilitary launch services: $5.4B next 5 years; $11B within 10 years	1,100 satellites currently in orbit, 300 nonmilitary birds to be launched by 1990. European Ariane expects to receive $650M in launch fees through 1986 = 26 satellites.
WEATHER & EARTH RESOURCES SATELLITES	• Specialized weather predictions • Oil exploration & mining data • Water management & snow cover measurements	Weather & earth resources services heavily used commercially. Free now. Reagan administration pushing for private commercialization. French & Japanese may soon launch superior space-based hardware.	
NAVIGATION SATELLITES	• Navigation services for ships, planes, surveyors, private cars • Time synchronization services	Navstar user sets should total $8B this century (mostly privately owned)	• 13 American navigation satellites in orbit. $1B committed to 21-satellite semi-synchronous constellation. • Russians, Europeans working on similar constellations.
MANUFACTURING IN SPACE	• Optical glasses • LSI substrates • Pharmaceuticals • Latex microspheres	Enormous potential. Pharmaceuticals alone may reach $23B this century.	Space-manufactured latex microspheres currently selling for $5M per pound; numerous manufacturing experiments have been conducted aboard Skylab, Spacelab, space shuttle, Russian space vehicles.
MANNED SPACE STATIONS	• "Getaway Specials" • Tethered payloads & subsatellites • Motion pictures in space	U.S. will soon complete design of $25B space station; 6-8 man level initially.	$1B European spacelab currently in operation. Soviets rapidly approaching capability for permanently manned space station.

*Space expert Gerard O'Neill envisions a $400B annual space industry by the year 2001.

The dream of manufacturing in space did not go up in flames with the space shuttle Challenger. The tragedy forced the National Aeronautical and Space Agency to postpone shuttle flights, and some contractors that build parts for the shuttle or use it to launch satellites could suffer for a while. But companies that hanker to produce exotic drugs and materials in zero gravity doubt the recent setback will crimp their long-term plans.

Brian Dumaine
"Still A-OK: The Promise of Factories in Space"
Fortune, March 3, 1986

3

SPACE-BASED MANUFACTURING

You probably don't think of them as a leader in high technology. They make Scotch Magic Tape, and those little yellow "Post-It" notes that seem to be stuck on everything these days. They make brown plastic tape for tape recorders. But they are also masters of organic crystals and polymer science, fruitful boulevards of research that are ushering us relentlessly into tomorrow's world of high technology. They are members of the research and production staff at Minnesota Mining and Manufacturing of St. Paul, Minnesota—the 3M Company, an organization with $7 billion in annual sales, looking toward space to lead its product line into the twenty-first century.

No other firm has a staff more ideally situated to play a leading role in space industrialization. They have the resources. They have the desire. They have the need. And they have a master plan for an aggressive program of scientific experimentation aboard the shuttle—and eventually aboard the space station. In a typical year, 3M brings to market one hundred new products, including adhesives so strong they are used to join aircraft wings.

3M is now forty-fourth among the Fortune 500; but in 1902 its only business was making sandpaper, and it was not very good at making that. The company faced bankruptcy several times, but somehow pulled through, and today it is known for an innovative outlook that attracts a superb staff of researchers. As Thomas Peters and Robert Waterman pointed out in their book *In Search of Excellence,* "3M has long focused on building, expanding, the opposite of restraining."

For every dollar in revenues, 3M spends 5 cents on new-product research. Small wonder its offices are "populated by feverish inventors and dauntless entrepreneurs who let their imaginations fly in all directions." Including space.

28

3M'S BOLD PLANS for MANUFACTURING in SPACE

In 1984, 3M's representatives approached NASA with a multimillion-dollar space commercialization plan stretching over ten years. It requested transportation for 3M equipment on board seventy-two shuttle flights.

Aviation Week was quite impressed with 3M's extraordinary request, which dwarfed anything being planned by Grumman, Lockheed, or any of the other old-line aerospace companies. "It is both the largest space commercialization project planned to date and the first formal proposal for private investment to assist in building the U.S. space station," wrote *Aviation Week*'s Craig Covault. "The 3M initiative could generate several hundred million dollars in commercial space activities and help draw other worldwide manufacturing companies into space commercialization."

For several years 3M's engineers had been interested in space research, although their initial concepts were quite modest and unimposing. But in April 1983 the interest and enthusiasm of their staff suddenly intensified when NASA astronaut Bonnie Dunbar and Dr. James I. Mueller of the University of Washington met with a panel of 3M representatives at a seminar in Houston. Dunbar, a former student of Dr. Mueller's, stimulated the panel's competitive juices by describing how European and Japanese business organizations were outdistancing their American counterparts in recognizing the commercial benefits of weightlessness—which could make new and interesting products economically practical.

Among her listeners was Dr. Christopher J. Podsiadly, who would later form a team of fifteen scientists and engineers at 3M devoted solely to designing scientific experiments to conduct in space. Many of his plans focused on organic chemistry, the chemistry of living creatures, which involves complicated interactions between the atoms of carbon and hydrogen. In particular, he wanted to do research on organic crystals.

A crystal is a bit of solid matter whose atoms are arranged in a simple, repetitive order. A snowflake is a crystal; so is a grain of salt, a sliver of ice, or a gemstone such as diamond or ruby. Stainless steel is composed of crystals, as are the dilithium pellets used in accelerating the Starship *Enterprise* to warp factor six.

Well-made crystals are far more important to our economy than you may realize. The most desirable properties of metals, alloys, ceramics, and other mineral products all depend on their underlying crystalline structure. The tiny slab of quartz in your digital wristwatch is a modern crystal. So are silicon and germanium substrates used in making chips for computers.

Crude inorganic crystals are easy to make. Drop a grain of pollen into a container of liquid sodium nitrate or copper sulfate and, within hours, you will be the owner of an intricate, if imperfect, crystal.* However, commercial-quality crystals are much more difficult to produce, in part because their container (or crucible) distorts their delicate crystalline structure and introduces contaminants while the crystal is growing to the proper size.

In space we can eliminate the container. Growing crystals are "levitated" by electromagnetic forces or acoustic waves so they do not touch anything. Zero-g processing also eliminates convection currents in the liquid mix, which, for modern crystals, must be heated to several hundred degrees. On earth the crucible is a gurgling, crackling caldron, but in space it is quiescent—even though it is the same temperature.

The characteristic properties of the *organic* crystals 3M scientists are making in space contrast sharply with the properties of ordinary *inorganic* crystals—which are made from completely different materials. Inorganic materials are hard and rigid, whereas organic materials are soft and pliable. The molecules of organic crystals are bound together into coils, rings, spiral structures, and branching chains, some of which are snarled and irregular. Moreover, their crystal structures are built on a massive scale. Some organic molecules are thousands of times larger and more complicated than ordinary inorganic molecules such as hydrogen peroxide and water—which can slip right through the more massive molecules in organic solids.

Important organic crystals include the enzymes that regulate most of our biochemistry, many pharmaceuticals, viruses in their quiescent state, and urea, an industrial substance used in producing chemical feedstocks, fertilizers, and animal feeds.

For more than eighty years, 3M scientists have been conducting laboratory experiments with organic crystals, polymers, and thin-film coatings. Now they are moving those experiments into space. What do they hope to build along the final frontier? New kinds of computer circuits, for one thing. According to *Aviation Week*, "The company expects its space shuttle and space station research to be in the forefront of new material breakthroughs that could supersede existing semiconductor-based electronics with a much faster generation of light-powered data-processing and storage systems."

Did 3M scale back its program of space research after the *Challenger* accident? Not at all. If anything, the program is even more ambitious than it was before. As *High Technology* magazine put it: "3M has already conducted three experiments aboard the shuttle and remains committed to its program of materials research in microgravity despite the fleet's temporary grounding. They are currently negotiating with NASA for quarters on 73 additional shuttle flights as part of R&D programs ranging from electronics to health care."

*Do not handle or taste the crystals you make. Many are poisonous.

3M'S EQUIPMENT MODULE FOR GROWING CRYSTALS IN SPACE

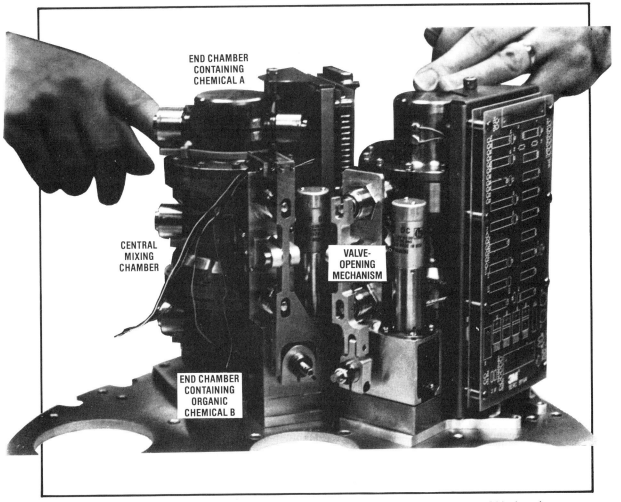

END CHAMBER
CONTAINING
CHEMICAL A

CENTRAL
MIXING
CHAMBER

VALVE-
OPENING
MECHANISM

END CHAMBER
CONTAINING
ORGANIC
CHEMICAL B

Two of the three football-size crystal-making chemical reactors flown into space by 3M aboard the shuttle are shown here. A long-term research program will be required before this effort will pay off, but company officials are betting they will gain a competitive edge in growing large organic crystals, a technology of importance to such diverse fields as data processing, communications, and health care.

How has 3M's space industrialization program affected the company's corporate posture? "It has already given 3M a competitive advantage in understanding the properties of certain organic crystals," concludes James P. Samuels, vice-president of research at Shearson-Lehman. A concrete example of this happy serendipity comes from 3M's vice-president for research and development, Lester Arough, who rejoices in his company's success in "growing a proprietary organic crystal during just seven days aboard the shuttle, despite years of thwarted efforts on the ground."

3M's success in space also translates into high morale at St. Paul. The company's scientists have such a close relationship with NASA, some of them are virtually assured of receiving invitations to fly on board the shuttle orbiter and the space station. The knowledge among staff members that their research might be rewarded with the ultimate space-age junket has, according to one company official, "stimulated a sense of adventure and excitement in their work."

This same spirit of adventure is also spreading outside the company. A few years ago, if engineering students thought of 3M at all, they regarded it as a rather mundane maker of Scotch tape. But today the company's pioneering spaceborne research is widely recognized at the best American universities. "Recruitment for graduating engineers has become much easier," says one executive, "especially for eastern schools like Harvard and MIT."

3M is today in the top 10 percent of the Fortune 500. But in the early days, success was not so easy to achieve. Fourteen years passed before the company paid its first dividend—6 cents a share. In the meantime, profits have grown at a steady pace. According to a company press release: "The stock, which once traded two shares for a shot of bar whiskey, has split seven times. One original share has become 384 shares, selling for about $75 each."

Early investors who casually drank down their 3M holdings saw only a fledgling company that made poor quality sandpaper. They could not visualize that someday it would become a major economic force. They certainly had no inkling that within four generations, it would blaze a trail for others to follow, straight up through the stratosphere.

THE ECONOMIC LURE of ZERO GRAVITY

Space offers a number of advantageous properties that can be exploited for financial benefit—hard vacuum, low vibration, zero g, wide-angle view, and complete isolation from the earth's biosphere. But our primary reason for building factories in space is to obtain long-term microgravity, or weightlessness.

Weightlessness can be created for brief intervals here on earth by building a drop tower, a long, vertical tube in which experimental specimens are released and allowed to fall until they crash into the ground below.

More than a century ago, drop towers were used to make the cannon grapeshot that filled the air over Civil War battlefields, and even today, smaller towers are used in producing millions of tiny glass beads for use on reflecting highway markers. Unfortunately, even the tallest drop tower can provide only a few seconds of weightlessness before the test specimen reaches the end of the tube. The grapeshot solidified into crude spheres within that brief interval, but most physical processes take much longer.

METHODS FOR OBTAINING WEIGHTLESSNESS

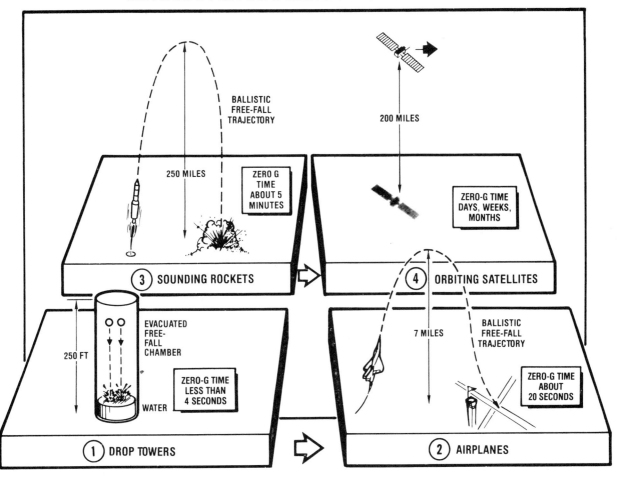

BALLISTIC FREE-FALL TRAJECTORY

200 MILES

250 MILES

ZERO G TIME ABOUT 5 MINUTES

ZERO-G TIME DAYS, WEEKS, MONTHS

③ SOUNDING ROCKETS

④ ORBITING SATELLITES

EVACUATED FREE-FALL CHAMBER

250 FT

7 MILES

BALLISTIC FREE-FALL TRAJECTORY

ZERO-G TIME LESS THAN 4 SECONDS

ZERO-G TIME ABOUT 20 SECONDS

WATER

① DROP TOWERS

② AIRPLANES

Drop towers, which have been in use since the middle of the nineteenth century, can keep a specimen in a weightless state for, at most, only a few seconds. Longer intervals of weightlessness can be achieved on airplanes or sounding rockets, but the duration is still limited to a few minutes. When we move the apparatus into space, weightlessness can be maintained indefinitely.

We can lengthen the free-fall interval to some extent by placing the specimen in an airplane that flies on a long gentle parabola. Sounding rockets can give us a little more time. But for weightlessness lasting hours or days, space is the only answer. Once an experimental specimen is in orbit it remains weightless until it comes back to earth.

The main barrier to the systematic exploitation of the weightlessness of space is affordable two-way transportation. Once transportation costs come down, the next gold rush can begin. "This high frontier, as some visionaries call it, could be the arena for the next industrial revolution," writes John S. DeMott at *Time* magazine. "The Center for Space Policy in Cambridge, Mass., predicts that by the year 2000, space industrialization could annually produce $27 billion in pharmaceuticals to combat cancer and emphysema, $3.1 billion in gallium arsenide semiconductors for electronics, and $11.5 billion worth of incredibly pure glass for optical purposes."

Similar projections have been made by the experts at Boeing in Seattle: "$7 billion for space-processed pharmaceuticals, $7 billion for semiconductor crystals, and over $11 billion for glass fibers." If these projections prove accurate, space-made products alone will involve more money than today's entire space program, including the NASA budget, the military space budget, and all of today's private profit-making ventures in space.

MICROGRAVITY RESEARCH ASSOCIATES

When the shuttle again becomes available, scientists at Microgravity Research Associates (Coral Gables, Florida) are planning to produce gallium arsenide crystals in space. Although gallium arsenide is difficult to fabricate, it has several properties that make it superior to silicon, the preferred material for most of today's semiconductor chips.

"Gallium arsenide is leaping from the high-tech doghouse to the high-tech penthouse," says Gene Bylinsky of *Fortune* magazine. "Most forecasters see gallium arsenide chip sales soaring from about $30 million this year to at least $1 billion in 1990. By the end of the century, gallium arsenide could account for one-third of the semiconductor industry's business—which is expected to spiral by then from last year's $15 billion to an astonishing $150 billion annually." Of course, an important fraction of this expanding need will be filled by high-quality gallium arsenide crystals made in space.

Unlike silicon crystals, crystals of gallium arsenide are made from two separate materials: gallium and arsenic. Today's gallium arsenide crystals are distorted and imperfect because of gravity-induced convection currents, which cause the heavier atoms to sink. This makes the crystal structure uneven and its electrical properties unpredictable and inconsistent. Only about 20 percent of today's commercially produced gallium arsenide is uniform enough to be made into wafers for chip production. By contrast, "all the material grown in space should be defect-free," according to Russell Ramsland, founder of Microgravity Research.

Most of today's "miracle chips" are made from silicon, but gallium arsenide offers much faster switching (by about a factor of ten), from a considerably smaller power supply. Low-power operation reduces heating and allows chip designers to stack circuits more densely within the material. Gallium arsenide is also more tolerant to radiation and temperature extremes. This makes it especially interesting to satellite makers and the military—both of which are already using substantial quantities of gallium arsenide made by today's crude and inefficient methods of production.

With the many advantageous properties of gallium arsenide, more and more uses for it are being found every day. Radar, high-frequency radio, and satellite communications are big users of gallium arsenide microchips, and the next generation of Cray supercomputers will use them to improve both processing and storage.

"Since speed is to electronics what money is to Wall Street, gallium arsenide should make possible not only supercomputers with capabilities undreamed of today, but also Dick Tracy–style wristwatch telephones that would receive and transmit signals via orbiting satellites," says industry observer Gene Bylinsky. "Gallium arsenide chips will be absolutely essential to direct broadcast satellites that beam TV programs to small rooftop antennas . . . they will also bring down the price of cellular car telephones, and they're at the heart of a collision-avoidance system now being developed for passenger cars."

Richard L. Randolph, president of Microgravity Research Associates, is convinced that the best supercomputers of tomorrow will perform billions of computations a second—roughly 10,000 times the computational rate of today's typical silicon-based machines. His company, which has been seeking venture capital from a number of sources, hopes to raise millions of dollars to beat the Japanese and the Europeans to a space-age bonanza: flaw-free gallium arsenide materials made in space.

His experts are planning to use the "epitaxy" method of growing large crystals with virtually no flaws. In the epitaxy method, an electrical current is passed through the molten material to grow the solid crystal in thin, flat layers. Microgravity Research has already signed binding agreements with Dr. Harry C. Gates of MIT, who holds patents on the process they plan to use.

The prospect of charging premium prices for space-made gallium arsenide crystals is very real. Today's technicians produce crude versions in large, heavy furnaces at temperatures of about 2,200 degrees Fahrenheit. Most are riddled with impurities and imperfections, but nevertheless they sell for $100,000 a pound. Flaw-free versions made in space should be considerably more valuable.

In April 1983, Microgravity Research Associates signed a Joint Endeavor Agreement with NASA for seven free rides for its crystal-growing apparatus aboard the space shuttle. On each mission the apparatus will produce 55 to 66 pounds of ultrapure gallium arsenide crystals. So far the company has raised more than $1.5 million from limited R&D partnerships, but additional funds are also needed.

PROTOTYPE CENTERS for the COMMERCIAL DEVELOPMENT of SPACE

If you or someone else in your organization has a clever idea for commercial development in space, NASA seed money may be available to help you get your enterprise started. In response to the wishes of President Reagan, NASA's experts are encouraging creative research by awarding contracts to "prototype centers" interested in space industrialization. So far, about a dozen of them have been capitalized to the tune of $500,000 to $1 million apiece for each of the next five years. Of course, the centers are expected, as part of the agreement, to raise money in similar amounts on their own.

"We have initiated the centers to stimulate further research and development in the space environment and to stimulate and encourage investment by individuals," says Jannelle Brown, a financial specialist at NASA's Office of Commercial Programs in Washington, D.C. The prototype centers will not pay for transportation on the shuttle, but their payloads will probably be subsidized, at least to some extent.

The University of Alabama in Birmingham, in conjunction with McDonnell Douglas, has already grown lysozyme crystals in space as a part of its participation in the program. Since the Birmingham center was formed in 1985, its researchers have been specializing in macromolecular crystallography. Corporate affiliates on this pioneering project include the Merck Institute for Therapeutic Research, Upjohn Co., Smith Kline, and the Schering Corporation.

Under a different agreement, researchers at Battelle Columbus Laboratories are concentrating on four generic materials processing projects: (1) metals and alloys, (2) glass and ceramics, (3) polymers and electronics, and (4) optical materials. Battelle's affiliates include Eastman Kodak, General Electric, Lockheed, Rockwell International, Case Western Reserve University, and Clarkson College.

The University of Alabama in Huntsville (in an effort separate from that of the Birmingham campus) is focusing on materials processing research with emphasis on innovative applications involving physical chemistry, material transport, and their interactions. Corporate affiliates include Boeing, John Deere, GTE, Teledyne Brown, and Union Carbide.

A number of other companies, including the Astronautics Corporation of America, Delco, Sundstrand, and the Snap-On Tools Corporation, have formed a group to study automation and robotics for space-based applications. Educational affiliates include Marquette University, the University of Milwaukee School of Engineering, and the University of Wisconsin.

Microgravity Research has a practical way of making a valuable product, patents to project it, and agreements with NASA for free transportation into space. However, company officials face a few serious problems, including an unusually long payout interval for any investment money they manage to raise. Consequently, according to their prospectus, they are seeking investment support primarily from "forward-looking individuals who have confidence in the opportunities offered by space, who believe in the business future of space-crystal growth, and are willing to wait an unusually long time for return on their investments." Fortunately, according to company founder Russell Ramsland, "such individuals can be found."

MAKING IRON and STEEL in SPACE-BASED FACTORIES

Offhand, tractor maker John Deere would not appear to be a likely outfit to conduct commercially oriented space research. But, in fact, John Deere's scientists and engineers are hoping to outdistance the competition by conducting spaceborne experiments to develop new insights into metallurgical science. Specifically, they are planning to study cooling and solidification of molten iron in zero g to perfect new techniques for improving foundry operations.

With $4 billion in annual revenues, Deere is our country's largest farm implement maker. Its foundries produce 600 million pounds of cast iron annually, a total second only to the foundries operated by the U.S. auto industry. Even small gains in efficiency or tiny improvements in the materials' strength could translate into enormous reductions in capital investments.

Interest in spaceborne research was suddenly aroused at John Deere when a staff scientist sawed some metallic meteorites in half for Chicago's Field Museum. Inside he discovered graphite nodules similar to the ones company metallurgists had puzzled over in their nodular iron products. Apparently, the graphite nodules had formed when the meteorite solidified in space. This suggested that direct observations of cooling and solidification in space might help researchers understand the complicated processes that occur when metal crystallizes. Armed with this information back on earth, they might be able to reduce costs, enhance production efficiencies, or improve the quality of the millions of tons of metals flowing from company foundries.

Cast iron has a long history stretching back into distant antiquity, but, nevertheless, some metallurgists believe it may be among the most complex alloys in existence. In the past few years, John Deere's scientists have conducted dozens of zero-g experiments in F-104 airplanes, but, with less than a minute of solidification time per test, they have been unable to learn much of anything significant. Carbon flotation in their nodular iron products is one intriguing area for basic research. When nodular iron cools, the carbon is pushed upward in the molten metal. Consequently, the top layers are weaker than the ones below.

"Anything that could be done to eliminate this effect would be highly desirable," said one John Deere researcher, who also noted that the simpler gravity-free environment of space may provide useful clues on detrimental effects of buoyancy and convection. Bethlehem Steel, which shares some of the same concerns, is working with John Deere on this fundamental research.

COMBUSTION PROCESSES and HIGH-STRENGTH TURBINE BLADES

Scientists at General Motors are watching John Deere's effort with keen interest, but they are even more interested in the effects of microgravity on thin-film coatings and combustion physics. One company plan calls for a series of studies in space on how coatings adhere to surfaces. Another calls for the burning of single isolated drops of fuel to gain baseline data on the behavior of combustion physics in zero g.

Researchers at Grumman Aerospace in Bethpage, New York, are studying the magnetization properties of manganese/bismuth alloys to see if they can improve the material's resistance to demagnetization using spaceborne fabrication techniques. Smaller, lighter, more powerful electric motors could be one result. Small motors are surprisingly important to our everyday lives. One study indicated that the average American household contains thirty fractional-horsepower motors. A more compact design would give us lighter power tools, for instance, and tools that last longer between replacements.

Other companies have been looking at the possibility of fabricating stronger, more temperature-resistant turbine blades. The blades would be grown in space as single crystals with the alignment of the crystal structure arranged so that the strongest axis would be in the direction of greatest need. Success would be especially beneficial to military aircraft, which often operate near the limits of their structural integrity. One study predicted that 15 percent fuel savings could result from space-made turbine blades. Aircraft performance could also be enhanced and maintenance costs reduced.

LAYING an EGG in SPACE

KFC, parent company of Kentucky Fried Chicken, is underwriting a different kind of orbital experiment in hopes of getting "more cluck for the buck." The concept was masterminded by John C. Vellinger, a twenty-year-old mechanical engineering student from Purdue University. His device, which won a competition with NASA when he was a student in high school, consists of a special incubator that will contain thirty-two fertilized eggs insulated against the shock of blastoff. Its purpose is to determine how weightlessness affects embryos during the development process.

TURBINE BLADES, MADE IN SPACE

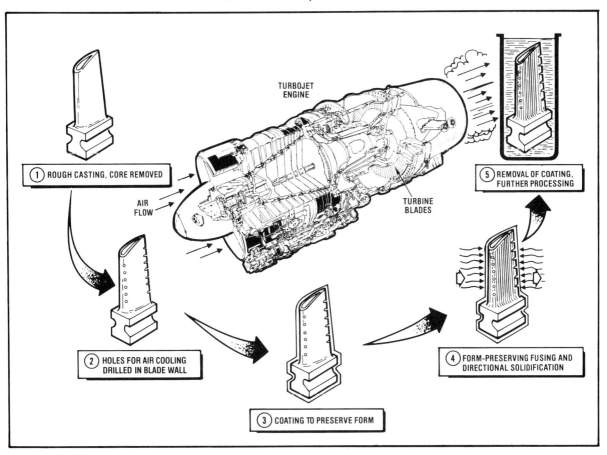

TURBOJET
ENGINE

AIR
FLOW

TURBINE
BLADES

① ROUGH CASTING, CORE REMOVED

② HOLES FOR AIR COOLING
DRILLED IN BLADE WALL

③ COATING TO PRESERVE FORM

④ FORM-PRESERVING FUSING AND
DIRECTIONAL SOLIDIFICATION

⑤ REMOVAL OF COATING,
FURTHER PROCESSING

The microgravity of space permits scientists to use "directional solidification," in which the individual crystals in certain metals can be aligned to provide increased strength in a particular direction. Turbine blades constructed in this way could resist far higher temperatures to increase the efficiency of jet engines and thermal powerplants. Expenses for routine maintenance and major overhauls would also be reduced.

"Such information will be vital if animals are ever to be bred in space," conjectures *Business Week*'s Otis Port, "or if coed space crews spend years traveling to distant planets."

CREATING NEW ALLOYS and UNIQUE OPTICAL GLASSES

Certain kinds of alloys and glasses cannot be made on earth because when they are mixed as liquids, buoyancy separates their constituent molecules. However, scientists can make those same substances with ease in the gravity-free environment of space. Shuttle experiments with zinc-lead, zinc-aluminum, and silver-germanium have already demonstrated that exotic alloys can be made successfully in space, and that they are much stronger than their counterparts produced on earth.

Westinghouse in Baltimore, Maryland, and Union Carbide of Oak Ridge, Tennessee, are looking into the possibility of making high-quality optical glasses aboard the shuttle. The lack of buoyancy there will allow molten glasses of various densities to be combined that will not combine on earth. Someday you may be wearing contact lenses made in space. With variable optical density (ability to bend light), more comfortable contouring of the lenses may be possible. Space processing may also permit finer, more consistent control in the porosity of the material for an improved flow of oxygen to the eyes, which become tired and irritated when lenses keep them from absorbing oxygen from the air.

With the advent of optical fibers capable of carrying enormous amounts of information, we are emerging from the age of electronics into the age of light. Last year American researchers spent at least $1 billion for research and development on new optical concepts. Unfortunately, their Japanese counterparts spent three times as much. "The optics boom has just started to explode," says Robert Spinrad, director of systems technology at Xerox. "Optics in the twenty-first century will be what electronics represents in the twentieth century." Space technology will not dominate this new revolution, but glasses made in earth orbit will surely play an expanding role.

Space-made glasses, for instance, may give us improved fiber-optics materials, and large-aperture lenses for low-light-level applications such as night-vision scopes for police helicopters. Improved camera lenses with less weight and wider field of view will also likely result, as will high-efficiency lenses and windows for the transmission of ultraviolet light. Laser fusion for electrical power production may also benefit, because with space processing, we may be able to make much more powerful glass lasers.

Most Americans seem hardly aware of the switch to optical computing that may soon take place. But nevertheless, the change will have far-reaching impacts on their lives. As Jeff Hecht of *High Technology* puts it: "The potential is enormous. Computers performing millions of billions of operations each second, a thousand times faster than today's supercomputers. Machines that mimic functions of the human brain. All-optical communications networks that relay signals at high speeds around the world without the electronic switches needed in today's fiber optic systems . . . what unites these visions is a vaguely defined concept called optical computing."

Increased processing speed is one strong motivation for making the switch to light-powered computing. The fastest available electronic transistors require several picoseconds (trillionths of a second) to switch between on and off or vice versa. Light beams, however, have been switched as rapidly as 0.008 picoseconds—or about 1,000 times more quickly. In addition, optical computing has other potential advantages, such as the ability to process several signals traveling simultaneously through the same transmission circuit, and vastly improved capabilities for interconnections using three-dimensional arrays of light beams.

MAKING TOMORROW'S MEDICINES in SPACE

Valuable drugs, drugs that can alleviate an amazing variety of deadly or debilitating diseases, are, unfortunately, commingled with other substances in the human kidney, the human pancreas, and the other hormone-producing organs of the human body. These drugs hold promise in the treatment of diabetes, dwarfism, hemophilia, heart disease, anemia, and a number of other medical conditions. For many years, pharmaceutical researchers have been frustrated in their attempts to gain access to these valuable substances, so powerful and so tantalizingly close. They know the substances are there. They have been able to separate some of them in experimental quantities for testing in animals and sick people, but they have not been able to produce them in sufficient quantities to treat large numbers of patients.

Fortunately, in the microgravity of space, scientists are devising ways to separate these drugs from the other substances with which they are intermingled. Researchers at the Astronautics Division of McDonnell Douglas (Huntington Beach, California) are using the microgravity of space to produce one of them, erythropeiotin, a hormone that stimulates red-blood-cell production in the human body. Erythropeiotin has the potential to prolong and improve the lives of millions of people suffering from anemia, certain forms of kidney disease, and other medical conditions that affect red-blood-cell production. Patients facing elective surgery will also be able to take erythropeiotin in advance of hospitalization to stimulate their bodies to produce extra red blood cells, thus minimizing or eliminating the need for transfusions during surgery. This could minimize allergic reactions, reduce hepatitis, and cut down on the spread of AIDS.

Small quantities of erythropeiotin made in earth-based laboratories are available now. But they are not widely prescribed because the drug is expensive, and because current production methods cannot filter out by-products harmful to humans. Marketing experts at McDonnell Douglas see a $1 billion yearly market for the new drug by the early 1990s. They are also convinced that their orbiting

PROMISING PHARMACEUTICAL PRODUCTS
LIKELY to BE MADE in SPACE*

PHARMACEUTICAL PRODUCT	PURPOSE	POTENTIAL ANNUAL U.S. PATIENTS
Beta cells	Provides potential single-injection cure for diabetes in young patients	3.2 million
Interferon	Induces immunity from virus infections (also a potential cancer treatment)	20 million
Epidermal growth factor	Helps in the treatment of burns and wounds	1.1 million
Growth hormone	Stimulates bone growth in young people	0.85 million
Antitrypsin products	Limits progression of emphysema (also enhances effectiveness of cancer chemotherapy)	0.5 million
Antihemophiliac products	Eliminates immunological reactions in hemophiliacs	0.5 million

*Nearly fifty other promising pharmaceuticals have been identified to date by Booz Allen & Hamilton's experts and others.

facilities can produce at least ten other valuable pharmaceuticals by the end of the next decade.

The production technique used, continuous-flow electrophoresis, separates a desirable biological substance from its surrounding medium by dribbling a fluid between two closely spaced panes of glass held within a powerful electric field. The various cells immersed within the liquid concoction are separated into parallel streams depending upon their individual electrical charges and their molecular weights.

Continuous-flow electrophoresis works on earth to some extent, but convection currents in the liquid created by gravity overpower the cell movements, thus severely limiting production efficiencies. In zero g, convection currents are eliminated. Experiments aboard the shuttle have demonstrated that the McDonnell Douglas apparatus can produce as much as 700 times more separated material than comparable units on the ground. Fourfold to fivefold increases in purity have also been observed.

A small demonstration model of the electrophoresis unit has already been operated on the shuttle by corporate payload specialist Charles D. Walker, who suc-

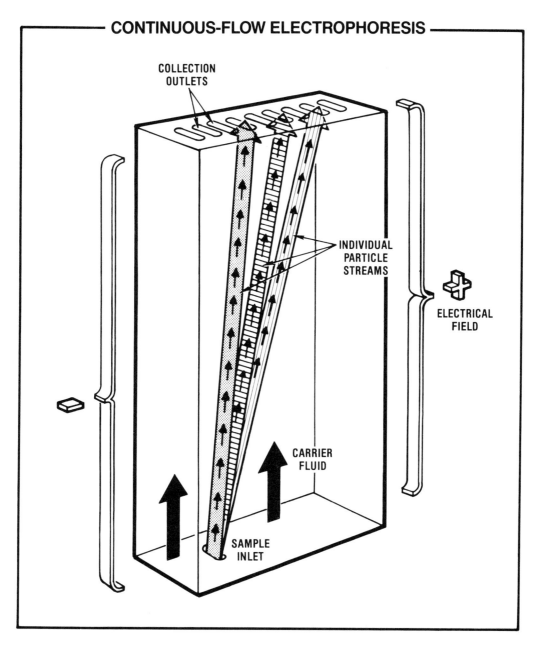

CONTINUOUS-FLOW ELECTROPHORESIS

COLLECTION OUTLETS

INDIVIDUAL PARTICLE STREAMS

ELECTRICAL FIELD

CARRIER FLUID

SAMPLE INLET

A small continuous-flow electrophoresis unit has been operated in the shuttle middeck by payload specialist Charles D. Walker and his colleagues at McDonnell Douglas to produce small quantities of valuable drugs in the weightlessness of space. A strong electric field perpendicular to the thin fluid sheet causes the various components in the liquid to follow separate trajectories in accordance with their electrical charges and their molecular weights. The process works on earth, but at a much lower efficiency, because gravity creates convection currents that tend to remix the components being separated.

cessfully produced test quantities of several drugs. When the shuttle is available to fly again, McDonnell Douglas specialists will install a larger 5,000-pound unit in the cargo bay to produce erythropeiotin at twenty-four times the rate achieved by their smaller experimental device. With larger quantities, they are hoping to obtain marketing approval from the Food and Drug Administration. Since a similar ground-made version of the drug is already available for testing, they are aiming for a two-year approval cycle for the version to be made in space.

Company officials at McDonnell Douglas were originally planning to develop their own free-flying pharmaceutical factory, but in the meantime, researchers from their consulting firm, Condon (San Francisco, California), have found a way to enhance production using genetic-engineering techniques. Thus the extra expense of a separate factory turns out to be unnecessary because ample quantities can now be obtained from the shuttle flights. Until 1986, the Ortho Pharmaceuticals Division of Johnson & Johnson was teamed with McDonnell Douglas. But company officials became convinced that they and their new partner, Amgen, a bioengineering firm, can make an adequate, if impure, version on the ground, and they withdrew from the agreement. Amgen also offered Johnson & Johnson two other genetically engineered drugs as part of the deal.

Experts at McDonnell Douglas are convinced they can make erythropeiotin cheaper in space and that the finished product will have much lower levels of contamination from other biological substances. Since some users will need to inject it on a regular, sustained basis, purity can be an important consideration.

The 5,000-pound electrophoresis unit can be used in separating various biological materials—cells, enzymes, hormones, and other proteins—in sufficient quantities and purities to enable more efficient treatment of many diseases. "The combination of genetic engineering and electrophoresis, in our minds, provides the ingredients of being able to make just about any natural hormone or enzyme that you can identify . . . in almost 100 percent pure fashion," says program manager James Rose. Already today in space biological cells from the human pancreas, kidney, and pituitary glands have been successfully separated.

McDonnell Douglas officials have encountered some problems in trying to find suitable American partners to join them in their quest to develop and market space-made pharmaceuticals. They would prefer an American company for domestic marketing, but this is not absolutely necessary. "If we cannot get a U.S. company to be our marketing partner, we will get a foreign company with a U.S. subsidiary," says John F. Yardley, president of McDonnell Douglas Astronautics. Several French and Japanese companies are interested in such an agreement and in developing space-made pharmaceuticals of their own.

SPACE-AGE ELECTROPHORESIS SEPARATION

Separating and purifying chemical substances has always been one of the keys for improving the quality of human life. Early man extracted metals from ores, for instance, wheat from chaff, and medicines from plants. Coke production, oil refining, water purification, and aluminum smelting all depend upon effective separation techniques. Today's most challenging separation problems are in the field of medical diagnostics and in the production of more effective pharmaceuticals.

Electrophoresis separation, in which electrical forces pull the constituent compounds out of a liquid solution, was first observed in crude form in 1807 by the Russian physicist F. F. Rouss, but it was not employed as a laboratory technique until 1937, when Arne Tiselius introduced a clever new approach. Tiselius first mixed the solution being analyzed with a pure solvent, then he subjected the resulting mix to an electric field as it sat on a flat, blotterlike material. The constituent molecules automatically migrated to different locations on the blotter in accordance with their molecular weights and their intrinsic electrical charges.

Unlike the Tiselius approach, continuous-flow electrophoresis separates the molecules in a fluid into useful streams of chemicals. Absorbent material is not used in continuous-flow electrophoresis. Instead, the fluid is sandwiched between two panes of glass held in an electrical field. The constituent molecules break into separate streams which can be collected in their purified state. This approach does not always work well in a 1-g environment because gravity causes convection currents within the liquid mix. In the microgravity of space it works much better. As a McDonnell Douglas advertisement in *Aerospace America* points out: "Electrophoresis is a slow, limited process on earth—but not in space. Operations on board the space shuttle show that, in a gravity-free environment, electrophoresis can separate precious substances 700 times more efficiently, and with much greater purity."

The 5,000-pound electrophoresis unit built by McDonnell Douglas will soon fly into space, where it will produce large quantities of erythropeiotin, a pharmaceutical that stimulates the production of red blood cells in the human body. Hundreds of thousands of patients suffering from anemia and kidney disease will benefit from the new technology. Other drugs can also be made using the same apparatus. Eventually, these may include a single-injection cure for some forms of diabetes, a drug to eliminate immunological reactions in hemophiliacs, and a juvenile growth hormone to treat dwarfism.

According to a study conducted by the financial experts at Booz Allen & Hamilton, over fifty medically important products have been identified for possible space manufacturing. They could provide us with dramatic improvements in the treatment of anemia, cancer, diabetes, emphysema, dwarfism, thrombosis, viral infections, and a number of other debilitating medical conditions. Promising examples include beta cells which are produced in the human pancreas. Large injections of beta cells could provide a single-injection cure for some forms of diabetes, thus alleviating the need for daily insulin injections and reducing the incidence of heart disease, blindness, and the early death often associated with chronic diabetes.

Another promising possibility is interferon, a powerful immunological agent manufactured by the human body to defend against a number of diseases, including viral infections and some forms of cancer. Space-based processing could provide us with large quantities of pure interferon at affordable prices for testing and treatment.

Battelle Laboratories of Columbus, Ohio, is interested in using zero gravity to grow collagen fibers for the repair and replacement of human connective tissues. Collagen is a fibrous material that occurs in the skin, bones, and tendons of vertebrates. It is used commercially in the production of gelatin and glue and in the tanning of leather. In humans its decomposition is connected with infirmities and aging.

Hewlett-Packard is another space-oriented company with the finances and the patience to bring medically important space-made products to market. In cooperation with the Genentech Corporation, Hewlett-Packard's researchers are exploring possibilities for performing genetic engineering in space.

Monoclonal antibody research experiments are being planned by the Lovelace Medical Foundation of Albuquerque, New Mexico. Their results may be directly applicable to the treatment of cancer and other deadly diseases such as malaria. In the monoclonal process, harmful cells, such as cancer cells, are fused with lymphocyte or other cells that produce antibodies to fight the disease. When cancer cells are used, for instance, the hybrid cells resulting from the fusion multiply like cancer cells, but they produce antibodies that can more easily identify and kill harmful cancer cells in the body.

A Lovelace production unit may eventually fly in the shuttle cargo bay, where it will make antibodies from the hybrid cells. Electrophoresis separation in space will provide researchers with much more of the useful drug—and in a purer state—than a similar unit located in the earth's strong gravitational field.

Materials-processing experts foresee significant business opportunities for the spaceborne processing of pharmaceuticals and biomedical substances despite today's shortage of flight opportunities following the grounding of the space shuttle. At the 1987 annual meeting of the American Astronautical Society, Louis Rancitelli, from Battelle Laboratories in Columbus, Ohio, said that his company is interested in using microgravity in space to process zeolite catalysts, a new kind of catalyst that could have applications ranging from biomedical implants to industrial processing. Zeolite can be grown in "long, fibrous, stringlike materials in space," said Rancitelli, "a substantial improvement over earth processing, where the material tends to truncate."

Space-made zeolite could be used as a "molecular sieve" for use in self-contained dialysis units, for instance, and for new drugs and superior glass for the electro-optics industry. In addition, according to Rancitelli, the "use of space-made zeolite could affect the entire economy of the automotive and petroleum industry."

At that same American Astronautical Society meeting, Myron Weinberg, a materials-processing specialist and aerospace consultant, predicted that emerging applications of new products made in space will be a dominant factor in the health-products market over the next twenty years. One of the important applications he foresees is "controlled-defect surface materials," which could, for example, be used to line a pumping assist device to prevent harmful blood clotting. The Jarvik artificial heart is a good candidate for the use of this technology.

Space processing may also allow the controlled growth of a single layer of cells to coat organs such as the human kidney, pancreas, or liver. A doctor could send a kidney into orbit, for instance, to be coated with cells that would help prevent its rejection when it is transplanted into a patient. Another product that could benefit from this technique is replacement material for human bone. The bone substitute would consist of a layered composite; the inner layers would provide strength and the outer layers would be designed to allow joining with other bones.

Weinberg also suggested that the controlled layering of cells possible in microgravity could be used to develop a treatment for AIDS. Single-cell antibodies that could destroy diseased cells could be attached to a special membrane, which would be returned to earth to treat AIDS victims.

Unfortunately, despite these optimistic projections of the economic potential of biological substances, one serious problem remains. If the United States continues to follow present trends, it will fall far behind Europe and Japan in space processing during the next decade. A NASA study conducted by astronaut and materials expert Bonnie Dunbar indicates that the United States is devoting less money and is providing itself with less access to space than are her major competitors, Europe and Japan. Both the Europeans and the Japanese are quietly purchasing dedicated shuttle and spacelab missions for spaceborne materials-processing experiments.

MOVING TOWARD the TWENTY-FIRST CENTURY

According to *Aerospace America*'s careful count, at least 350 private companies are poised to take advantage of the new potentialities of space. Industry giants including Eastman Kodak, Union Carbide, Bethlehem Steel are mingled with smaller outfits like Eagle Engineering and Microgravity Research. Broad-ranging participation is being encouraged because government officials see important opportunities to improve the country's balance of trade, morale, and productivity.

Unfortunately, researchers and political leaders in other countries, including Germany, France, Great Britain, Japan, and the Soviet Union, are just as perceptive as those in the United States. Soviet experts, in particular, are eyeing the possibilities for international trade via manufacturing in space. Compared with about a hundred American experiments in materials processing, scientists in the Soviet Union have performed more than 1,600 experiments during an impressive 100,000 man-hours in earth orbit.

In 1986 at the 37th Congress of the International Astronautical Federation in Innsbruck, Austria, Soviet representatives engaged in some of the most open discussions of Soviet space technology ever heard in a public forum. Speaking before an audience of 1,000 delegates from all over the world, the chief spokesman on space processing, Liya Regal, an outgoing woman in her forties, painted an impressive picture of Soviet accomplishments.

In blunt, clear English she told Western researchers about her country's crystal-growing experiments in space. She was also proud of the fact that Soviet materials and biological-processing experiments have produced specimens with much better properties than comparable earthbound experiments. Their main goal of this stage is to design onboard facilities for material production in space for manned and unmanned space stations. This should be our goal too. For if it is not, we will inevitably trail competing countries that are not at all myopic when it comes to the enormous potential of space.

YOUR PARTICIPATION in SPACE INDUSTRIALIZATION

The easiest way for you to participate in the coming era in space industrialization will probably be to develop a new product or process that can benefit from the microgravity of space. How about a new technique for making jewelry aboard the space shuttle? Any measurable gain in quality, brightness, or luster would likely be a winner, because many people would enjoy owning a souvenir from space. The Soviets and the Japanese are becoming specialists in growing whisper-thin layers of diamond on other flat surfaces. Eventually, this new technology may allow them to produce carving knives and razor blades that virtually never show signs of wear. Are there any advantages to be gained by transferring this process into space?

How about producing contact lenses in orbit with variable optical densities or special porous structures? How about motion-picture films showing the intriguing characteristics of weightlessness for use in teaching high school students physics and chemistry? Do you have any ideas on promising new uses for high-quality crystals? Optical lenses? Or high-strength permanent magnets?

If you let your imagination soar, you may be able to test your concepts in space at surprisingly affordable rates. For as little as $3,000, NASA will carry your 50-pound experimental payload into orbit. Dozens of these "Getaway Specials" have already been transported onboard the shuttle. Many have carried experimental modules equipped to study physical processes in the microgravity of space. Chapter 8 provides further information and describes specific examples. In the meantime, before you get that far, take an occasional break and keep thinking about new and interesting possibilities for manufacturing in space. You may be able to help this and future generations have a better life, and, if you are skillful enough, you may enhance your own financial status too.

4

COMMUNICATION SATELLITES

Nearly two million American families have purchased backyard dish antennas capable of picking up television programs from space. Some simple models are selling for as little as $1,000 each. Many buyers live in rugged terrain where television reception by other media is poor or nonexistent, but one-fourth of the new space-age antennas have been installed in urban areas already served by commercial cable television. Until recently, their owners enjoyed cost-free admission to a wonderland of sports, news, and entertainment. "For an investment averaging about $3,000, dish owners gained access to 75 to 100 channels of satellite programs at no charge," observed *Popular Science* magazine, "including shuttle launches, children's shows, most major sports events, and about 650 movies a month."

Unhappily, in January 1986, two of the most coveted movie channels, Showtime and Home Box Office, began scrambling their programs in response to complaints from cable TV operators who were attempting to market the same signals available free to anyone with a satellite dish. Suddenly dish sales collapsed, until howls of protest caused Congress to provide assured access to cable transmissions—at affordable, if more than neglible, fees. Many dealers folded before the market rebounded to 350,000 dishes per year, but now that the crisis has passed, industry sources are confidently predicting much stronger sales as satellite designers shift from C-band transmissions (4 to 8 billion cycles per second) to the more efficient Ku-band (12 to 18 billion cycles per second).

These higher-frequency transmissions will create a sensation in the industry as consumers begin to understand that they can be picked up with antennas that are smaller, cheaper, and less susceptible to terrestrial interference than conventional transmissions at lower frequencies. In the next few years, unit prices could drop

50

SATELLITE DISHES SPROUT AROUND THE LANDSCAPE

Backyard dish antennas capable of picking up television programs from space have been purchased by about two million of America's families. As higher-frequency Ku-band transmissions become increasingly popular, the size and cost of tomorrow's antennas will shrink, thus opening up important new markets for renewed industry growth.

below $500, and as they do millions of antennas will begin to sprout like wild mushrooms across the American landscape. Some of the newer ones may measure only 2 or 3 feet across, and eventually even smaller versions will probably be available.

THE GROWING MARKET for TODAY'S COMMUNICATION SATELLITES

Many space industrialization projects are still perched on the drawing boards, but communication satellites have already sparked a mature, $3-billion-a-year industry that is flourishing in today's competitive marketplace. Practical, everyday applications include telephone and television relay, electronic teleconferencing, computer networking, and direct-broadcast TV.

Communications 21, an industry consulting firm in Redondo Beach, California, predicts healthy growth over the next few years as the hardware needed to pick up satellite signals become smaller and more affordable and as enthusiastic users spread the word on the personal benefits of the new technology. A Communications 21 report entitled "World Satellite System Scorecard and Forecast" quantifies capital requirements in the industry: "In the last two decades 82 communication satellites have been launched at a total cost of $3.3 billion," the report estimates in strangely unemotional terms. "Capital requirements for construction and launch of 183 satellites between 1985 and 1990 may be as high as $9 billion. By the year 2000 a total of 418 communication satellites may be launched at a cost of $25 billion."

Each of today's satellites carries as many as two dozen "transponders," electronic devices that receive packets of information from earth stations and then amplify them for retransmission back to earth. A modern transponder can handle 500 to 1,000 simultaneous telephone conversations or a single channel of color TV.

In 1975 about 175 transponders were in use aboard commercial communication satellites. Today there are slightly less than 1,000, and by the beginning of the next century, at least 3,000 transponders will be relaying messages through larger, more sophisticated communication satellites. Thus, in only a quarter century, our space-based communication capabilities will have expanded by a factor of seventeen, while requiring fresh infusions of capital of $25 billion from both private individuals and well-heeled institutional investors.

Communication satellites are, in essence, high-altitude relay stations in the sky. They pick up signals from earth and then send them back on a different frequency. These modern electronic marvels handle three different kinds of information:

1. Sounds (music and spoken words)
2. Television pictures
3. Computer data

Communication satellites are affecting ordinary people in surprisingly varied ways. Listen to Mozart on your FM radio or watch *The Paper Chase* on cable TV and you may be witnessing a real-time broadcast relayed through space. You probably already knew about that. But did you know that if you walk into a Safeway, J. C. Penney's, or Holiday Inn, you are just about as likely to encounter space-based communications? Listen to classical music on your car radio and chances are it got to you by communication satellite. Most international telephone calls also follow similar routes through space.

This chapter discusses the impact of some of these budding technological miracles. It also suggests a few ways in which you may participate for fun and profit. We

TODAY'S GROWING INVESTMENTS IN COMMUNICATION SATELLITES

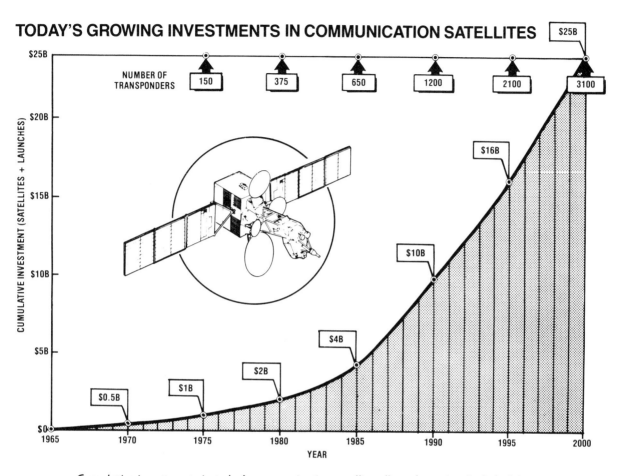

Cumulative investments in today's communication satellites (launch services included) have grown to about $7.5 billion, with current expenditures running at about $1.2 billion each year. According to figures published by Communications 21, an industry consulting firm, the cumulative total will probably approach $25 billion within twelve years. In that same twelve-year interval, the number of spaceborne transponders will triple to 3,000 to provide users with the capacity equivalent of 3,000 channels of TV or nearly two million simultaneous telephone conversations relayed through space.

start with a new programming technique for stereo radio that successfully marries satellites with computers to make nearly everyone in radioland a happy winner.

STEREO MUSIC in the AGE of SPACE

In recent years, terrestrial telephone lines capable of carrying high-quality audio signals have become considerably more costly. The costs for large music libraries and talented announcers with deep booming voices have also spurted upward. These trends, and the ready availability of compact disks, have driven some of our smaller, more specialized radio stations to the brink of insolvency. Fortunately, communication satellites are coming to the rescue.

The Beethoven Satellite Network is a prime example of how satellites are helping solve these tricky economic problems—while providing enjoyment for millions of people in all fifty states. Every night the Beethoven Network offers its listeners classical music in all four time zones from midnight to daybreak. WFMI originates the programs, which feature superb announcers who select quality music from a library of more than 40,000 classical recordings. The programs are sent by satellite in real time to all the stations in the network. "It's a cost-effective way to reach a loyal and responsive audience," explains David Levin, director of program development for the Beethoven Network. Specialized all-night programming becomes economically attractive when production costs can be spread over a dozen small stations even if they have only a few hundred listeners each.

Some audio networks are combining satellite technology with computer controls to add a "local" flavor to their programs, which are being beamed to a total of 600 radio stations throughout the United States, the Virgin Islands, Bermuda, and the West Indies. Most of the programs originate from a centrally located broadcast facility, but at each location, listeners are made to feel that the voices coming through their radios originate locally. Unless you have a broadcast background and excellent ears, you would probably never realize that the program is actually being broadcast nationwide.

Commercials, weather forecasts, and regional announcements are all prerecorded and transmitted to the station ahead of time. Then, during the broadcast, subaudible tones are transmitted to insert the desired "local" announcements. For instance, each disk jockey tapes twenty-five or thirty weather forecasts for insertion at the local level. Because there are only so many ways the weather can vary, this is enough to provide for hundreds of broadcast locations. The same announcers also record dozens of local spots on sports, health, family relations, and entertainment.

Satellite Music Network (SMN) of Dallas, Texas, is one of the most successful of the new stereo networks. It was formed in August 1981, with programming for three FM stations. Within two years, the initial funding of $1.5 million—which was furnished by the three original partners—had tripled to $4.5 million. When they realized that more capital was needed, they quickly convinced fifty-five investors from the Dallas–Fort Worth area to pump in another $2.5 million. Later, they raised additional money from a public offering of warrants and common stock. For a while their stock was hovering around $4 a share, but in 1985, it appreciated to $24 a share.

THE INTELSAT 5

Imagine a mechanism ten times as complicated as a family automobile designed to operate flawlessly in a punishing environment for seven full years—without servicing. Its name is Intelsat 5, fifth-generation descendant in a long line of distinguished machines. It is assembled from 118,000 separate parts, many of them flimsy and delicate, but redundancy and clever design combine to give it a long lifetime of useful service.

The Intelsat 5 is a modern communication satellite. Built by Ford's Western Development Laboratories, it weighs 2,100 pounds and measures 51.5 feet wingtip-to-wingtip (the height of a five-story building). It retails for more than $40 million or about $20,000 per pound—triple the current price of 24-karat gold. The Intelsat 5 is considerably more capable and cost-effective than any of its forerunners. It can handle 12,000 telephone conversations plus two channels of high-quality color TV.

Most communication satellites are in the shape of huge snare drums rolling through space. Like a toy gyroscope, such a satellite remains stable because of its high rate of spin. Mechanical or electronic devices are used to "despin" its antennas so they are always oriented toward the earth. The Intelsat 5, however, does not rotate as it moves around its orbit. Its orientation is maintained by spinning flywheels inside and tiny rockets on the outside that keep its communication antennas in an earth-seeking orientation. Automatic mechanisms guided by infrared sensors continuously swivel its winglike solar arrays toward the sun. This approach is trickier and more expensive than spin stabilization, but for large satellites it can provide more transmitter power per pound of spacecraft and more flexible communications. However, despite the apparent advantage of the Intelsat 5's design and construction, its successor, the Intelsat 6, with three times more capacity, is using the simpler drumlike design.

Many other specialty markets in broadcast radio could be served by inexpensive stereo transmissions. John Hodge at Leaming Industries, a manufacturer of stereo equipment, estimates that some "90 percent of the homes in this country can get stereo broadcasts." Most listeners are surprisingly faithful to their favorite stations, but, in John's opinion, "they do not necessarily get the service they desire." Accordingly, he predicts "a huge increase in satellite-delivered 'niche' radio networks."

Possibilities for new, nationwide services are easy to conceptualize. For instance, America's 55 million single adults, who already have their own newspapers and magazines, could easily support their own radio network. So could the millions of individuals who work the graveyard shift and sleep when others are awake. There are no guarantees for success in such a venture, but entry into the market is relatively easy, and capital requirements are quite modest compared with other nationwide enterprises on a similar scale.

MOBILE COMMUNICATIONS

We live in the age of telecommunications in a prosperous country with one-third of the world's telephones, but 11 percent of our country still does not have reliable access to the kind of phone services most Americans take for granted. As *Aerospace America* put it, "half a million households have no telephone service because they live in areas too remote and of too low population density for terrestrial systems." Mobile communications based in space may eventually alleviate some of the isolation these individuals feel. Models for tomorrow's mobile communication systems are already in use in two forms: mobile cellular radio in urban areas, and the Inmarisat system, which links large commercial vessels on the high seas.

Between 1985 and 1987, Inmarisat has doubled its user base to 7,000 vessels, and, now that the system has achieved routine operation, Inmarisat antennas will probably be installed aboard 10,000 to 11,000 vessels by 1990. A special directorate in London manages the system, which includes two-way telephone services, telex, data exchange, facsimile, and "group-call" broadcasts to the ships in a particular fleet or those in a particular geographical region.

Inmarisat started with only three satellites, but its constellation now includes five more in low-altitude orbits. To date, the various participants have invested a total of $330 million in the satellites, the ground control equipment, and the user sets aboard the individual ships.

Cellular radio now serves about 500,000 users nationwide, and the experts are forecasting as many as two million installations by 1990. Moreover, according to *Aerospace America,* "decreasing prices could eventually attract 10 to 20 million subscribers." But despite large capital investments ranging up to $20,000 per channel, most experts contend that, at most, only about 10 percent of the land area in the United States will ever be served by cellular radio.

With the successful experience of Inmarisat and cellular radio available to guide them, a dozen private companies, including Hughes Communications, Omninet Skylink, and Globesat, are developing mobile communication systems to allow trucks, trains, and airplanes to communicate with one another using satellite relays. Ideally, a mobile system would be interoperable with Inmarisat, cellular radio, and today's conventional telephone systems. If you are using your cellular telephone and your car passes beyond its coverage area, the satellites would acquire your signal automatically, thereby providing uninterrupted service. Then, when you reach another metropolitan area, the satellite would "hand off" your call to the local transmitters.

Large mobile systems using satellite relays are projecting per-channel costs in the same ballpark as terrestrial cellular systems. Target markets include interstate trucking firms, railroads, emergency medical services, rental cars, and public utilities, as well as maritime and air industries.

Omninet's design calls for 30-foot antennas—the largest ever sent into space for commercial use. These huge, dish-shaped antennas will work like giant lenses, picking up extremely weak signals and concentrating them for retransmission to another terrestrial location. By making their satellite antennas larger, the system designers can use smaller antennas on the ground and simpler, less powerful transmitters. This design philosophy is called "complexity inversion." Demand for Omninet's system, which includes navigation services using signals from the Navstar navigation satellites, is projected at 2.4 million user sets. Of these, 2.1 million will include voice communication and 1.3 million will include navigation.

Omninet's basic service is slated to cost $27 a month plus 25 cents for each minute of usage. This low rate is possible because the designers are planning to employ new signal-modulation techniques to shrink channel widths to one-sixth their normal size. "Multibeam" feed horns will break the signals into a fan of pencil-thin beams for convenient frequency reuse. "It's . . . like cellular radio in space," explains company president Richard Anglin, Jr. Frequency reuse makes the service cheaper, and it reduces the need for heavily regulated transmission frequencies.

PLACING TELEPHONE CALLS from COMMERCIAL JETS

"Airfones," which have already been demonstrated aboard 150 commercial jetliners, are another form of mobile communication. Today's Airfone system, which is operated by Western Union, does not use satellites; the calls are relayed through one of forty stations on the ground. But company president John D. Goekan believes that future versions will take advantage of satellite relays for both domestic and international service. Goekan bristles with irritation when critics attack his Airfones as a "luxury" service for wealthy travelers and an unnecessary burden on the frequency spectrum. In his opinion, the Airfone system is no more of a luxury than conventional telephone service, and no more of a "frequency hog" than cellular radio.

Airfones are easy to use. When your plane reaches cruising altitude, you merely insert any major credit card into a slot to release the cordless phone from its cradle. You can then take the phone back to your seat for a chat with your family, friends, or your business colleagues. Its transmissions are picked up by a long

MAKING TELEPHONE CALLS ABOARD COMMERCIAL JETLINERS

Western Union's portable "Airfones" have gained enthusiastic acceptance from busy businessmen aboard commercial airline flights. A credit card releases the portable cordless phone so the user can take it back to his seat for privacy and comfort. Today's calls are being routed into our conventional telephone networks through forty ground-based relay stations. But in the future, Western Union officials are planning to simplify their system by relaying Airfone conversations through communication satellites.

antenna loop that runs overhead along the full length of the cabin. When you return the phone, your credit card is automatically released. Calls cost $7.50 for the first three minutes.

Eventually, a "pocket telephone," somewhat similar in concept to the Airfone, may be available to the general public for use anywhere on or near the earth. In 1977 a special space industrialization team at Rockwell International developed the plans for practical pocket telephones using large multibeam antennas in space. Each satellite was designed to serve 250,000 users at a per-call cost of about 20 cents—to and from any points in this hemisphere. Safety was one strong selling point. At any time, from any place, you could press a single button to summon an ambulance or the police.

SAFEWAY'S PROFITABLE USE of BROADCAST SATELLITES

Broadcast International of Salt Lake City, Utah, is using multichannel satellite broadcasts for a much more mundane purpose—and making a profit in the process. The company employs communication satellites to send twelve channels of music, shopping tips, and consumer information into 800 Safeway Stores coast to coast. Most of the time, the broadcasts, which are "programmed" by the In-Store Satellite Network, consist of high-quality music for soothing Safeway customers into a comfortable buying mood. But special information on food preparation is also included, together with announcements of current specials and paid advertisements—mostly from food-processing companies and their vendors.

"Consumer reaction has been positive," says Felicia Delcampo, spokeswoman for Safeway, "because there is a lot of emphasis on consumer information and helpful hints. The ads are quite helpful and we see the music as a bonus to our customers." But customer satisfaction is not the only goal of the broadcasts. Safeway also makes a profit from the sale of advertising time. Compared with other advertising media their charges are quite modest; 0.1 cent per listener compared with typical per-listener charges of 0.3 to 0.8 cent for conventional radio and television broadcasts. Moreover, the demographic mix is excellent, and the potential customers have a verifiable interest in the food products being marketed; otherwise they would not likely be strolling through a Safeway Store.

In-Store Satellite Network, which sends twelve sound channels into each store, takes pride in the flexibility and responsiveness of its programming. When one store manager, for instance, asked that the rock song "New Attitude" be broadcast into his facility twice a day, the network's programmers were delighted to accommodate his request. The extra channels also permit individual stores to sell ads to their own vendors. Some of the network's competitors distribute their in-store programs on audio tapes, but satellite distribution provides sharper and clearer music and the opportunity to make last-minute changes in the programming.

A SHORT HISTORY of COMMUNICATION SATELLITES

Active "repeaters" are the only popular kind of communication satellites in current use. But in the early days of space, electronic amplifiers were so bulky and unreliable most designers were convinced that passive "reflectors" with no failure-prone parts were a better approach. In 1960 the Echo balloon, a 100-foot plastic sphere coated with aluminum, was launched into space. At first it reflected 98 percent of the radio waves hitting its surface, but gradually it lost its inflating gases and became prune-faced and nonreflective. Four years later, a larger balloon replaced it. The new version was stressed to remain spherical even when its gases leaked out into space. The new Echo worked as advertised, but the days of passive communication satellites were strictly numbered, primarily due to headlong advances in solid-state electronics.

The first Telstar, an active "repeater," reached its low-altitude orbit in June 1962. A faceted sphere 3 feet in diameter, it weighed 175 pounds and used 3,600 solar cells to produce 15 watts of electrical power (about the same as a small Christmas-tree bulb). Most of its transmissions were picked up by giant 85-foot antennas such as those at Goonhilly Downs and Andover, Maine.

In 1964 the first true geosynchronous communication satellite, Syncom 3, was blasted into a 22,300-mile orbit. A 50-pound cylinder with five slender "cat whisker" antennas, it relayed "live" telecasts from the Tokyo Olympics.

The following year the "Early Bird" (Intelsat 1) became the world's first commercial communication satellite managed by the Intelsat consortium. A squat rotating cylinder weighing only 85 pounds, it could relay 240 two-way conversations or one low-quality television channel. Today Intelsat uses sixteen geosynchronous satellites to interlink 112 sovereign countries. The newest model, the 4,400-pound Intelsat 6, can handle 30,000 two-way telephone conversations plus two channels of high-quality color TV. Thus, in just twenty years, the communications capacity of a typical communications satellite had grown by a factor of 1,200 and more. Moreover, in that same interval, hardware costs per channel have dropped to 1 percent of their former value.

Ike Egan, president of Broadcast International, is pleased with the effectiveness of his company's satellite distribution system. The Payless Drugstore chain is another customer for his services, and he is negotiating with several other retail companies. Eventually, Egan and his colleagues are planning to use the same satellite links to handle the stores' data and for management-training courses on video.

The use of commercial-laden audio broadcasts via satellite into specialized facilities scattered across the country awaits much more broad-ranging applications. How about a network for bookstores, laundromats, or personal computer outlets? Come up with a new idea and you, too, can have your own space-based business.

SPACE-AGE DATA DISTRIBUTION

"Radio will increase," observes Harley Shuler of Western Union, "but data is really growing." As a matter of fact, one expert confidently predicts that data transmissions from space will require the equivalent of 400 transponders by 1992, although data of all types use only forty or fifty today. If these projected growth rates do materialize, data distribution will then occupy half as much satellite capacity as the total for all types of services today—including television, telephone, video conferencing, and today's smaller amount of data distribution!

Equatorial Communications Services, which concentrates on data transmission (much of it timely stock-market information), provides one of the most spectacular success stories among smaller companies in the field of business communications. Low-speed data transmission and inexpensive receive-only earth stations have brought in most of the profits at Equatorial Communications.

Even in 1982, its first year of operation, the company made impressive profits on revenues of $9.6 million. Consequently, in September 1983, the company's financial officers were able to tap the public equity market for $33.9 million in new capital for business expansion while they were shipping 1,000 2-foot earth stations per month.

Unfortunately, growth can sometimes create special problems for a young company, especially if projections for runaway growth fail to materialize. After several years of expanding profits, Equatorial Communications began to encounter serious sales and schedule problems. The company is well positioned in a growing market—the number of Ku-band stations installed is expected to expand perhaps a thousandfold by the early 1990s but its portion of that market has not been growing at the pace company officials once anticipated. To survive in a highly competitive field, they are having to slim down and restructure expenditures.

Other expanding data-distribution services include computer networking, electronic paging, and remote printing for advertising circulars, magazines, and newspapers. Each day, for instance, the entire *Wall Street Journal* is transmitted via satellite to eleven regional printing centers spotted around the country. Each center then prints and ships its own edition. The national newspaper *USA Today* is distributed countrywide in the same way, while it is still fresh and new. Unlike the rather staid *Wall Street Journal, USA Today* is famous for lively color pictures and shimmering graphics.

GLOBAL PAGING SERVICES

Global paging services could also benefit from the broad reach of orbiting satellites. *Aviation Week* estimates that 2.5 million paging devices are currently being used by doctors, lawyers, business executives, and parish priests. Moreover, on one of her daytime talk shows dealing with prostitution, Oprah Winfrey was shocked and amused to learn that high-priced call girls use paging services to cut their time in transit and thus increase profits.

Of course, today's paging systems are mostly confined to specific urban areas. Users who want broader coverage must subscribe to a number of services in several different locations. An attempt to cover a larger area is being masterminded by a small publicly traded company called the AT&E Corporation. Their engineers have found a way to turn a standard wristwatch into a paging device called the "Receptor."

The electronic devices enabling watches to receive messages can be furnished to watchmakers for as little as $6 each. Presumably, they will cooperate because this extra feature would help them sell additional watches. FM radio stations in urban areas throughout the world would broadcast simple "telegram" messages such as "Come home" or "Call 943-6815." An electronic display on the watch would flash the appropriate message.

Service charges of $5 monthly plus 25 cents for each message are envisioned by the system's creators. Whenever a subscriber is to visit another city, he would phone in his itinerary so his messages could be properly routed. So far, investors have put up $13 million in various private placements and public offerings.

Although this system might eventually make a profit, a simpler concept using satellite relays seems more likely to succeed. It merely awaits a clever inventor who can use low-data-rate transmissions through commercial communication satellites to handle the message distribution. Moreover, it is likely to be much more popular with users, who will not have to notify anyone if they decide to slip off to Honolulu or the South of France for a quick holiday.

ROUTING COLOR TELEVISION SHOWS THROUGH SPACE

Seventy percent of the business for today's domestic communication satellites comes from cable TV. But television images of other types are also beginning to make substantial contributions. For instance, Holiday Inns and several other major hotel chains receive their in-room movies from communication satellites. Airwave ministers, including Oral Roberts and Rex Humbard, are also heavy users of satellite transmissions.

Other big organizations are also beginning to make use of satellites. The American Bar Association and the American Law Institute, for example, have signed an agreement with COMSAT General Corporation for a continuing legal-education network. Initially, a single uplink at COMSAT headquarters in Washington, D.C., will relay signals through satellites to 10-foot antennas at twenty-five universities and law schools scattered around the country. But eventually the network, which will be shared with professionals in the medical and accounting fields, may involve as many as 2,000 installations at as many locations.

In a similar cooperative venture, J. C. Penney's department stores and the Private Satellite Network plan to install 6-foot earth stations in one hundred shopping malls nationwide. Among other things, the new network will distribute management training courses developed by the Penney chain. In addition, Penney's executives are planning to market "video-conferencing services using shopping-mall motion picture theaters . . . gourmet cooking classes, and family financial planning instruction." Upscale ideas like this will also help enhance the Penney image.

ELECTRONIC TELECONFERENCING

Video conferencing is becoming routine at several hundred organizations whose executives see it as a powerful way to keep widely dispersed forces informed of new policies, new product lines, and new developments that may affect the bottom line. Enthusiastic users include Digital Equipment Corporation, the Ford Motor Company, TRW, Merrill Lynch, and the U.S. Army—which in one study reported a saving of $1,700 for each student trained via satellite.

Most people tend to assume that conferencing by satellite will reduce travel, but studies have shown that heavy users of video conferencing end up traveling more than they did before they started using the service. Apparently, they make contacts electronically, then follow up with personal visits. They also change, but do not reduce, their travel patterns. As *Aviation Week*'s James Ott put it: "Heavy users tend to reserve teleconferencing for programs and projects, while increasing travel to scientific and technical meetings."

The major airlines are largely unconcerned about the effects of teleconferencing on business travel. In fact, they gladly use teleconferencing themselves, wherever it seems appropriate. Boeing Aircraft, for instance, speeded certification of the Boeing 757 by linking the engineers at its two locations at Seattle with satellite transmissions. Moreover, in response to requests from the airlines, Boeing is testing seat-area telecommunications services for the airplanes now being designed for use in the 1990s and beyond.

After conducting a survey of ninety-four U.S. corporations, Frost & Sullivan concluded that revenues from teleconferencing will grow nine and a half times between 1983 and 1992. Thus, in just nine years, revenues of $370 million would top $3.4 billion as prices drop and more companies discover the many practical and financial benefits of electronic video conferencing.

ORBITAL OVERCROWDING

"It has taken man thousands of years to crowd the earth," observed space writer Barry Rosenberg, "but the prime geosynchronous orbit above the equator, the only place where communication satellites can be located without the use of costly tracking stations, is filling up quickly."

Today there are only about a dozen dozen satellites hovering at the geosynchronous altitude, a circular arc 165,000 miles long. Therefore, it may seem ludicrous that today's mission planners would be worrying about the population explosion at geosync. On the average the satellites are nearly 1,200 miles apart. But, in fact, if we don't develop effective preventive measures, we will soon be faced with serious satellite overpopulation. Collisions are not the main difficulty, although as you will learn in chapter 10, they are a definite possibility. The biggest problem is that, when our satellites are too close together, messages directed toward one of them tend to spill over onto its neighbors in space.

So far, in the seemingly vast arena of space, "squatter's rights" have usually prevailed. This means that when a satellite has been launched into orbit, it preempts a specific location and certain specific transmission frequencies, which are then unavailable to future users—until the satellite dies. Naturally, shrill cries of protest originate from Third World countries incapable of launching satellites of their own, especially if their territory is directly under the satellite in question.

These arguments are voiced every few years at major frequency-allocation conferences. In 1979 in Geneva, Switzerland, for instance, Third World representatives insisted that the available orbital slots and transmission frequencies should be apportioned administratively once and for all. Delegates from the United States and Western Europe contended that premature allocations would waste resources and create barriers to innovative research. Some compromises have been achieved, but by and large, Third World attitudes toward administrative apportionment are gaining favor with regulatory bodies as their representatives become better organized and more technically attuned to the issues involved.

Fortunately, there are technical ways to alleviate orbital overcrowding. Higher-frequency transmissions are helpful to some extent, because a ground antenna of a given size sends out a smaller, more directional beam if it is transmitting at a higher frequency. Early communication satellites could be positioned along the geosynchronous arc no closer than 3 to 4 degrees, because they operated at relatively low frequencies. More recently, however, these heavily used frequencies were doubled, and aerospace engineers are eagerly exploring the feasibility of doubling them once again. This will require expensive new equipment—in space and on the ground—but it will allow as many as 360 new geosynchronous satellites to be positioned as close as 1 degree apart. Unfortunately, these higher-frequency transmissions, whose waves are only about one-thirtieth of an inch long, are absorbed by falling raindrops. However, this problem, too, is yielding to technical solutions such as higher-power transmissions and multiple receiving sites at widely dispersed locations connected by fiber-optics cables.

Multibeam satellite antennas are another promising way to conserve available frequencies. A multibeam antenna transmits a fan of pencil-thin beams often so slender that by the time they reach the ground, their footprint covers an oval only a few dozen miles wide. As a result, the same frequencies can be used and reused in several different areas on earth.

Another conservation method, called bandwidth compression, is based on the fact that in most instances, there are only minor frame-to-frame changes in the individual pictures of a TV show. Consequently, efficiencies can be enhanced by transmitting only those small portions of the picture that have changed since the last frame rather than transmitting a complete new picture. This technique, which requires a great deal of computer processing, produces acceptable-quality pictures with the equivalent of sixty voice circuits instead of the 600 normally required.

When it flies again, the space shuttle may give us another way to reduce the overcrowding at geosync: orbital antenna farms. An orbital antenna farm is a large platform equipped with several antennas each operating on a different frequency and each devoted to a different service. Onboard switches would interlink the messages being received by the various antennas. The platform could be owned by a single large company, or smaller organizations could lease portions of it while sharing electrical power, thermal control, and other utility services. This same concept is employed in a large shopping mall where lighting, air conditioning, parking, etc. are shared, but each individual store is rented by a specific tenant.

GLOBESAT'S "MIGHTY MITE"

Still another way to control the population explosion at geosync is to position communication satellites—in large numbers—at completely different locations in space. Globesat, Inc., of Logan, Utah, has been pursuing this concept since 1984. Its designers are convinced that "the hardware and launch costs to establish a 50-satellite communications relay system in 250- to 400-nautical-mile orbits would be about 10 percent of the cost of one geosynchronous satellite." *

Small, multipurpose satellites will be packaged in 19-inch polyhedrons that can be launched by the shuttle in inexpensive "Getaway Special" canisters. In one concept, the orbiting satellites would tape-record computer data and retransmit it at the appropriate times from their low-altitude orbits to ground stations worldwide.

By concentrating on small satellites in a widely proliferated constellation, Globesat can take advantage of recent advances in electronics design. Moreover,

*A nautical mile is about 15 percent longer than a conventional statute mile.

SOME PROMISING CURES
FOR ORBITAL OVERCROWDING

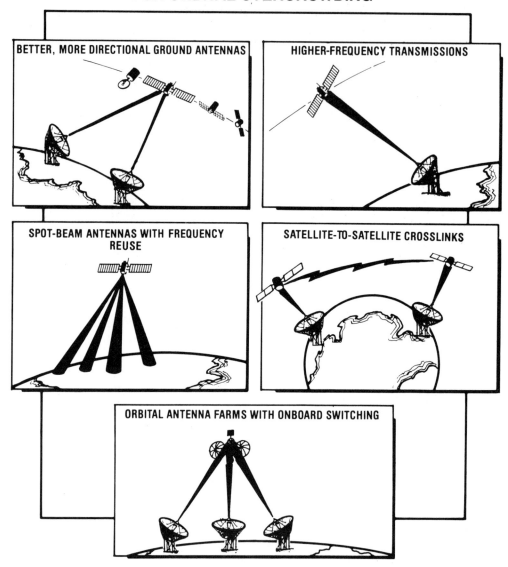

Scientific projections indicate that if something isn't done soon, our growing population of geosynchronous communication satellites will saturate the airwaves as early as 1995. Fortunately, various technical solutions—improved ground antennas and higher-frequency transmissions—will allow us to pack more satellites into the geosynchronous arc. In addition, multibeam antennas, orbital antenna farms, and satellite-to-satellite crosslinks will help increase the capacity of each satellite so fewer of them would be needed to handle the desired volume of communications.

by placing large numbers of cheap satellites in low-altitude orbits, the designers can use an inexpensive method of attitude control called gravity-gradient stabilization. Once a satellite is in orbit, it automatically extends a telescoping boom upward away from the earth. Gravity pulls harder on the lower half of the "elongated" satellite than it does on the upper half, thus forcing it to maintain a permanent vertical orientation as it swings around the earth. This clever technique is used for other low-altitude satellites such as the advanced Nova version of the Transit navigation satellite, but it is not practical at geosync because, at that higher altitude, the tug of gravity is forty times weaker and consequently the gravity gradient has virtually no effect on satellite dynamics.

Despite its small size, Globesat has already masterminded the launch of a satellite from the shuttle cargo bay. It was called Nusat, and both the Federal Aviation Administration and the Department of Defense used it to adjust the elevation of the radar beams they employ for air traffic control. The test results were inconclusive, but nevertheless, the Department of Defense contracted with a small company, Defense Systems, Inc., of Morgan, Virginia, to develop another small satellite, the Flomr, for monitoring remote military sensors.

Globesat's engineers had hoped to follow up Nusat and Flomr with a real-time communication system for mobile telephone users. In their request for frequency allocations with the FCC they proposed a constellation of fifty of their 110-pound satellites launched into 57-degree orbits to cover all latitudes between ±73 degrees. Coverage of the polar regions could be achieved by ten additional satellites in 90-degree orbits.

Each of the fifty Globesat communication satellites in the constellation could provide several hundred voice circuits with coverage available 98.8 percent of the time at a randomly selected location on earth. Costs for the proposed communication system are surprisingly modest. According to Globesat's Lawrence Megill, the fifty randomly distributed satellites "could be built and launched for an estimated $25 million." Thus, the total cost of all fifty of them would amount to only 10 percent of the cost of one advanced geosynchronous satellite.

In addition to communications, Globesat envisions other uses for their "mighty mite," and they are also open to outside suggestions. In the meantime, company officials are providing services to several customers for the design and integration of "Getaway Specials" to ride aboard the space shuttle. They are also working on the design of a canister-borne project for a major aerospace company investigating the effects of meltdown on substances in zero gravity.

COMPETITION from OPTICAL FIBERS

Intelsat, an international consortium of communications users, currently operates sixteen communication satellites carrying two-thirds of the world's transoceanic communications. With the recent addition of Rwanda and Mauritius, the membership of that global consortium has reached 112 sovereign nations. In addition, twenty-seven of them lease transponders aboard Intelsat satellites for domestic or regional communication services.

Growth rates have been truly impressive, but there is no cause for complacency among the managers at Intelsat or its major American partner, COMSAT. Fiber optics cables are the biggest threat to the preeminence of today's communication satellites. A fiber cable is composed of a bundle of hair-thin glass rods each of which is capable of carrying the same amount of information as a much thicker copper cable.

AT&T's new TAT-8 fiber-optics cable will have the capacity equivalent of 40,000 two-way conversations. Although this is only slightly more than the capacity of Intelsat's newest communication satellite, the Intelsat 6, the TAT-8 has a projected life of twenty-five years compared with only seven years for a typical communication satellite. Some experts maintain that, when fixed costs, operating costs, and useful life are all taken into account, voice circuits on the new transatlantic fiber-optics cable should cost only about half as much as Intelsat charges for similar services.

Much of the difference stems from the pricing philosophy adopted by Intelsat in its formative years. At that time, Intelsat officials decided to charge the same amount for all its circuits regardless of the volume of traffic being attracted on that particular route. This pricing philosophy has helped Third World countries gain economical access to satellites, by, in effect, subsidizing the services they receive. Unfortunately, it also allows Intelsat's competitors—which do not operate under the same self-imposed constraints—to skim off the most heavily used communication routes such as the North Atlantic. A more competitive pricing philosophy would rankle Third World customers, but it would also foster more equitable competition on all routes, popular and unpopular alike.

Another, less politically controversial response to cable competition is to develop smaller, cheaper satellite dishes in mass-production quantities to allow satellite transmissions to be delivered closer to the ultimate point of need. This minimizes the costs associated with the distribution of the signals, which can be more expensive than the original satellite relay.

Participants at a recent conference, Satellite and Fiber Optic Communications, in Vancouver, Canada, concluded that fiber can be a formidable competitor for heavily used trunk routes, but they maintained that satellite relays are clearly superior for point-to-multipoint applications such as television distribution. Satellite links are also more flexible. "Once you lay a cable, whether it's optical fiber or not, you can't move it very well," explains Robert B. Gamble of AT&T's Communication Services Group, "but you can easily put in another [satellite] earth station."

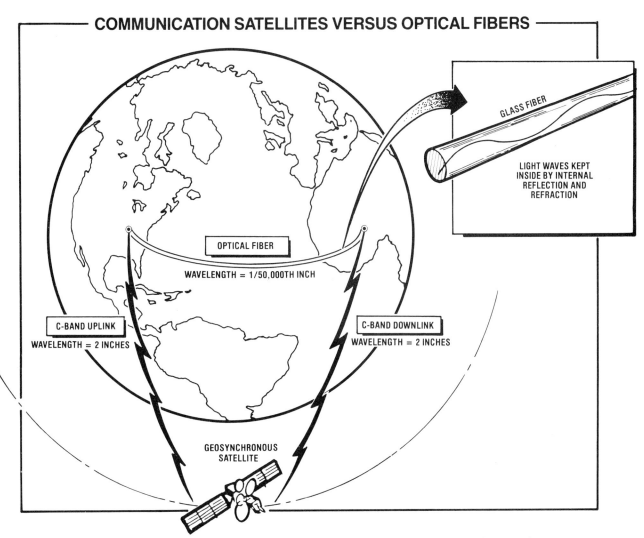

COMMUNICATION SATELLITES VERSUS OPTICAL FIBERS

GLASS FIBER

LIGHT WAVES KEPT
INSIDE BY INTERNAL
REFLECTION AND
REFRACTION

OPTICAL FIBER

WAVELENGTH = 1/50,000TH INCH

C-BAND UPLINK

WAVELENGTH = 2 INCHES

C-BAND DOWNLINK

WAVELENGTH = 2 INCHES

GEOSYNCHRONOUS
SATELLITE

Fiber-optics cables can be formidable competition to communication satellites, because their shorter optical wavelengths can carry huge amounts of information from one location to another at affordable rates. The optical wave stays near the center of the optical fiber because the hair-thin fiber is designed to bend and reflect light waves internally. Industry experts believe that fiber optics will likely capture about 12 percent of the communication market that would have otherwise gone to communication satellites.

Traffic estimates for the North Atlantic corridor show projected usage for satellite circuits slowing from a compound growth rate of 12 percent per year to 8 percent starting in 1990. Of course, most mature industries would be happy with an 8 percent rate of growth. At that pace, usage rates will triple over the next twelve years despite competition from optical fibers.

According to projections stitched together by the Communications Center in Clarksburgh, Maryland, "Fiber optics systems will take over about 12 percent of the satellite communications market." It is a noticeable loss, but, in an industry that has been growing at a breakneck pace, a gradual 12 percent loss is not a particularly serious threat. "That little wound heals very quickly," says company president Walter Morgan, a respected authority in telecommunications. In his view, the controversy is somewhat overblown: "Long-haul telephone services are at most risk in the competition," he says, "but other areas of space communications will quickly expand to fill the void."

Even that small portion of the satellite business will not be conceded without a fight. Providers of satellite communications are already finding ways to become more competitive with fiber. In November 1986, for instance, COMSAT officials announced a new method of station-keeping for communication satellites. By allowing a satellite to drift in orbit in yo-yo fashion (northward and southward) while executing a special tilt maneuver to obtain the same earth coverage, they can reduce on-orbit propellant consumption as much as 90 percent. In some cases, this will double the satellite's useful life, thus substantially reducing the cost of its services. Licensing the patents on the new "COMSAT maneuver" will also bring in extra revenues to help make COMSAT more competitive.

THE STRATEGIC IMPORTANCE of the GEOSYNCHRONOUS ARC

In 1865, when President Abraham Lincoln was assassinated, twelve days passed before the news reached the streets of London. A hundred years later, when President Kennedy suffered a similar fate, people all over the world got the story within minutes. In the two decades since then, the ease of sending information over long distances has grown even more dramatically, primarily because of geosynchronous communication satellites. In effect, these satellites have become the "supertankers" of telecommunications, carrying vast amounts of information over great distances more reliably and far more cheaply than traditional landlines, microwave relay towers, or coaxial cables.

It would be almost impossible to overestimate the importance of our country's geosynchronous communication satellites. Indeed, as Rockwell International's space industrialization expert, Dr. Charles Gould, has observed, "At the rate we are going, the real estate at geosync may soon be as important to the United States as the Panama Canal, the San Francisco Harbor, or even the Straits of Hormuz." He made his assessment only a decade ago, in 1977, but the prophecy it contains may already have come true.

5

SURVEYING THE EARTH'S RESOURCES

He was neither an archaeologist nor a professional space scientist. He was an Oklahoma businessman named Ron Frates with a catlike curiosity and a Sherlock Holmes approach to sticky technical problems. In 1984 he read an article describing the painful tribulations of a gang of archaeologists hacking their way through the jungles of the Yucatan Peninsula in search of the ruins of an ancient Mayan civilization.

He was impressed by their tenacity. But their basic approach seemed strangely anachronistic in the age of space, an age in which he and his Oklahoma colleagues were using pictures from earth-circling satellites to search out fresh supplies of oil and to keep watch over the timberlands assigned to their care. "I thought it was kind of dumb," he later commented, "to go down there and thrash around in the jungles. I knew a thing or two about remote satellite sensing, and I thought it would be a good way to become an instant archaeologist."

Starting with $250,000 of his own money, Frates proposed a bold plan to Stephen Prucha and John Dykstra, staff members of Maryland's Earth Satellite Corporation, which had been helping him with spaceborne oil exploration. From Landsat's false-color pictures, they would try to piece together subtle clues of ancient Mayan settlements hidden under the dense jungle foliage just north of Belize.

It turned out to be painstaking work that often made them reach for the Visine. But eventually they discovered the aerial Rosetta stone of the Yucatan—almost imperceptible coloration changes in the jungle where Mayan villagers had skinned back the earth to form square reservoirs thirteen centuries earlier. The

71

trio's excitement mounted exponentially as they quickly located 112 promising sites for later exploration.

After checking and rechecking their results, they packed up a bundle of Landsat photographs, a signed permit from the Mexican government, and a Navstar receiver borrowed from Raytheon. Then they flew to Mexico and joined Mayan archaeologist Dr. Ed Kurjack of Western Illinois University. Once there, they helicoptered inland from the Caribbean port city of Chetumal, guided by a constellation of six Navstar navigation satellites circling overhead.

The first day they found nothing except thick, straight trees. But early on the second, they amassed conclusive evidence that their satellite-based methods of archaeology were clearly superior to the brute-force approaches Frates had read about the previous year. Skimming over the jungle canopy, they could see a nearly continuous expanse of low rock walls, carefully piled together by ancient Mayan workers. One stretched on for nearly 40 miles. "The walls were just spectacular," exclaimed Frates. "We found zillions of miles of them all over the Yucatan. They leave you with the impression that, at one time, there must have been millions and millions of Mayans in that area."

Their co-traveling archaeologist from Illinois could hardly contain his enthusiasm. "Kurjack was so excited," quipped Stephen Prucha, "he nearly fell out of the helicopter." The walls, which were entirely unexpected, presented tantalizing new clues concerning the life-style of the Mayan villagers sixty-five generations earlier. Until Ron Frates and his noisy expedition clattered over the jungle, most experts were convinced that the area's ancient residents used only slash-and-burn agriculture, a primitive form of cultivation still practiced in many Third World countries where land is abundant and villagers thinly settled.

In a slash-and-burn economy, ownership of individual farming plots is meaningless, because land is never in short supply. So enclosing the fields would be a waste of time and energy. "These walls seem to indicate small pieces of property tenaciously held over long periods of time, which, to me, means a far more intensive agriculture and a far greater population than we had hypothesized," Dr. Kurjack later told a reporter. He declined to make specific population estimates, but other experts guess that, at their peak, as many as 15 million Mayan natives may have been scratching out a living in the area.

Guided by their Navstar receiver, the space-age archaeologists visited many of the promising sites they had spotted in the Landsat pictures. One of them was apparently Oxpermul, a settlement that had been discovered in the 1930s, then lost again because archaeologists in those days had no way of pinpointing its location accurately enough so they could come back later for a closer look.

Another high point of the expedition came a day later when they flew over an astonishing sight: the top of a stone pyramid peeking through the jungle canopy. Using an old hoist they had borrowed from a Texas junkman, they lowered Ron

Frates down onto the smooth, flat rocks. He was impressed with what he saw, but next time he would probably prefer to get there by foot or train: "It's not a very pleasant way to go," he later commented, "because the damned prop wash sets you spinning around and around."

At another jungle-covered site there was no place to put the helicopter, so they reeled two crew members down to clear a landing site. Unfortunately, their chain saw broke, and they had to scamper back up again.

Ron Frates was pleased with the results of his hastily organized archaeological expedition, but he was even more delighted with its exceptional efficiency. "We were able to map the extent of the Mayan civilization in the Yucatan in about five days," he concluded when he got back home. "Working on foot it would have taken at least one hundred years."

THE VIEW from SPACE

As an earth-resources satellite repeatedly crosses the equator and moves up over the poles, it takes a series of closely spaced "snapshots" of the ground using television-like scanning techniques. Hanging there in the blackness of space, it picks up both visible and invisible radiation. Our eyes are sensitive to visible light only, but different objects, when illuminated, emit radiation in other parts of the electromagnetic spectrum—including the infrared and the ultraviolet bands. Each object—corn stalk, oak tree, copper mine, corrugated tin roof—reflects sunlight in a specific spectrum of characteristic "colors" called its "spectral signature."

The electronic sensors onboard the satellite "see" the world much as our eyes do, but they are more sensitive and they get a broader view. An infrared device, for instance, is sensitive to certain wavelengths of reflected light, but it also responds to energy emitted as heat. Under certain conditions, such a sensor can actually detect the warm rectangle left behind on the pavement where a car was parked the night before.

Infrared sensors were first used during World War II when Allied bomber crews had trouble distinguishing between natural vegetation and the camouflage often used in covering gun emplacements. Fortunately, pictures made with special infrared film revealed the reflective difference between living plants and cut branches or strips of cloth draped over the enemy artillery.

By calibrating their spaceborne measurements with "ground truth" data—careful observations of the spectral reflectivity of known objects in the field of view—scientists can learn to identify a number of economically important objects in satellite images: copper ores, icebergs, fish breeding sites, earthquake fault lines. Agriculturists, topographers, and meteorologists use these calibrated signatures to track farmland use, choose damsites, map unknown regions, and predict snowmelt levels in mountainous terrain.

SURVEYING THE EARTH'S RESOURCES

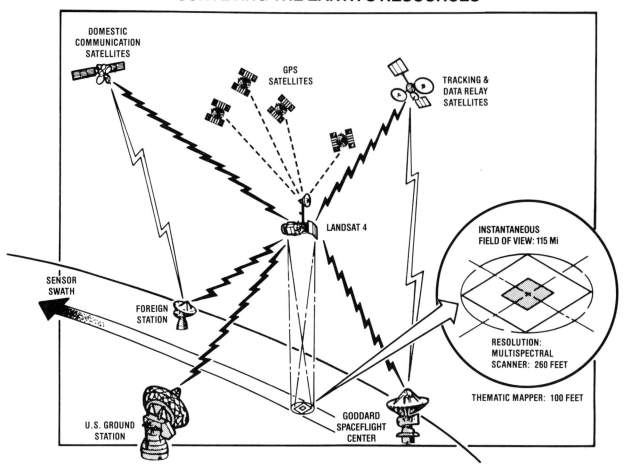

The Landsat earth-resources satellite interacts with three other types of satellites as it curls around the earth. It determines its position using signals from the constellation of eighteen Navstar navigation satellites, and it communicates with users on the ground by means of the tracking and data-relay system and commercial communication satellites. It also transmits images of the scenes it views from space directly to terminals that are within line-of-sight range.

An earth-resources satellite is within sight of 15 percent of the earth at any given time. Consequently, it can gather topographical data with stunning efficiency. Several years ago, when Australian topographers were planning to map the Great Barrier Reef with airborne cameras, they estimated that the task would require thirty years at a cost of 30 million U.S. dollars. Luckily, the age of space has given them an opportunity to make the maps at a substantially lower cost. Using images from remote-sensing satellites, the job will take barely three years and cost only

$3 million. The maps will also be more accurate—and certainly more timely—than the ones they were planning to construct using pictures shot from high-flying planes.

THE REMOTE-SENSING BUSINESS

According to Boston's Center for Space Policy, remote sensing could be a $2 billion annual business by the end of this century, but money is already changing hands in surprisingly large amounts. Industrial customers willingly pay $730 for multispectral images from the Landsat, and high-resolution pictures from its thematic mapper retail for $4,400 each. Preprocessed and annotated pictures fetch higher prices still, and computer tapes bring in as much as $20,000 apiece. Remote sensing is not yet on a par with communications from space, but it is quietly becoming a lucrative business for value-added companies and consumer-oriented entrepreneurs.

Almost 30 percent of today's remote-sensing market is dedicated to oil, gas, and minerals exploration—mostly in remote, inaccessible areas. But scientists are quietly uncovering hundreds of other practical uses as they sift through a modern avalanche of satellite data. Wilbur E. Garrett of the National Geographic Society estimates that "more than a million scenes have been transmitted from earth-sensing satellites in space." Among other things, these million-plus false-color images have helped our experts find "oil in Sudan, tin in Brazil, copper in Mexico, and uranium, zinc, copper, and nickel in the United States." Those same scenes were also helpful to the team of cartographers who recently discovered a previously unknown island off Canada's Atlantic coast. Appropriately, they christened it Landsat Island.

Despite woeful complaints from some industry spokesmen, the market for remote-sensing images is, in fact, increasing. Charles Wilson, manager of the Earth Resources Data Center in Michigan, projects growth rates of at least 10 percent a year for the foreseeable future. "Oil companies have really been buying large-area mosaics," he maintains, and "they have been buying them in large numbers." His contention is supported by growth rates in his own company, which has contracts totaling some $27 million annually.

Most value-added companies work for standard fees, but other imaginative forms of payment are being explored by a few daring entrepreneurs. For instance, Geospectra Corporation, a relative newcomer to the remote-sensing industry, is experimenting with oil-field "overrides"—percentage payments taken from oil actually found. Already Geospectra holds a 1 percent gross override on 300,000 acres leased by oil companies for petroleum exploration. Key customers include Exxon and the Utah International Mining Company.

Coal, oil, and other minerals are all located through remote sensing in essentially the same way. First, the experts search the images for telltale geological features such as outcroppings and fault lines. Then, when promising features are found, they try to develop a tectonic history of the region stretching back millions of years. This, coupled with a careful geobotanical study of the local vegetation, helps them locate valuable—and exploitable—mineral resources tucked under the earth's crust. This is no business for the faint-hearted. It's more like a high-tech table-stakes poker game in which millions change hands at the blink of an eye.

Many industrial applications are trade secrets, but satellite measurements are known to have been used in assessing spoiled mining land in Missouri, surveying the timber forests of Idaho, constructing soil maps in northern India, plotting transportation arteries in Ethiopia, and predicting crop-destroying locust swarms in Asia and Africa.

"EXPERT SYSTEMS" and GEOPHYSICAL EXPLORATION

Go anywhere you like and, when you get there, plant yourself on solid ground. Now look down at the dirt beneath your feet. The first cubic mile of it will contain, among other things, a billion tons of aluminum, 500 tons of iron, and 75 tons of pure gold with a total value of $1,160.9 billion. That figure, however, does not include recovery costs, which will be far more than $1,160.9 billion by the time you have extracted the valuable minerals.

Economical exploitation requires minerals in high concentrations, which occur in only a few isolated pockets on the globe. Until recently, these valuable "mother lodes" were found mostly through extraordinary luck or brutalizing work. Today, however, satellite observations coupled with "expert systems" can help us in the quest. An expert system is a special computer program that attempts to duplicate some of the "thought processes" employed by experienced human experts working in the same field.

Expert systems are at the heart of the "Prospector" program, which analyzes geophysical data entered on geological maps or obtained through a dialogue with the user. When the program has processed the data, it produces full-color contour maps that estimate the probability of finding ores at various levels of concentration. In 1981 Prospector found a new molybdenum deposit in Canada worth millions of dollars. It also found promising deposits of copper in the United States. Other successful applications are rumored, but mineral exploration is shrouded in secrecy, so their authenticity has been difficult to verify.

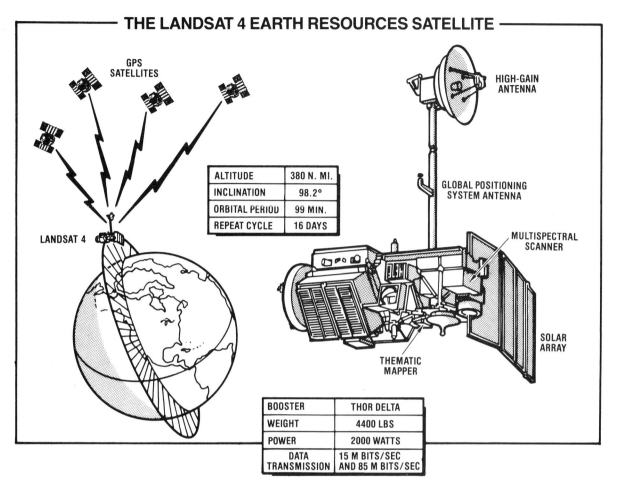

THE LANDSAT 4 EARTH RESOURCES SATELLITE

GPS SATELLITES

HIGH-GAIN ANTENNA

GLOBAL POSITIONING SYSTEM ANTENNA

MULTISPECTRAL SCANNER

SOLAR ARRAY

THEMATIC MAPPER

LANDSAT 4

ALTITUDE	380 N. MI.
INCLINATION	98.2°
ORBITAL PERIOD	99 MIN.
REPEAT CYCLE	16 DAYS

BOOSTER	THOR DELTA
WEIGHT	4400 LBS
POWER	2000 WATTS
DATA TRANSMISSION	15 M BITS/SEC AND 85 M BITS/SEC

From its vantage point 435 miles above the earth, this 4,400-pound Landsat satellite views Vermont-size regions with two kinds of optical sensors: the multispectral scanner, with a resolution of 260 feet, and the thematic mapper, with a resolution of 100 feet. Advanced versions of the satellite find their positions in space by picking up signals from the Navstar navigation satellites. Some of the measurements are transmitted directly to the ground, others are relayed through tracking and data-relay satellites hovering overhead at geosync.

THE ANATOMY of the LANDSAT

From its 435-mile polar orbit, the Landsat earth-resources satellite images the planet earth with two different instruments: the multispectral scanner and the thematic mapper. Both take successive "snapshots" spanning an area about the size of a small state. The multispectral scanner, which operates in four spectral bands, can distinguish features as small as 260 feet across (about the size of a football field). The thematic mapper, which takes its measurements in seven spectral bands, has a resolution of 100 feet (a little bigger than a tennis court).

The multispectral scanner uses television-like scanning techniques to break the scene into individual picture elements (pixels), each of which is assigned a single number ranging from 0 to 255 to indicate its average shade of gray—in that particular band of the frequency spectrum. The thematic mapper uses mechanical scanning techniques. As the satellite moves along its orbit, a swiveling mirror rocks back and forth seven times each second. This causes the incoming light to illuminate rows of light-sensitive photodetectors similar to the one in the "electric eye" of an Instamatic camera. The multispectral scanner produces 15 million bits (ones and zeros) of pictorial information every second. The thematic mapper, with its higher resolution and its larger number of spectral bands, produces 85 million bits.

Landsat's spectral bands were carefully selected for their specific information content. Writers on the staff at *National Geographic* provide us with this explanation of how today's researchers cull meaning from its spectral bands:

> The blue band helps distinguish vegetation from bare soil and penetrates clear, shallow water, revealing its depth to the chart maker. The green band identifies healthy vegetation and penetrates turbid water. The red band distinguishes one crop from another and delineates cultural features such as cities and highways for demographers and land planners.

NASA's Goddard Space Flight Center in Greenbelt, Maryland, managed the first few Landsat satellites, but during the Carter administration, management responsibilities were transferred to another branch of the federal government, the National Oceanic and Atmospheric Administration (NOAA) in Washington, D.C. Four years later, one final change was made. During the Reagan administration, the Landsat became the property of a private, profit-making company, EOSAT, specifically formed for that purpose.

THE FREE-MARKET APPROACH

"Now is the time to transfer this program to the private sector. The American people have invested more than $1 billion in the system," said Commerce Secretary Malcolm Baldrige, "and we hope to see this investment capitalized into private-sector jobs and opportunities here and overseas." However, despite his carefully reasoned endorsement, the transfer was not easy to accomplish, primarily because the U.S. government had been losing a great deal of money on the Landsat.

Of course, government services have never been established to make a profit, and Landsat was no exception. Nevertheless, after long, tedious months of haggling, the government did sell Landsat to a private, profit-making company, the

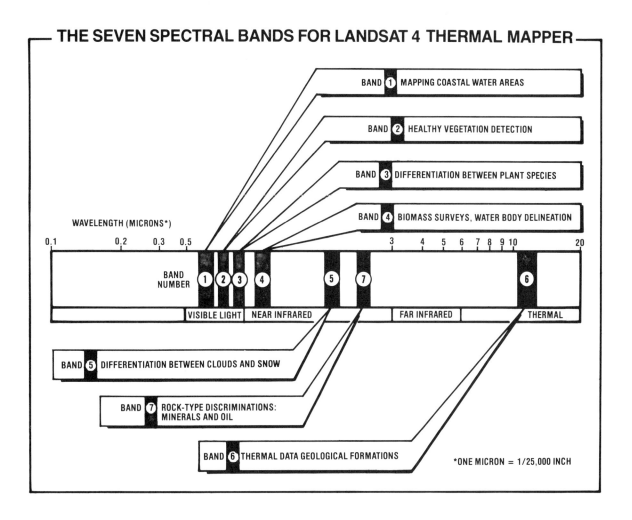

THE SEVEN SPECTRAL BANDS FOR LANDSAT 4 THERMAL MAPPER

BAND ① MAPPING COASTAL WATER AREAS

BAND ② HEALTHY VEGETATION DETECTION

BAND ③ DIFFERENTIATION BETWEEN PLANT SPECIES

BAND ④ BIOMASS SURVEYS, WATER BODY DELINEATION

WAVELENGTH (MICRONS*)

BAND NUMBER

VISIBLE LIGHT   NEAR INFRARED   FAR INFRARED   THERMAL

BAND ⑤ DIFFERENTIATION BETWEEN CLOUDS AND SNOW

BAND ⑦ ROCK-TYPE DISCRIMINATIONS: MINERALS AND OIL

BAND ⑥ THERMAL DATA GEOLOGICAL FORMATIONS

*ONE MICRON = 1/25,000 INCH

The Landsat's thematic mapper views the earth in seven different frequency bands with wavelengths ranging from 1/2,000 to 1/50,000 of an inch. Three of them are in the visible portion of the spectrum, three are in the infrared portion, and one is in the thermal portion. All together, they collect and transmit 100 million bits of useful information (the information equivalent of 25 college textbooks) every second they are in operation.

EOSAT Corporation, a joint venture between RCA and Hughes Aircraft. EOSAT agreed to conform to all applicable laws, make the data available for international use, and launch at least the next satellite in the series, Landsat 7. For its part the government agreed to provide $250 million in subsidies spread over several years, to continue to operate Landsat 5 (which was already in orbit), and to develop other Landsat vehicles. Seven companies participated in the competitive bidding, and four of the losers—Geospectra, Space America, Miltope, and Eastman Kodak—are planning to stay in the remote-sensing business with varying roles.

Despite a few snags in their working relationship with the government, EOSAT's officials are convinced that remote sensing can be a lucrative enterprise. According to EOSAT's vice-president, David Thilboult, the biggest advantage of privatization is the new company's ability to advertise and market its wares in far more aggressive ways than any government bureau could ever manage to do. He and his colleagues are planning to spend $75 million for advertising and marketing. Their surveys indicate that as a result of aggressive advertising campaigns, EOSAT should experience a 40 percent increase in image sales to oil and gas companies alone— the largest and most vigorous part of the remote-sensing market.

However, EOSAT officials are convinced that the biggest sales jumps will occur in the 1990s when new processing techniques will greatly improve the consumer's ability to interpret the information and use it in economically attractive ways. In the 1990s, annual revenues for EOSAT's services are projected in the $50 million range, with ten to twenty times that amount being raked in by all the participants in the earth-sensing game. These include, in particular, the value-added companies that analyze, enhance, and interpret raw Landsat data, sometimes for hefty fees. Geophysical and urban-planning data will continue to be important, but in the latter part of this century, say company officials, most of EOSAT's business will be coming from agriculture and related industries.

In 1976 only eight companies had invested in in-house data-processing facilities capable of analyzing Landsat and other satellite data; however, only four years later, eighty companies worldwide had made the necessary investments. In addition, hundreds of other organizations are using information from the Landsat satellites furnished to them by value-added companies and data-processing centers operated by various governmental agencies both domestic and international. International examples include America's EROS Data Center, Canada's CCRS, Australia's CSIRO, Japan's RESTEC, and France's Spot Image.

The easiest way for you and your colleagues to enter into a remote-sensing enterprise is to develop a market-niche value-added service specifically targeted for a narrow group of users: pecan farmers, shrimp-boat captains, electrical utilities, state fair planning commissions. Another approach may be to develop specialized software: artificial-intelligence programs, color graphics modules, user-friendly interrogation routines, and the like. A more difficult route, which is being pursued by a few brave entrepreneurs, consists of developing a new breed of more capable earth-sensing satellites for tomorrow's more competitive world.

TAKING INVENTORY of the WORLD'S CROPS

For years, researchers in America and in other parts of the world have been using remote-sensing images to predict worldwide grain yields, especially those from the "breadbasket" regions of the Soviet Union and the United States. Similar

SPACE AMERICA'S PRIVATELY OWNED REMOTE-SENSING SATELLITES

Three brash young companies, American Science and Technology, AEROS Data Corporation, and Space Services, Inc., have hammered together a new consortium called Space America with a bold dream: they are hoping to launch a series of privately owned earth-scanning satellites. Each satellite they launch is slated to cost only about $30 million—about one-tenth the current price of the government's Landsats. "When we said we would produce a system for an order of magnitude less than NASA, people laughed," says Diana Josephson, president of Space America. Well, the snickers have died down now, and aerospace professionals are taking the fledgling little company quite seriously.

"Enter a new contender—Space America—in the growing saga to commercialize space," announced the respected trade journal *Space World*. "This newest venture is a combined effort of three young companies to offer a nongovernmental remote-sensing satellite service dedicated to monitoring earth's three major shortages—food, water, and energy—and to make money."

Space America's dynamic young executives are driven by the same entrepreneurial spirit that led the founders of Space Services, Inc., to launch the Conestoga rocket, the first one ever put together by a private profit-making company. As Max Faget, a founder of Space Services, put it, they were "trafficking in the place where the right stuff meets the green stuff." Conestoga launches will cost about $20 million each. According to another Space Services founder, former astronaut Donald (Deke) Slayton, private launch services could be a $2.3-billion-a-year business in about ten years.

Space America's first satellite will consist of 600 pounds of remote-sensing equipment, poised in a polar orbit 565 miles high. It will have a five-year useful life and will feature solid-state electro-optical sensors producing three-dimensional stereoscopic images with a resolution of 140 to 260 feet. The three-dimensional effect will be provided by two identical sensors mounted on the fore and aft of the satellite. Three-dimensional images are especially useful for geological mapping and agricultural applications.

The officials at Space America are especially proud of the data-processing system they are developing to be used in connection with their family of earth-resources satellites. It will feature fancy color graphics and artificial-intelligence routines to allow the computer to respond "Star Trek" fashion to questions asked by the user.

images are used for a variety of commercial purposes, some global in scope, others on a surprisingly small scale.

Who would have anticipated, for example, that the manager of the Hudson Fertilizer Company in Murray, Kentucky, would decide to use images from space to improve sales for his chemical fertilizers? Farmers in the Bluegrass State seem forever strapped for cash, so they resist making any extra fertilizer purchases—unless they see convincing evidence of solid financial returns. For years, officials at the Hudson Fertilizer Company have had fairly reliable methods for determining soil fertility, based on a number of variables, but they wondered if they could get more convincing results by using data gathered from space. Accordingly, they approached the agronomists on the faculty at Murray State University, a land-grant college in the city of Murray, to see if it might be possible to use images from Landsat's thematic mapper to pinpoint regions of unusually low fertility. In the first stage of the project the researchers concentrated on the 1986 wheat crop, but they are now planning to expand the program to include others such as alfalfa, corn, and soybeans.

Individual farmers are also using Landsat data to measure and predict the probable productivity of their competition. "Knowledge of crop yields obtained by remote sensing can mean the difference between profit and loss for a farmer," says Frank Lamb, founder of Cropix, a company that uses a large number of Landsat images. He goes on to explain that in 1983 in the Columbia Basin, potatoes sold for $80 per ton early in the year, but $130 when lower-than-expected yields were known to everyone by the completed harvest. For Lamb's farm alone, advanced knowledge of the depressed yields, as obtained from satellite images, provided him with a $750,000 difference in revenues.

Some of the images from earth-resources satellites are being used to detect illegal diversions of irrigation water. State officials in Arizona, for instance, are taking vengeance against water "rustlers" by electronically matching Landsat data to detailed aerial maps and other measurements they gather on the ground. Dennis Sundie, who heads Arizona's remote-sensing enforcement program, maintains that the program has been quite successful. "We buy $10,000 of Landsat data to catch an illegal field of crops anywhere in the state," he says. So far, satellites have given officials the confidence to write a dozen citations for illegal water use in Arizona.

Earthsat, another company that markets enhanced Landsat data, provides a typical crop-forecasting service, a monthly printed report called *CROPCAST*. For $12,000 a year, it also offers an interactive data base called CROPDIAL accessible by personal computer. The system is so flexible it can stack as many as twelve layers of information to form multiple, interacting images on the screen. It also enhances the contrast of the Landsat images by digital processing techniques. Colors highlight specific data categories for easy recognition by the user.

Scientists may someday have the tools to predict probable yields for most of the world's major crops, thus bringing about profound changes in global markets for food. They are already using Landsat data to help famine-aid groups such as the U.S. Agency for International Development respond more quickly and effectively to heartbreaking emergencies that sometimes leave large areas of the world without adequate food.

One of the worst of these tragedies, locust plagues, can be just as devastating today as they were 3,000 years ago when Moses used them to such good effect against the Pharaoh of Egypt. Crops and rangelands valued at $30 billion per year are susceptible to the ravages of desert locusts, which, at their worst, mow down everything in sight. Locust-susceptible regions cover a total of 12 million square miles in sixty countries. When conditions are good, these regions supply food for more than one-fifth of all the people in the world. When they are bad, as in biblical times, families often end up without enough food.

The migration of swarming locusts is influenced primarily by the moisture content of the air and the ground where the crops are planted, factors that can be inferred with reasonable accuracy from remote-sensing images. When properly processed, this information can be used to predict probable migration routes to help the experts plan more effective programs of pesticide spraying. Detection and measurement of swarming locusts was first successfully demonstrated in 1981 in Algeria. Ground confirmation was supplied through United Nations monitoring stations in Rome.

MONITORING the EARTH'S OCEANS

The fisheries of the world are another important source of food that can be monitored effectively with space-based sensors. Several specialized ocean-monitoring satellites have already been launched, and others are in the works. Nimbus-7's Coastal Zone Color Scanner, which went into orbit in 1978, was one of the first. It imaged ocean colors and the reflection of solar energy from the ocean's surface to help scientists estimate chlorophyll levels and locate nutrient-rich upwellings. Water conditions of this type correlate strongly with local concentrations of plankton, microscopic organisms found in abundance in fish-breeding grounds.

Water temperature measurements also help commercial fishermen locate the most favorable fishing grounds. They usually catch specific species of fish when water temperatures fall within surprisingly narrow bands. Salmon, for example, are usually caught in waters that lie between 49 and 51 degrees Fahrenheit; and most abalone are caught at temperatures between 60 and 64 degrees. One study showed that careful use of nimbus water-temperature charts reduced the average fishing vessel's search time by 20 percent. So far, however, the $1,000 cost of each chart discourages widespread use by commercial fishing vessels.

IMAGE-ENHANCEMENT TECHNIQUES

Only one private company, EOSAT, is today supplying satellite-based measurements of land-use patterns on the earth. However, more than forty profit-making organizations are analyzing and enhancing the images being produced. The purpose of enhancing raw Landsat data is to make it more useful to potential customers, which today include crop analysts, petroleum geologists, topographers, hydrologists, and commercial fishing fleets. Because EOSAT officials are so intent on protecting their markets for raw Landsat data, they have designated the "unenhanced" products they provide as "trade secrets" in all purchase agreements. This means that the images cannot be resold unless they are enhanced and/or processed in various specific ways. Of course, EOSAT also forbids duplication of Landsat computer-compatible tapes.

The companies that offer enhanced Landsat data, such as Earth Resources Data Analysis Systems, Inc., or MARS Associates, Inc., often offer hardware and software packages that are used to merge data from a variety of sources into a single composite image. They also use image-enhancement techniques, specialized computer processing procedures that eliminate static and bring out finer details in the pictures.

MARS Associates, which sells $1.2 million worth of remote-sensing data annually, offers a specialized package that merges remote-sensing data with the tectonic history of a particular region to help scientists determine which mineral formations are under tension, and, therefore, offer the best conditions for commercially exploitable deposits of oil and natural gas. Results are closely guarded trade secrets, but MARS Associates is doing a brisk business with oil exploration companies.

Dr. Ron Lyon at Stanford University is working on a mobile remote-sensing device that can access earth-resources data from anywhere on the globe. It uses a personal computer and a 1-meter banana-shaped antenna to collect remote-sensing images directly from satellites and process them in real time to extract useful information. Dr. Lyon has joined forces with a group of San Francisco businessmen to form the Earth Data Corporation. Says Paul Minto, one of the company's cofounders, "We are designing an inexpensive processing system that allows for frequent resampling of satellite data." This is a cautious understatement, since the transmissions are not merely sampled, but also processed in a number of interesting ways.

TOMORROW'S INTERNATIONAL COMPETITION

The sponsors of Landsat and other proposed domestic remote-sensing satellite systems are bracing themselves for intense international competition. The Japanese, for instance, are planning to launch several maritime satellites, including a weather satellite named GMS-4 in 1989 and an earth-resources satellite in 1991. In addition, the French Spot satellite is already in orbit and sending quality images back to earth. Domestic companies will also feel competition from the Canadian government, which in 1991 is planning to launch an earth-sensing satellite called Radarsat.

The Japanese are no longer depending on the United States for copy-cat space technology. They are building their own launch vehicles and their own satellites. If all goes well—and it usually does for the tenacious Japanese—they intend to launch a total of sixteen satellites devoted to earth observations by the year 2000. They are particularly interested in using satellite data to predict earthquakes, volcanos, and tidal waves, disasters that plague their small islands.

As a major seafaring nation, Japan is particularly troubled by sea ice, which affects commercial operations in the Okhotsk Sea. Spaceborne surveys of currents, water temperatures, and plankton distribution could help Japanese fishermen catch more fish and increase the cruising efficiency of their vessels. Japan's environmental agencies are planning to use satellite data in surveys of rivers and lakes and in monitoring both marine and atmospheric pollution.

The French and the Japanese decided to build their own earth-sensing satellites, in part because the Landsat's resolution was not good enough for their purposes. Of course, military reconnaissance satellites are much more sensitive. Their actual capabilities are classified, but William Spann, president of Metrics Inc. (Atlanta, Georgia), believes, "We have satellites in the U.S. that can count golf balls on the green."

Locating lost golf balls from space will probably never be economically practical, but future earth-sensing satellites could have such good resolution that rather than scanning the entire earth indiscriminately, their operators could, on customer demand, aim the sensors toward designated "targets" of interest on earth.

FUTURE TRENDS in IMAGING from SPACE

Six hundred years ago when the Black Plague raged across the European continent, there were only about 500 million inhabitants on the planet earth. Today our population is eight times bigger—and growing. Worldwide increases currently average 1.9 percent per year. Inevitably, in the next decade nearly a billion additional passengers will board our planetary spaceship. Like their predecessors, these new arrivals must be packed into a thin, life-supporting rim called the biosphere.

Any effective program for studying the complex iterations in the biosphere will necessarily involve measurements of the earth and the space around it as an integrated whole. Thus, we will need observations of our weather, climate, oceans, and atmosphere and we will need ways to study the dynamics of the solid earth and the biochemical cycles of all the major nutrients.

Unmanned remote-sensing satellites will form the backbone of this effort, but manned flights will also make important contributions. Astronauts aboard Skylab and the space shuttle have already carried out several experimental assignments of this type. In 1984, for instance, those aboard the shuttle used a new imaging radar to make a stunning archaeological discovery: ancient riverbeds buried under millions of tons of sand undulating in long, lazy curves under the Sahara Desert.

Researchers were, at first, convinced that the unusually dry conditions in the Sahara had allowed the radar waves to penetrate so deeply into the soil. But later experiments in other regions, including the Andes Mountains of Peru, showed that soil moisture was not the key. Soils of several different types are surprisingly "transparent" to spaceborne radar waves.

Some experts are convinced that tomorrow's remote-sensing satellites can help us build a stable and prosperous world free from the worst ravages of hunger and want. As John McElroy of *Spaceflight* magazine puts it: "The peaceful daily observation of the earth's atmosphere, oceans, and land from a polar platform—provided through international cooperation attended by a multinational crew of astronauts—is one of the dreams for the age of space."

Take a large, almost round, rotating sphere 8,000 miles in diameter. Surround it with a murky, viscous atmosphere of gases mixed with water vapor. Tilt it back and forth with respect to a source of light and heat. Freeze it at the ends and toast it in the middle. Fill most of its surface with a liquid that feeds vapor into that atmosphere as millions of gallons of it slosh up and down to the rhythmic pull of its natural captive satellite. Then—if you can—try to predict the conditions of that atmosphere over one small area 50 miles square for a period of one to three days.

Agenda of Weather Radar Symposium
sponsored by Raytheon, January 1963

6

WORLDWIDE WEATHERWATCH

During the Great Depression, when Americans heard Al Jolson singing "April Showers," they trusted his predictions about as much as the daily weather forecasts they had been hearing on the radio. Millions relied on pseudoscientific sources for weather information: groundhogs, spiderwebs, *The Farmer's Almanac,* even their own aching arthritic joints. "Everybody talks about the weather, but nobody does anything about it," they all agreed. Certainly nobody had found a reliable way of telling them how to dress for tomorrow's weather.

And yet, many midcentury Americans were convinced that our country's scientific experts could at least predict the destructive paths of major typhoons and hurricanes. In September 1938, when a big-city daily heaped almost embarrassing praise on the skills of the government's professional meteorologists, no one phoned in to offer a rebuttal, despite the article's overconfident, almost haughty, tone: "Due to our admirably organized meteorological services, the East Coast will always be kept informed of the path of any hurricane," it stated with impassioned optimism. Unfortunately, after an unmercifully brief interval, that haughty confidence would be shattered beyond belief.

Only hours after the morning edition hit the streets, a tropical hurricane off Cape Hatteras bashed into the Atlantic Seaboard, sweeping away everything in its path. After describing the awful devastation it brought to coastal communities, the Associated Press carried this bruising assessment: "The greens and the commons of New England will never be the same again. Picture postcard mementos of the oldest part of the United States are gone with the wind. The day of the 'biggest wind' has passed and a great part of the most picturesque America, as old as the Pilgrims, has gone beyond recall or replacement."

What had caused our most talented meteorologists to be so badly mistaken on that dismal September day? According to their calculations, the hurricane was expected to "whirl out into the Atlantic," where it would spend itself churning up harmless waves. Unhappily, hurricanes do not always "whirl" as science antici-pates. Instead of ambling along the continental shelf, this one suddenly veered freakishly shoreward, covering over 600 miles in twelve fateful hours.

Winds as high as 186 miles an hour chose the worst imaginable spot to make a left turn, a turn that carried the hurricane over some of the country's heaviest population centers dimpling the shoreline between Boston and New York. Sud-denly, the beaches of Connecticut and Rhode Island became a soggy burial ground for old and new construction. In the words of one contemporary account, "High tide rose 12 to 25 feet . . . inundating the land and washing buildings out to sea."

Wind-driven water, with buckshot fury, killed 680 people, seriously injured 700 more, and damaged $400 million worth of property. It smashed 26,000 family cars, splintered more than 2,000 private boats, destroyed 15,000 buildings. And it flattened, snapped, or uprooted 275 million trees.

It also flattened America's faith in the science of meteorology. "A sophisticated population died by the hundreds with little or no knowledge of what raw shape death took when it struck from the sky," wrote one observer when the hurricane finally subsided. "In the long and laudable annals of the government's weather forecasts, that day's record makes what must be the sorriest page."

Later the East Coast hurricane that failed to "whirl" as expected was declared the worst natural disaster in American history. Chicago and San Francisco had hosted more famous natural disasters. But Mrs. O'Leary's cow destroyed only 200 lives and $200 million worth of property; and San Francisco's "fire" claimed only about 450 Californians and jarred $350 million worth of homes and offices into useless rubble.

Could the "biggest wind" ever again sneak ashore to devastate unsuspecting Americans? Not likely. Today with weather satellites aloft, experts easily track any hurricane lurking off the Atlantic coast. And when skyborne disaster does strike, Americans in the hundreds are routinely saved by quick evacuations.

Picture-postcard shorelines can still be menaced by nature's fitful tantrums, but people everywhere now know in advance when the "biggest wind" is whirling toward the shore. Everybody still talks about the weather. And, even today, nobody can do anything about it. Except leave.

HOW DO SATELLITES HELP US PREDICT TOMORROW'S WEATHER?

When we examine the complex web of interrelated factors affecting the earth's atmosphere—clouds, winds, rain, sun, moon, airborne aerosols, even gravity and the earth's rotation—we should be amazed that our meteorologists can predict anything at all useful about tomorrow's weather. Weather prediction is a three-dimensional problem involving intractable systems of partial differential equations, a single one of which once caused the great Isaac Newton to complain to his friend Christopher Wren that "it makes my head hurt and I can think of it no more."

Most of the information that goes into these equations is still gathered by people and instruments on the ground. But today's satellites are providing us with cost-effective methods of gathering supplementary data on precipitation, temperatures, water vapor, ambient pressures, soil moisture, and snow cover. The spaceborne measurements most crucial to accurate long-term weather predictions include the positions and shapes of the jet streams and the temperature profiles of the ambient air.

Satellite measurements help our experts model the atmosphere's behavior by providing crude but important information that would otherwise be nearly impossible to obtain: cloud-cover observations in the Indian Ocean, for instance, and wind-velocity measurements over sparsely populated islands. Although the quality of satellite data is not usually on a par with comparable data gathered on the ground, it covers a broader area. Moreover, we can get it more frequently and at a substantially lower cost. In 1966, rather skimpy coverage for much of the northern Pacific and the oceans of the Southern Hemisphere was provided by weather ships at an annual cost of about $160 million. Compare this with the annual outlay for today's coverage of the entire globe (four times daily) by two Nimbus weather satellites for $100 million a year.

METEOROLOGICAL FEATURES VISIBLE from SPACE

Satellites give us information on cloud patterns and jet streams that cannot be obtained in any other practical way. These relatively inexpensive "observation posts" in the sky routinely spot hurricanes and tornadoes while they are forming over remote oceans. These simple but effective observations save hundreds of millions of dollars each year and the lives of at least dozens, sometimes hundreds of people.

In the early 1960s, observations from TIROS 1 helped scientists discover cloud structures not previously known to exist: spiral cloud patterns, small-scale eddies, and convective cells, all of which eventually served as "red flags" to alert meteorologists to the formation of deadly tornadoes, hurricanes, or, on more favorable days, soft April showers that affected Al Jolson in such touching and tender ways.

Water-vapor patterns, which are delineated by dark and light regions in the pictures from high-flying satellites, can provide our meteorologists with an extraordinarily clear picture of the atmosphere's complicated patterns of atmospheric circulation. Although the equations involved are horrendously complicated, the understanding we have of the underlying phenomenon is based on a surprisingly simple rule of thumb: moist air rises, dry air descends.

Jet streams, rivers of wind snaking through the sky at heights of 30,000 to 40,000 feet, have a powerful influence on our weather. They are practically invisible from the ground, but satellite photos reveal weather features that indicate when and where jet streams are racing forward at speeds as high as 200 miles an hour. Sharp boundaries of moisture (dark regions) cutting across a satellite picture, for instance, often highlight jet-stream boundaries in the upper atmosphere. They had been suspected previously, but their existence was known for sure only during World War II when Allied pilots reported fierce headwinds over the Sea of Japan. Sometimes these winds were so powerful they actually stopped the forward progress of B-29 formations on the way to bomb Tokyo.

Meteorologists can enhance their knowledge of jet streams by tracking the drift rates of clouds whose heights are crudely estimated from air-temperature measurements gathered by satellite. These measurements are not as accurate as direct measurements of the trajectories of drifting balloons released from weather stations, but they do give at least some information on rapid air movements over remote, inaccessible regions.

Accurate monitoring of winds aloft can save high-flying jets appreciable amounts of time and fuel. Westbound pilots seek out hefty tail winds, but when they return in the opposite direction, they prefer an altitude shrouded in still air. According to one estimate, a typical airline can expect to save at least $1 million a year if its pilots and support crews use satellite data to harness the winds aloft.

SEVERE STORM FORECASTING

Each year, 400 Americans are struck by lightning. About 150 of them die, and most of the rest end up with terrible headaches. Tornadoes and hurricanes snuff out another 300 lives, mostly on the Atlantic Seaboard and along the Great Plains. Fortunately, the GOES satellite, America's high-altitude sentinel in the sky, has dramatically enhanced our ability to understand and predict dangerous weather.

Researchers at the University of Wisconsin's Space Science and Engineering Center have estimated annual weather-related losses to agriculture in the $12 billion range. Their studies also show that these losses could be cut by $5 billion through accurate five-day forecasts generated from satellite-based weather observations.

Much of this damage is rather unspectacular: delayed plantings, rotted wheat, equipment bogged down in the mud. However, according to the National Center for Atmospheric Research (Boulder, Colorado), freak storms adversely affect at least 30 million people annually and cause $1 billion worth of damage to private property in much more dramatic ways. Part of this damage could be averted if we could develop more accurate forecasts and disseminate them in efficient ways. Timely and accurate information on current snow cover, for instance, could help America's meteorologists develop more accurate predictions of flooding, which costs our citizens an average of about $1 billion per year.

MAKING MONEY from TODAY'S WEATHER SATELLITES

A few investors are already making big money from today's space-based weather observations. Commodity traders, for example, armed with color-coded satellite weather maps, have a big advantage in stock-market trading, and farmers with access to long-range weather predictions can plan planting and harvesting to maximize return on investment. They can also optimize their expenditures for fertilizer, irrigation water, and part-time crews.

People everywhere have always wished that they could control the weather, but in the main, their attempts have produced only the most pathetic results. In prehistoric times, for example, hopeful natives sacrificed young virgins to the gods of wind and rain, but often their crops wilted and died anyway. In the sixth century B.C., the Greeks built the Tower of the Winds on the Acropolis, but powerful winds continued to sweep across the Athenian plain. Even the American Indians engaged in rain dances for endless hours, but America's east and west are still separated by the great desert. Since the 1950s, meteorologists have attempted to control the weather in a more scientific manner. On occasion, they have succeeded in creating badly needed rain by seeding certain kinds of clouds with crystals of silver iodide.

Eventually, large-scale weather modification guided by satellite observations could have a beneficial impact on the world's major sources of food and fiber. In the meantime, cloud seeding promises to provide simpler but important results. In one study founded by the National Science Foundation, researchers concluded that improved cloud seeding in a single area, the upper Colorado River Basin, could augment the local snowpacks enough to provide $13 million in annual benefits.

A number of private companies are already processing and disseminating meteorological information collected from satellites. The raw data they use is available to nearly anyone, but these "value-added" companies reduce it to a more useful format for other people who must make decisions based on foreknowledge of tomorrow's weather. Most of their regular clients are engaged in agriculture, entertainment, or transportation.

Aviotex of Costa Mesa, California, for instance, has ferreted out a small but lucrative market among America's 700,000 private pilots, who willingly pay for accurate weather information. Before Aviotex opened shop, private pilots were forced to rely upon the Federal Aviation Administration to provide them with weather forecasts over the phone. The FAA was a terrific fair-weather friend, but when the weather deteriorated, dozens of calls clogged the lines and callers might be put on hold for forty-five minutes waiting for a brief weather report.

The computerized process developed by Aviotex combines satellite and radar images with videotext in a system that displays color-coded maps matched to important flight information. Pilots can store flight plans in the system—which they can access through computer terminals or television monitors in hotels, airports, or their own homes. Users pay $30 per month plus 60 cents for each minute of computer time.

Aviotex executives are also trying to gather extra revenues by soliciting advertising for fuels, maintenance services, car rentals, hotels, and clothing and supplies for pilots. Most of the early business Aviotex attracted was on a small, personal scale, but recently company executives made a $2.5-million-a-year deal with the Canadian government to install their computer-based systems in thirty-five of Canada's busiest airports. Based on this and other promising possibilities for new business, Pascal Tlahvi, chairman of Aviotex, is projecting $20 million in annual revenues within the next two years.

Given accurate storm warnings, fishermen can save money in a number of different ways. In particular, advanced disaster warnings can help prevent damage to boats, minimize injury to crews, and reduce waste of fuel and supplies. One government study, which dealt with the benefits of satellite-based weather forecasts on 200 albacore fishing vessels, showed a $580,000 annual savings in fuel costs alone. One fisherman told the study team that he had "caught an extra $10,000 to $12,000 worth of tuna as a result of using satellite data."

In a larger study involving various types of commercial boats, the National Marine Fisheries Service concluded that 1,000 West Coast fishing vessels saved 10 percent on their fuel bills when they had timely access to satellite weather data. If these same per-boat savings could be spread across the entire American fishing industry, annual benefits would add up to $2,440,000.

The agriculture and transportation industries represent far larger opportunities for economic benefits. Pictures made by today's weather satellites provided a $1 million saving the first year they were used by the Waialua Sugar Company in Hawaii. Advance knowledge of the weather is essential to sugar-cane harvesting, because the fields are deliberately set on fire to release the sugar from the cane. Wind can cause violations of federal air-pollution standards, and, once burning is complete, rain can destroy the fallen stalks in the fields. In a typical harvesting operation, 50 to 100 acres of cane fields are ignited at one time, thus leaving $250,000 worth of sugar cane lying on the ground at the mercy of the weather.

The production manager at the Waialua Sugar Company, who holds the responsibility for making the daily harvesting decisions, has many sources of information, but his personal favorite is the pictures he gets from weather satellites. "I look at the weather maps and listen to what they are saying on the broadcasts," he said, "but when I look at the satellite pictures, I can really see what's coming." Each season the Waialua Sugar Company plants about 15,000 acres in highly perishable sugar cane. If all goes well, its total value is about $40 million. But if the rain falls at inopportune times, Waialua can end up with a soggy mess.

ROUTING SHIPS ACROSS the HIGH SEAS

"Only a man who has commanded a ship at sea can know the burden of responsibility borne by a modern ship's master." So states a colorful pamphlet published by Oceanroutes, a space-age enterprise that helps large commercial vessels pick their way through dangerous weather. "For he knows that despite the clear calm of any moment on the sea, there lurks ahead the threatening storm, the pall of fog, the edge of ice. . . . Many morning watches will find him huddled behind a wind screen after a night of staring into the foggy murk. Because always the responsibility for crew, and cargo, and ship is his."

The master of a ship does, indeed, have worrisome responsibilities, but they are getting easier now that the experts at Oceanroutes are available to lighten the load. For a fee averaging $700 per voyage, they provide efficient real-time routing information to help harried ship captains find the safest, most efficient trajectories across the sea.

America has a surprisingly long history of trying to route oceangoing vessels for increased efficiency. One of the earliest researchers was Benjamin Franklin, politician, statesman, inventor, entrepreneur. In 1768, six years before he and his fellow rebels gathered for the First Continental Congress, Franklin, who was then working in London as Deputy Postmaster General for the American colonies, learned that packet ships sailing from Falmouth to New York typically required two weeks longer than merchant ships traveling the longer route from London to Rhode Island. His curiosity was sparked by this tantalizing puzzle, and soon he was contemplating a number of likely causes, including the uneven patterns of the ocean's circulation.

In a later conversation with Nantucket sea captain Timothy Folger, Franklin learned that there was a powerful stream of water curving along America's Atlantic Coast skirted by large whales—who instinctively swam around its edges. Often, whaling ships would slip into the Gulf Stream, only to be separated from their fellow whalers as the current quickly carried them away. The Yankee ship captain also told how he and other American whalers had tried to advise British sailors to avoid the midocean stream, but to no avail. "We have informed them that they are stemming the current . . . and advised them to cross it and get out of it," Folger recalled, "but they are too wise to be counseled by simple American fishermen."

As he crossed the Atlantic in 1775 on a voyage from London to Philadelphia, Franklin conducted the first scientific study of the mysterious coastal current. All

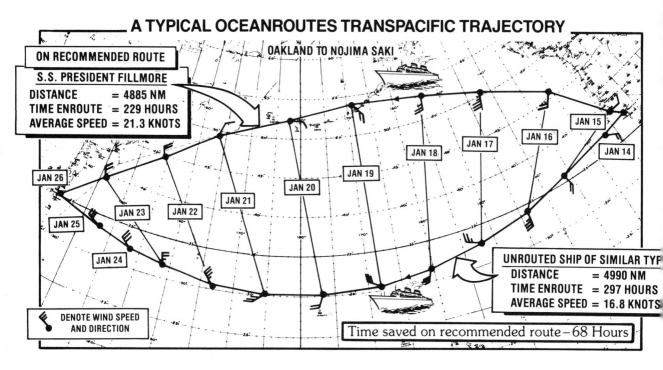

A TYPICAL OCEANROUTES TRANSPACIFIC TRAJECTORY

OAKLAND TO NOJIMA SAKI

ON RECOMMENDED ROUTE

S.S. PRESIDENT FILLMORE

DISTANCE	= 4885 NM
TIME ENROUTE	= 229 HOURS
AVERAGE SPEED	= 21.3 KNOTS

UNROUTED SHIP OF SIMILAR TYP

DISTANCE	= 4990 NM
TIME ENROUTE	= 297 HOURS
AVERAGE SPEED	= 16.8 KNOTS

DENOTE WIND SPEED AND DIRECTION

Time saved on recommended route – 68 Hours

Researchers at Oceanroutes (Palo Alto, California) develop safe and efficient trajectories like the one at the top of this figure for large oceangoing vessels. They use computers to process data from weather satellites and other sources. Each optimum route takes into account real-time weather conditions, the physical characteristics of the ship, and the wishes of the ship's master—who gets an updated trajectory twice each day. Inmarisat satellites provide some of the communication links, and those in the partial Navstar constellation provide some of the positioning information. The cost of the service for a typical voyage is $700, a fee that is repaid thirty to forty times over by shortened travel times and more efficient maritime operations.

along the way he measured the speed and temperature of the waters, carefully marking down the readings in his scientific journal. Later he combined this new knowledge with the practical observations of Captain Folger to produce a navigational chart of the Gulf Stream and the surrounding waters. Though it was a bit oversimplified, it was, by the standards of its day, a remarkably accurate document showing acute powers of observation and deduction.

Seventy-five years later, Matthew Fontaine Maury of the U.S. Navy expanded upon the work of Franklin and other nautical observers in a brilliant scientific treatise, *The Physical Geography of the Sea.* "The ocean has its system of circulation," he wrote in that widely influential book, "which is probably as complete and not less wonderful than the circulation of the blood through the human system." Navigators of sailing ships who used Maury's charts dramatically shortened the duration of their voyages. According to one estimate made a decade after it came off the press, the charts and sailing directions Maury had compiled saved millions of dollars for Britain alone.

Oceanroute's researchers expand on the work of Franklin, Maury, and their more recent colleagues by gathering data from weather satellites and other useful sources. They process it in real time on high-speed computers, and transmit the results through Inmarisat satellites (and other communication channels) twice a day to oceangoing vessels. From their comfortable offices in Palo Alto, California, and at several other locations around the globe, they work with a thousand ships in a routine month. Each recommended route is worked out for that particular ship "on that specific voyage, with the given cargo load, status of trim and draft, with the ship's own distinctive speed and sea-handling characteristics."

The computer program they use emphasizes emerging weather, but it also takes into account currents and fog, choke points and navigational hazards, and sea ice in northern regions. Some cargoes, such as oil and fruit, are temperature-sensitive; others, such as automobiles and heavy machinery, may shift under heavy waves. Still others have time-critical deliveries. The program successfully takes these and other factors into account whenever it makes routing recommendations.

According to Alan Cima at Oceanroutes Headquarters in Palo Alto, California, a typical shipping concern saves $30 to $40 for every $1 spent on data from Oceanroutes.

If hazardous weather threatens to close in anywhere along the way, the ship's master is alerted and given an instant recommendation for a new course to keep crew and vessel out of harm's way. If rerouting is impossible, he is notified of the force and duration of hazardous winds and waves. So far in 43,000 crossings aided by Oceanroutes information, travel times have been reduced an average of four hours in the Atlantic, eight in the Pacific. Operating a large oceangoing vessel costs as much as $1,000 an hour, so time savings alone translate into substantial reductions in cost. In addition, other expenses are also reduced.

In the early 1960s when Oceanroutes services were not yet available, the cost for repairs of weather-damaged ships ran from $32,000 to $53,000 in an average year. Today those costs have dropped to only about $6,000. Cargo damage has also decreased. One international auto dealer told Oceanroutes researchers that his damage claims for cargo had dropped over $500,000 per year. Another big Oceanroutes customer discovered that damage claims were running less than half those in the industry as a whole.

According to Alan Cima, Oceanroutes has captured about 80 percent of the market, despite the fact that three commercial competitors and six governments duplicate some of their services. His fellow employees total about 200 worldwide, a number that is likely to grow as satellite links become more widely available and shipping concerns find more uses for the services they provide.

AMERICA'S WEATHER SATELLITES

Some of America's meteorological satellites are launched into geosynchronous orbits 22,300 miles above the earth; others barely skim over the ground, usually in near-polar orbits at altitudes of only a few hundred miles.

A satellite in a geosynchronous orbit hovers over one particular spot above the earth's equator. From its high vantage point in space it can "see" about 44 percent of the globe. Resolutions are not very good, but the instruments on a geo-synchronous platform are able to observe large-scale weather patterns over ex-tended periods of time. Most of the weather maps that flash across your TV screen on the nightly news come from geosynchronous satellites.

A low-altitude satellite that barely glides over the atmosphere can "see" only a small fraction of the earth, typically about 15 percent at any given moment. Its instantaneous view is rather limited, but it sweeps around the earth in a little over an hour and a half, so within a day it scans most of the earth, gaining a detailed, close-up view of the clouds and weather patterns below.

In 1960, America's first dedicated weather satellite, TIROS 1, was launched into a low-altitude orbit tipped 60 degrees with respect to the equatorial plane. TIROS 1 was a simple pillbox-shaped device weighing only 270 pounds. It soon demon-strated its value when it tracked Hurricane Esther on her vicious rampage off the North Atlantic coast. Over the next few years, TIROS 1 detected dozens of devas-tating storms and, as a result, is credited with saving several hundred lives.

William Widger, a private pilot who used the weather data from the TIROS satel-lite, eloquently described some of the benefits he derived:

Enclosed is the TIROS weather map given me on my departure on May 4, 1962. . . . It is so accurate as to be almost unbelievable. Not only was the cold front located exactly, but, with a 150-mile scan on radar, its North-east/Southwest positioning was clearly definable. . . . In my estimation we have found the answer; let's send up more TIROS satellites!

Today improved weather satellites are helping thousands of pilots pick their way through blackened skies. They are also providing the data for reasonably accurate crop forecasting in our own country and in Europe, South America, the Soviet Union, China, and West Africa—where famine often sweeps across the land. Spaceborne measurements of temperature, pressure, humidity, rainfall level, and wind characteristics are fed into a computer model that also includes soil and plant-growth characteristics to forecast soil moisture, likely plant condition, and stress levels, all of which have a strong influence on annual crop yields.

The Nimbus satellite, which supplements the TIROS, is equipped with an ad-vanced vidicon (TV) camera and a high-resolution infrared radiometer to mea-

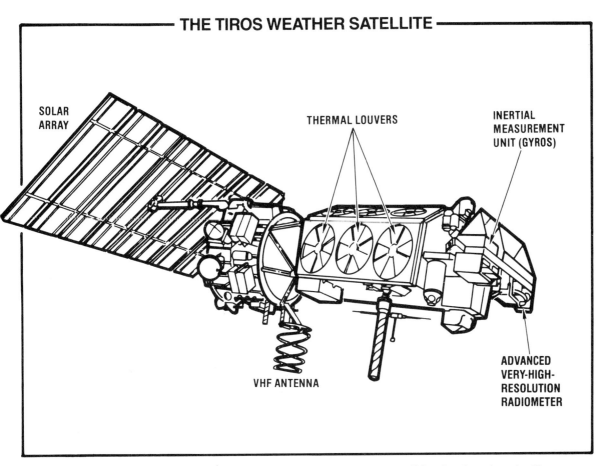

THE TIROS WEATHER SATELLITE

SOLAR ARRAY

THERMAL LOUVERS

INERTIAL MEASUREMENT UNIT (GYROS)

VHF ANTENNA

ADVANCED VERY-HIGH-RESOLUTION RADIOMETER

This TIROS weather satellite rides aboard a Thor-Delta booster into 435-mile orbit, where it will turn on its television cameras to begin observing weather patterns all over the globe. TIROS is powered by solar cells mounted on its curved cylindrical body and is equipped with two different kinds of television cameras. The scenes it observes are stored on tape recorders for later trans- mission to users on earth.

sure reflected radiation from the earth's surface and from the tops of clouds. More recent versions of the Nimbus have, in addition, been equipped with ocean-color imagers to give oceanographers and fishermen reasonably accurate information on ocean temperatures. The orbital location of the Nimbus satellites is also differ- ent. They are launched into near-polar orbits to provide a more comprehensive view of the earth, including the Arctic and the Antarctic, where ground-based weather readings are very sparse.

Recently, researchers discovered that Nimbus 7 was giving them interesting information on the ozone layer over the South Pole. Atmospheric ozone is a spe- cific type of oxygen molecule that shields us from harmful ultraviolet radiation. According to one popular interpretation of the Nimbus data, the layer of ozone over the South Pole has been thinning by as much as 40 percent each year. Typ- ically it reaches its thinnest level in the month of October, then begins to thicken again. Researchers worldwide are trying to discover the causes of ozone thinning—which could have unknown effects on health, weather, crop production, perhaps even our survival. We know that without the ultraviolet shield provided by the ozone layer, skin-cancer deaths would rise. So would the incidence of cataracts. According to one study quoted by Isaac Asimov ("Danger: We're Losing Our Shield of Life," *TV Guide,* February 20, 1987), "over the next 80 years or so, there may well be up to 40 million cases of skin cancer among Americans alone, and 800,000 deaths." Humans can stay inside, wear hats, and carry sunshades out of doors, but the real danger is to the microscopic life forms that live in the soil and the uppermost layers of the sea. To them extra ultraviolet rays could be truly deadly.

The GOES satellites, which are launched into geosynchronous orbits, supplement the Nimbus coverage. The details they "see" are not nearly as fine as those observed by the Nimbus satellites, but GOES provides a broader view. The GOES instruments were selected to provide infrared images of global cloud cover, measure precipitation, gauge wind speeds, and estimate snow cover and sea-surface temperatures. From their high-altitude geosynchronous orbits, the GOES satellites help us track severe storms, especially over remote ocean basins. Since this program was instituted two decades ago, no storm has ever crashed upon our shores undetected.

Unfortunately, on May 3, 1986, a Delta rocket carrying GOES-G into orbit exploded. Most Americans had never heard of the GOES satellites, but suddenly our dependence on them for severe storm warnings received heavy coverage in the evening news. "It is very critical to have two of those [GOES satellites] rather than the one we have now," said William O. Borner, director of the National Meteorological Center. "With two satellites you always feel more comfortable." He then went on to worry aloud about the possibility of losing the remaining GOES satellite. "There is a great feeling of unease for having no satellite. That could be catastrophic to the weather service in this country."

With only one GOES weather satellite in operation, we lacked adequate storm-warning capabilities over much of the North Atlantic, the Caribbean region, Alaska, and the southern islands of Hawaii. This unfortunate situation could have affected shipping in those areas, and under a worst-case scenario it could endanger the lives of the local inhabitants.

Fortunately, on February 26, 1987, a perfect launch from Cape Kennedy carried a $55 million replacement for the GOES into orbit above the cape. "This feels terrific!" said Bud Litton, a spokesman for the National Oceanographic and Atmospheric Administration (NOAA), moments after the satellite's $40 million Delta rocket roared away from its pad. "It's something to keep everybody jumping for joy from Hawaii to Maine," added Jamison Hawkins, a meteorologist from NOAA

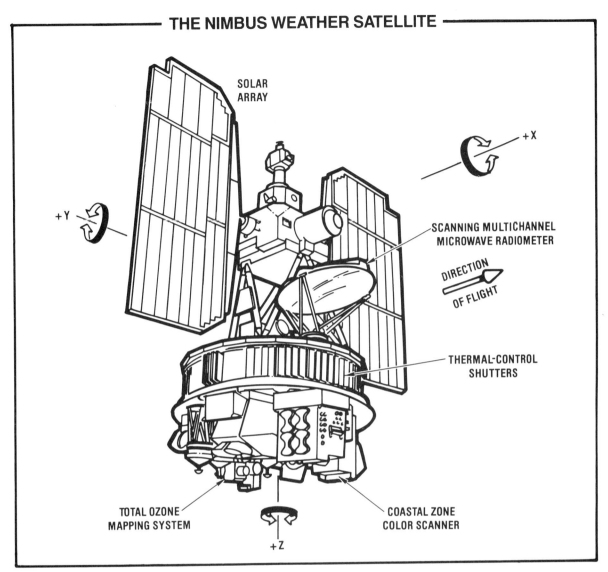

THE NIMBUS WEATHER SATELLITE

SOLAR
ARRAY

+X

+Y

SCANNING MULTICHANNEL
MICROWAVE RADIOMETER

DIRECTION
OF FLIGHT

THERMAL-CONTROL
SHUTTERS

TOTAL OZONE
MAPPING SYSTEM

COASTAL ZONE
COLOR SCANNER

+Z

This Nimbus weather satellite is flying into orbit from Vandenberg Air Force Base aboard an Atlas booster. Unlike many simpler satellites, Nimbus features flat-panel solar arrays that automatically swivel to track the sun. The rows of thermal control shutters open and close automatically to maintain a nearly constant internal temperature. This is necessary because the instruments and the electronic devices inside operate most efficiently when they are kept close to room temperature.

headquarters. If all goes well the new GOES satellite will be checked out and operational by the end of April, just in time for the annual hurricane season that normally begins around the first of June.

The television-like images streaming down to receivers on the ground cover about one-third of the earth's surface every thirty minutes. Scientists can analyze these images to measure the movements of clouds, which provide important insights into how the atmosphere is circulating on that particular day. GOES also collects data from instrumented buoys, tide gauges, seismometers, and oceangoing vessels, and it distributes the results to meteorologists at other distant locations.

Each year millions of dollars are spent to measure the depth of the snow cover in mountainous areas of the United States. These measurements are computer-processed to help our experts estimate the probable volumes of runoff water so they can decide how much water to impound and how much to release from catchment basins and reservoirs. Release too much, and supplies could turn out to be inadequate for irrigation, hydroelectric power production, and industrial consumption. Release too little, and destructive flooding may occur later in the season.

A study conducted in the 1970s indicated that accurate snow-cover data obtained from the GOES satellites produced 5 to 10 percent improvements in runoff predictions, thus providing a $36 million annual savings for the western United States. More accurate water impoundment can also reduce political tension in the water-starved West.

The new NOAA series of low-altitude weather satellites travel around the earth 14.3 times every twenty-four hours. The combination of the NOAA's orbital motion and the earth's rotation causes each one of them to pass within view of the entire earth's surface twice each day. The aim of these satellites is to predict the weather with reasonable reliability at least thirty-six hours in advance. Experts are hoping this can be accomplished with soundings (height measurements) in addition to conventional scanning techniques that produce flat (two-dimensional) images of clouds, snow cover, and the like.

NOAA-G, which was launched on September 17, 1986, is equipped with a global search-and-rescue system called SARSAT which allows its users to signal whenever they need help. Earlier versions of SARSAT have been in use for about fifteen years. In its first three years of operation SARSAT was credited with saving about 350 lives. Most of the potential victims had been lost in ships or planes, but in one rather odd instance a young racecar driver, who had been tearing across Africa at 140 miles an hour, was rescued by satellite.

SELLING OUR SATELLITES to PRIVATE INDUSTRY

In 1983 the Reagan administration devised a plan to sell both the Landsat earth-resources satellites and a number of weather satellites to private industry, which it believed could manage the operations for improved efficiency. Under a special "privatization" directive, the Department of Commerce was to start serious negotiations with firms to find a buyer, but unfortunately this effort was almost immediately immersed in raging controversy.

Initially, the major industrial participant in the discussions was COMSAT, the Washington firm that already runs our major communications satellites for profit. According to Paul Maughan, head of COMSAT's Earthstar team, the group was willing to take over both the Landsat and the weather satellites as a package deal. In his opinion, they could have reduced the staff and put more modern technology in both future satellites and the ground stations to streamline their operations. With both types of data for sale, the COMSAT team would have been able to approach the market on a grand scale, with a solid chance of making a profit.

According to Peter Marsh *(The Space Business):* "COMSAT offered to pay the government $300 million for five weather satellites and one Landsat satellite already in orbit, 'spares,' and other space hardware on the ground plus earth stations." At first it sounded like a rather attractive deal for America's taxpayers, but there was more to it than that. "COMSAT also proposed that the government should guarantee to buy data from the new operation for fifteen years, agreeing in advance to pay out some $325 million per year." However, as Marsh puts it, the proposal was "seen in some quarters as rather cheeky, to put it mildly." Why cheeky? Because the proposed arrangement could "entail the government handing over more cash for the data under the new arrangement than it does at present through ownership of the satellites."

Another criticism of the "privatization" scheme stemmed from the fact that it might jeopardize the arrangement under which the United States "swaps" data from its meteorological satellites with other foreign entities such as Japan, the USSR, and the eleven countries of the European Space Agency. Toward the end of 1983, critics of the sale won out. Congress voted to stop the President from going ahead with the scheme to sell weather and earth-resources satellites as a package deal. However, the sale of Landsat alone went ahead as planned.

INTERNATIONAL COMPETITION and COOPERATION

The United States is aiming toward broad international cooperation for the TIROS, which, like so many other federal programs, is experiencing sharp budget pressures as a result of Gramm-Rudman legislation. Under this new expenditure-limiting bill, the United States will be hard pressed to maintain a two-satellite TIROS system. Coverage cutbacks would affect business enterprises and researchers in many foreign countries, including Australia, France, Italy, Japan, Norway, and West Germany, to name only a conspicuous few. In response to this ticklish situation, they are banding together in hopes of finding a way to share expenses. Japan, for example, is formulating plans to contribute sensors, structures, and an operational ground system. Norway would like to contribute ground support. Australia is considering a contribution of sensors and a special device that provides powerful mathematical processing for the images.

Today's NOAA satellites already carry French-built relay equipment to transmit their data. The French have also created a commercial agency to promote international utilization of their Argos system, which is jointly operated by the French Space Agency, NASA, and NOAA. This agency, which is attempting to turn a profit, was created with a $2.1 million joint investment by the French Space Agency, the French Oceanographic Institute, and a pool of French banks.

The SARSAT search-and-rescue satellite is another international project built on an impressive scale. All together, it involves the cooperative efforts of eleven sovereign nations. The Canadians and the French have provided a search-and-rescue satellite aided by additional payloads carried aboard both American and Soviet satellites. The signals they pick up from travelers requesting help are relayed by American and Russian ships to receiving stations in France and several other countries all around the world.

Currently, Fairchild and the Jet Propulsion Laboratory are teamed with the French on a new oceanographic satellite called Topex. When it reaches orbit in 1991, Topex will measure the average heights of the oceans to an accuracy of a fraction of an inch. Armed with this precise information, meteorologists and climatologists may be able to produce long-range weather forecasts and detect the disastrous El Niño weather phenomenon that occurs every few years.

Meanwhile, half a world away in Shanghai, China, international cooperation is appearing in another form as American aerospace experts help the Chinese with their first weather satellite, to be launched into a 500-mile near-polar orbit in the early 1990s. The new Chinese satellite is being masterminded by the Shanghai Institute of Satellite Engineering. Its imaging system, a television-based device similar to the one on America's TIROS, is being designed and built at the Shanghai Institute of Satellite Engineering. The American aerospace industry will supply only one major component, a tape recorder, to work in tandem with the one built by the Chinese.

The Chinese weather satellite will also carry three radiometers. One will be designed to respond to infrared illumination; the other two will operate in visible portions of the spectrum. During its anticipated orbital lifetime of one to two years, the Chinese satellite will transmit data to any country that has data-reception capabilities compatible with American weather satellites.

FUTURE SATELLITES and THEIR ENHANCED CAPABILITIES

One of the most exciting weather projects for the future, the Global Atmospheric Research Program (GARP) is designed to increase our understanding

USING WEATHER SATELLITES to SAVE LIVES

If a special weather satellite had not been available when Serge Goriely's four-wheel-drive Citroën whipped out of control in a remote African desert, he might not be alive today. Goriely, a twenty-one-year-old professional racecar driver, suffered a fractured skull and lay motionless beside his crushed vehicle after it crashed, rolled over several times, and threw him out on the dust.

Fortunately, his car was equipped with an experimental search-and-rescue beacon that was automatically activated when his car went off the road. Immediately, it began sending a distress signal into space for relay back to Paris, where it was picked up only seventeen minutes later. A doctor was promptly flown to the scene of the accident, arriving there seventy-nine minutes after the crash. He patched Goriely back together, then admitted him to a nearby hospital for several days of recuperation before his colleagues knew for sure that he would live long enough to join the 344 others whose lives had been saved by SARSAT.

Teams of technicians in the United States, Canada, France, and the Soviet Union, and seven other participating nations work together to make sure SARSAT stays on the air. Emergency beacons—space-age cries for help—stream up to the satellites from planes, boats, and even battered racecars for immediate retransmission by American and Russian satellites. Relay stations on the ground then pass the information on to rescue centers assigned to dispatch appropriate help. The satellites are designed to relay specially coded messages that tell who (or what) is in trouble and the approximate location of the distress beacon.

Before the SARSAT system was available, average notification time for a missing aircraft was thirty-six to forty-eight hours. However, if lives are to be saved, rescue must usually be accomplished within twenty-four hours. With four active SARSATS in the constellation, an emergency signal from Africa, or any other remote location, can always be picked up by ground monitoring systems within one hour.

of the physical processes taking place in the universe. Satellites will be an integral part of this ambitious effort, which has been receiving enthusiastic worldwide support.

Another possible breakthrough will involve the use of a pulsed laser for measuring global winds by the Doppler shift of light reflected from particulates floating in the air. The new Global Horizontal Sounding Technique could also be of comparable importance. In that effort satellites will be used to track constant-altitude balloons as they are carried along by winds above the Southern Hemisphere.

EL NIÑO and the TOPEX SATELLITE

Freezing rains sweep across Florida's orange crop. Hail in Kansas damages winter wheat. Prolonged drought in the San Joaquin Valley burns the lettuce. What in the world could be causing this? El Niño!

In just the past decade scientists have learned that El Niño, a periodic depression in the waters of the South Pacific, strongly influences weather patterns throughout the Pacific Basin and, to a lesser extent, throughout the world. El Niño is centered in a small patch of ocean off the coast of Peru, where 13 million tons of anchovies, slender finger-length fish, are harvested in an average year. Few are eaten directly by humans, but Peruvian anchovies constitute one-fifth of the world's annual catch of commercial fish. Unfortunately, when El Niño cuts across the Pacific, every seven years or so, anchovy harvests plummet, soybean futures rise, and the price of chickens in the small towns of South Carolina rises by 40 percent or more.

The Peruvian fisheries are so productive because cold water pushes up to the surface carrying a rich load of nutrients to feed tiny microscopic plants. El Niño disrupts the upswelling patterns by sloshing warm water eastward across the Pacific and southward along the Peruvian coast, idling fishermen and starving millions of coastal birds.

Fortunately, alert meteorologists have trained themselves to read El Niño's probable future. "The region forms the core of the heat engine that drives the world's weather and climate," explains oceanographer William Patzert of the Scripps Institute.

The Topex satellite now being developed under the sponsorship of NASA's Jet Propulsion Laboratory and the French government will provide much of the information needed to predict the next El Niño. Topex will carry a sensitive radar altimeter capable of measuring the heights of the oceans to an almost unbelievable accuracy—somewhere between three-eighths and three-quarters of an inch! Topex will orbit in a 750-nautical-mile polar orbit swinging around the earth every 104 minutes.

Pinning down El Niño will help the poor people of Peru, but it will also benefit many others living in distant lands. El Niño's curious predictability has helped convince today's weather experts that if they can understand all the interactions among the earth's many forms of energy—sun, waves, tides—they may eventually learn to predict average weather patterns days, weeks, even months in advance.

Armed with these and other valuable pieces of information, the scientists of the world may eventually develop effective weather-modification techniques. Someday, cloud seeding might consistently trigger rain in drought-stricken areas and dissipate hurricanes, tornadoes, and devastating floods. Successful weather modification would provide enormous economic benefits—especially to Third World countries where food is often in short supply. Harvests could be accentuated, transportation and shipping could become far more efficient, and the most devastating effects of freakish weather could be largely alleviated.

7

SPACE-AGE NAVIGATION

Eighteenth-century British sailors exhibited an almost haughty disdain for accurate navigation. When asked how to guide a ship from London to the New World, one limey navigator is said to have replied: "Sail south until the butter melts, then turn right."

Britannia's seamen, with a little judicious help from the lowly bumblebee, ruled the waves for several profitable decades, but they paid for their lack of navigational expertise with precious ships and expensive cargoes, and on occasion they paid extra with their own lives.* The Maritime Museum at Greenwich holds a special display depicting some of the tragic results of inaccurate navigation. In 1691, for example, several ships of war were lost off Plymouth when the navigator mistook the Deadman for Berry Head. Another devastating incident occurred in 1707 when Sir Cloudsley Shovel was assigned to guide a British flotilla from Gibraltar to London. After twelve days shrouded in heavy overcast, he ran aground at the Scilly Islands. Four ships and 2,500 men were lost.

These and similar disasters at sea moved Parliament to establish the British Board of Longitude, a special study group composed of the finest scientists living in the British Isles. They were ordered to devise a practical scheme for determining the locations of ships sailing on long journeys. After a heated debate, the board offered a prize of 20,000 English pounds to anyone who could develop a method for fixing a ship's position within 30 nautical miles after a transoceanic voyage lasting six weeks.

*The two nineteenth-century biologists Karl Vogt and Ernst Haeckel once observed that the British Empire owed its power and wealth largely to bumblebees. They reasoned that the true source of England's influence resided mainly in its superb navy, whose sailors were fed with beef "which came from cattle that subsisted on clover," which would not grow without "pollination by bumblebees."

One proposal put forward by contemporary astronomers would have required that navigators take precise sightings of the moons of Jupiter whenever they were eclipsed by the planet. If trials had demonstrated the workability of this novel approach, special astronomical guides would have been furnished to the captain of every flagship or perhaps every ship in the British fleet. The theory was quite elegant; but unfortunately, no one was able to tell the navigator how to make the necessary observations under the rugged conditions existing at sea.

An alternate approach called for a series of "lightships" to be anchored along the principal shipping lanes on the North Atlantic. The crew of each lightship would fire luminous "star shells" at regular intervals timed to explode at an altitude of 6,400 feet. A ship in the area could calculate the distance to the nearest lightship by timing the duration between the visible flash and the sound of the exploding shell.

Still another approach would determine position by combining sextant sightings of the stars with precise time measurements. Accurate time is necessary because the earth's rotation causes the stars to sweep across the sky 15 degrees every hour. A one-minute timing error translates into a 15-nautical-mile uncertainty in longitudinal position. Unfortunately, measuring time accurately aboard ship presents another set of tricky problems. One imaginative individual, whose name has long since been forgotten, advocated the use of a special patent medicine said to involve some rather extraordinary properties. Unlike other popular nostrums of the day, "the Power of Sympathy," as its inventor called it, was applied not to the wound, but to the weapon that inflicted it. *The World of Mathematics,* a collection of articles dealing with the history of technology, describes how this magical remedy was to be employed as an aid to maritime navigation:

> Before sailing, every ship should be furnished with a wounded dog. A reliable observer on shore, equipped with a standard clock and a bandage from the dog's wound, would do the rest. Every hour on the dot, he would immerse the dog's bandage in a solution of the Power of Sympathy and the dog on shipboard would yelp the hour.*

As far as we know, this method of navigation was never actually tested; so we have no convincing evidence that it would have worked as advertised. However, in 1761, after forty years of painstaking labor, a barely educated English cabinet-maker named John Harrison successfully claimed the 20,000-pound prize. Harrison's solution involved the development of a new shipboard timepiece, the marine chronometer, which was amazingly accurate for its day. On a rolling ship in

* *The World of Mathematics* (New York: Simon & Schuster, 1956).

nearly any weather, it gained or lost, on average, only about one second every twenty-four hours.

Harrison's marine chronometer was a marvel of clever design. He constructed parts of it from bimetallic strips to compensate for temperature variations, he mounted it on swiveling gimbals to minimize the effect of wave-induced motions, and he rigged it with special mechanisms so it could be wound while it continued to keep accurate time. Harrison built four different versions of his chronometer during the last forty years of his life, all of which can be seen today in Britain's Maritime Museum.

By 1761, he was a broken man, enfeebled by long hours of painstaking labor. He was only sixty years old, but he did not have enough strength to prove he was worthy of the prize. So he asked his son, William, to sail from London to Jamaica to test the capabilities of the fourth version of the marine chronometer. During the entire journey, which lasted approximately six weeks, the chronometer lost less than one minute. It also demonstrated a navigation accuracy of 20 nautical miles. Disputes raged for years thereafter, but eventually, after several other demonstrations, John Harrison was awarded the entire 20,000 pounds by the British Board of Longitude.

For the next two centuries, sextant measurements timed by precise marine chronometers represented the only reliable means of fixing position in unfamiliar waters. The sextant is still used on the ground, at sea, and in space, but today radio-navigation techniques are more commonly employed.

Radio navigation was perfected in the early years of World War II when British researchers found that in a typical bombing raid against the Nazi war machine, only about 3 percent of the bombs were landing within 5 miles of their intended targets. By war's end, England's bomber crews had substantially improved their accuracy by relying upon Decca and other precise radio-navigation techniques. Radio navigation is a method whereby the position of a user's craft is determined by picking up radio signals broadcast from multiple transmitters.

THE ADVANTAGES of RADIO NAVIGATION from SPACE

Ground-based transmitters are adequate for many practical applications. In fact, according to a survey conducted by the IEEE (Institute of Electrical and Electronics Engineers), at least 1,385,000 navigation receivers are in use in the United States; by IEEE reckoning, 95 percent of them rely upon signals from ground-based transmitters. However, if accurate *global* navigation is the goal, positioning the transmitters on the ground entails certain serious disadvantages. High-frequency radio waves can provide accurate navigation, but they travel in straight lines. They do not reach beyond the horizon, and so coverage is strictly limited. By contrast, certain low-frequency signals hug the ground or are reflected by the ionosphere, so they can be received over vast areas, but do not yield good accuracy.

Fortunately, a practical solution is available: if we move the transmitters into space aboard orbiting satellites they can provide wide-area coverage with accurate high-frequency radio waves.

In 1959 the 3¼-pound Vanguard satellite, America's "beeping grapefruit," accidentally demonstrated one form of space-based radio navigation when researchers realized that its orbital motion created Doppler-shift effects that differed sharply depending on the location of ground-based observers. The most familiar example of Doppler shift is the change in pitch of the whistle of a moving train. As the train approaches, the sound waves from its whistle are compressed, thus producing a higher pitch; but as the train recedes, they are stretched out, and the pitch drops. This interesting phenomenon, as applied to radio waves rather than sound, became the basis of the Transit, our first space-based radio-navigation system. In 1964 the first Transit satellite was sent into orbit to aid in submarine navigation. Five of the Transits are in orbit today broadcasting the navigation signals used by receivers aboard thousands of maritime vessels.

A Transit receiver finds its position by observing the Doppler shift pattern of a satellite as it moves across the sky. Each specific location on earth produces a unique Doppler-shift variation. Given this information, computer processing fixes the user's longitude and latitude.

THE NAVSTAR GLOBAL POSITIONING SYSTEM

The Transit navigation satellites are in low-altitude orbits 665 miles above the earth, so they cannot provide continuous navigation coverage for their users. In fact, on the average a typical user must wait an hour or so to get a position fix. However, a new constellation of satellites, the Navstar Global Positioning System (GPS), now being installed in space, will provide global coverage at all times. It will also provide accurate, instantaneous navigation.

When it is fully operational in three or four years, the Navstar Global Positioning System will involve eighteen to twenty-one satellites launched into six orbit planes each tipped 55 degrees with respect to the equator. All of the satellites will be placed in 11,000-nautical-mile orbits, where they will require twelve hours to travel around the earth. Because the *Challenger* accident delayed the shuttle program, expendable Delta boosters built by McDonnell Douglas will carry most of the early Navstar satellites into space. The redesigned shuttle will share some of the later launches.

Like most of its competitors, the Navstar GPS is a radio-navigation system that uses passive triangulation. Each satellite broadcasts prearranged timing pulses blanketing the full disk of the earth. When the receiver picks up a timing pulse, it

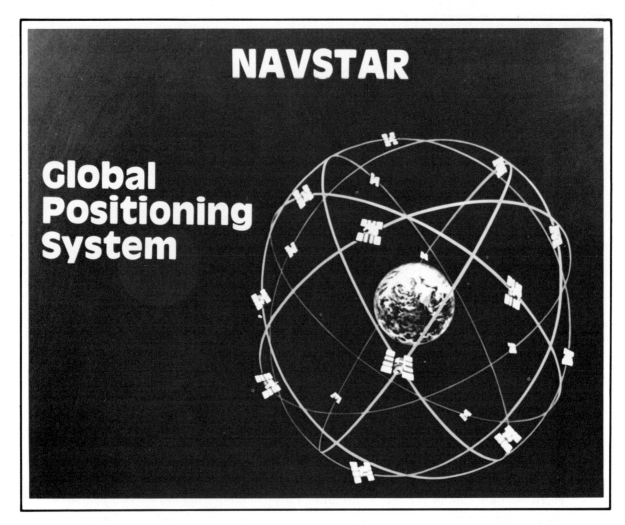

NAVSTAR

Global Positioning System

When it reaches full operational status in the early 1990s, the Navstar constellation will consist of eighteen to twenty-one navigation satellites in twelve-hour orbits, 11,000 nautical miles above the earth. By picking up signals from the satellites, a Navstar receiver can fix its position to an accuracy of 50 feet anywhere in the world. Tens of thousands of receivers capable of determining the locations of boats, planes, trucks, trains, and family Chevrolets will be owned and operated by ordinary private citizens. Industry experts are projecting a market for $2 billion worth of receivers by the year 2001.

multiplies the signal travel time by the speed of light (186,000 miles per second) to get the range to the satellite.

In theory, three range measurements of this type could be used to nail down the user's location in three dimensions. In practice, however, information from a fourth satellite is used to compensate for any clock errors in the receiver. Thus the receivers can be equipped with inexpensive quartz-crystal oscillators rather than precisely synchronized atomic clocks. A crystal oscillator, which is smaller than

Each Navstar navigation satellite is constructed from 65,000 separate parts. Yet it is designed to operate six full years or 450 million miles without servicing. The solar cells mounted on its winglike solar arrays generate 710 watts of electricity to power the transmitter and the other satellite subsystems. Internal temperatures are maintained within narrow bands by thermostatically controlled louvers and insulation blankets wrapped around some of the critical components.

the head of a twopenny nail, would require nearly three years to gain (or lose) one second. Although this may seem impressive by ordinary standards, the atomic clocks on board the satellites are 10,000 times more stable and accurate.

Indeed, the key to the Navstar's extraordinary precision lies in the ability of the satellite's atomic clocks to keep amazingly accurate time. In a radio-navigation system even the smallest timing errors are intolerable, because a radio wave travels 1 foot in a *billionth* of a second. Consequently, every billionth-of-a-second timing inaccuracy creates at least a 1-foot error in navigation. To achieve the desired 50-foot accuracy worldwide, the satellite clocks must always be mutually synchronized to within 13 billionths of a second. Navstar's designers achieved this difficult goal by constructing miniature atomic clocks that are so accurate they would require 72,000 years to lose or gain a single second—and by resynchronizing them from the ground at least once every day.

In the 1970s, when preliminary concepts for the Navstar navigation system were first being investigated, a typical atomic clock was about the size of a household deepfreeze—far too big and heavy to fly into space. However, space-age miniaturization techniques have slimmed down today's atomic clocks to only 30 pounds, or even less. Each modern Navstar satellite is equipped with four mutually redundant atomic clocks: two cesium clocks and two rubidium clocks. If one fails, another is switched on to take its place.

MAKING MONEY from NAVSTAR NAVIGATION

So far, only about 500 Navstar receivers have been sold to civilian users, at prices ranging from $16,000 to $139,000 each. Sales have been constrained because so few Navstar satellites have been launched into space. In the past few years only about six of them have been in operation at any given time. However, the full eighteen-satellite constellation should be in place within three or four years, and when it is, the marketplace will explode.

According to projections published in the *Wall Street Journal,* as many as 250,000 Navstar receivers will be snapped up in the next thirteen years by transportation companies, research laboratories, and ordinary private citizens. In addition, the Army, Navy, Air Force, and Marine Corps are planning to purchase 20,000 battle-hardened receivers costing at least $20,000 each.

In 1985, aerospace consultant Phil Diamond of Washington, D.C., was commissioned to evaluate the commercial market for tomorrow's family of Navstar receivers. According to his projections, as many as 200,000 of them will probably be sold in the remainder of this century—if the price is right. Diamond's surveys indicate that mobile users—ships, boats, planes, trucks, trains—will constitute the bulk of tomorrow's navigation market. However, surveyors, astronomers, and research laboratories will also buy substantial numbers of Navstar receivers.

Diamond and his colleagues concluded that if the cheapest receivers remain at today's price of $16,000 (an extremely unlikely possibility), about 40,000 will be sold in the next thirteen years with total revenues of $1.05 billion. But if prices drop—as they surely will—the market will expand to include enormous numbers of users who cannot now afford accurate navigation. If prices do reach affordable levels, large numbers of delivery trucks and other commercial vehicles, for instance, may find Navstar navigation economically attractive. Diamond estimates

HUNTING for DINOSAURS with the NAVSTAR

Most applications for Navstar receivers are proposed with profits in mind, but a few innovative users are interested in things other than money, like spending a sweaty weekend hunting for dinosaurs. Consider, for instance, the adventure of Dr. Roy P. Mackal, a research biologist from the University of Chicago, and his colleague Dr. Herman Regusters, an engineering consultant at Cal Tech's Jet Propulsion Laboratory. During a visit to the Congo in the early 1980s, Mackal interviewed more than thirty pygmies who pumped him up with vivid descriptions of a strange, hippopotamus-size beast called a *mokele mbembe*.

According to their account, the giant animal, which spent most of its time immersed in swampy waters, had a "reddish-brown body, a long neck, a relatively small head, and a long, powerful tail." When Mackal showed them drawings of a variety of animals they all agreed that their *mokele mbembe* was most like the brontosaurus—the largest animal ever to walk the earth. The *mokele mbembes'* favorite hangout was a big lake also frequented by the local fishermen, who had, according to a *Science Digest* article, "erected a barrier across one of the rivers feeding the lake in order to keep the beasts out." But one of the monsters attempted to break through, "so the pygmies speared it, cut it up, and ate it."

Mackel became even more interested in returning for a careful search when he learned that several Western observers had also picked up traces of the oversized animals in the jungles of the Congo. In the 1770s, for instance, French missionaries had reported seeing "the tracks of a clawed animal the size of an elephant," and about two centuries later, "two separate German expeditions hinted at the existence of the elusive monster."

When he returned to the Congo in 1982, Roy B. Mackal carried video cameras and sonar devices designed to monitor the underwater movements of the *mokele mbembes*. He was hoping to find them paddling around in the swollen streams during the rainy season when water levels would likely rise enough for their families to venture out of their hiding places in the jungle and come downriver in search of food.

Mackal had planned to carry a Navstar receiver to help him locate the swampiest regions as revealed on false-color images obtained from the Landsat earth resources satellites. He tried to borrow a receiver from the military, but, unfortunately, all available units were tied up in the military test program. He went to the Congo anyway, but found no *mokele mbembes*. The conclusion thus seems obvious: if only a Navstar receiver had been available, public zoos all around the world would now have on display families of brontosaurus-like creatures supposedly long since extinct.

that at a retail price of $2,000 each for the cheapest receivers, at least 200,000 sets could be sold with total revenues reaching nearly $2 billion.

Dr. Keith McDonnell, an expert on the GPS at the Federal Aviation Administration in Washington, D.C., recently published estimates indicating that nonmilitary sales have, so far, totaled only about 500 receivers. But how large will the ultimate market turn out to be? And how much will tomorrow's receivers cost, when Sony produces them and they are on sale at Radio Shack and Sears?

We can gain some insight into the probable outcome by examining what has happened to the costs and sales of the Transit navigation receivers, which also pick up signals from space. In 1973, when 1,000 Transit receivers had been sold, the simplest ones cost $27,000 each. Seven years later, when 25,000 of them had reached the marketplace, the simplest models were selling for less than $2,000 apiece.

Today's cheapest Navstar receivers retail for $16,000 each. But if a total of 200,000 of them are sold in this century, how inexpensive might the cheapest models be? Some industry experts bravely mention retail prices as low as $500 each. If their estimates turn out to be accurate, new and exciting uses—backpackers, private boats, family cars—seem certain to emerge.

A typical receiver of today is about the size of a small electric typewriter, but a much smaller model, the "Virginia Slim" receiver, is appearing on the horizon. The Virginia Slim, which is sponsored by the U.S. military, will be about as big as a pack of king-size cigarettes. Once military dollars perfect the best design, civilian versions will almost certainly follow at affordable prices, and when they do, you will be able to carry an infallible guide in your vest pocket!

The Navstar satellites are being financed by the U.S. military, but the signals they transmit are available without charge to anyone at any time.* So far about twenty private companies, including Texas Instruments, Magnavox, Litton Industries, Rockwell International, and Stanford Telecommunications, have announced plans to build and market Navstar receivers. Promising commercial applications include nearly anything that moves: fishing vessels, cargo boats, private planes, trucks, trains, jeeps, helicopters, submarines, tanks, automobiles.

Rental markets with low capital requirements may also become big business. Consider this moneymaking possibility:

Each year thousands of tourists rent houseboats for a lazy cruise on the Delta just south of San Francisco. What if you could develop special software to display a young couple's boat on a TV screen displayed at the appropriate place on an image of the river? To enhance the sales potential, be sure to include color-coded contours showing the depth of the water and colorful markers for all the major tourist

*The navigation accuracy for nonmilitary users is purposely degraded, but it is still better than that of any competing technique.

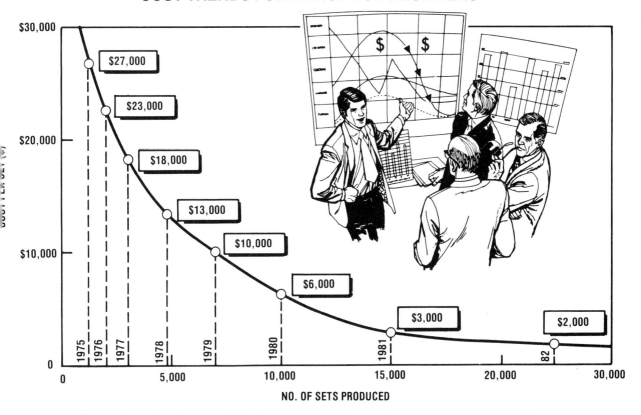

COST TRENDS FOR NAVIGATION RECEIVERS

Cost per unit ($)

$30,000

$27,000

$23,000

$20,000

$18,000

$13,000

$10,000

$10,000

$6,000

$3,000

$2,000

0

1975 1976 1977 1978 1979 1980 1981 82

0   5,000   10,000   15,000   20,000   30,000

NO. OF SETS PRODUCED

Historical trends in the price of the cheapest available Transit navigation receivers are traced in this graph. In 1973 when only 1,000 of them had been sold, the cheapest models were available for $27,000 each. Seven years later when 25,000 of them had been sold, their price had dropped below $2,000. Today only about 500 Navstar receivers are in use among civilians, and the least expensive models cost about $16,000 each. Seven years from now when thousands of them have been sold, what might be their price? After carefully studying the pace of evolving technology, some experts are projecting single-unit retail prices in the $500 range.

attractions. Program in instructions for running the boat, and you may be on the track of a promising business.

How about a different kind of program for those adventuresome souls who ride burros into the Grand Canyon? Would it be a good idea to include a tape-recorded commentary of the local terrain triggered by the location of the receiver? How about an emergency locator beacon in case the explorers have an accident or get lost along the way? How about a nationwide family of electronic maps showing old placer mines, gold-panning sites, abandoned ghost towns? Try one of these ideas, or think of a different possibility of your own, and you too can create a profit-making rental business using space-age navigation.

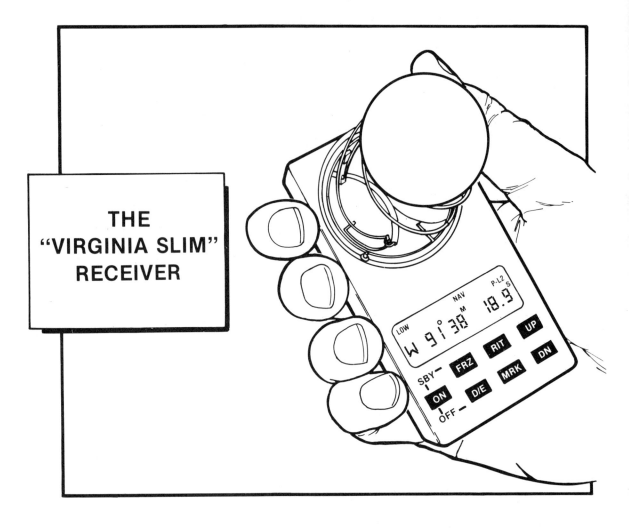

THE "VIRGINIA SLIM" RECEIVER

Most of the Navstar receivers now in production are about as big as portable electric type-writers. However, five companies are working under military contract to design special "Virginia Slim" receivers smaller than a king-size pack of cigarettes. Once the military places these miniature units into production, civilian versions will almost certainly reach the commercial marketplace; and if a big-volume demand does materialize, prices will probably drop to a few hundred dollars each.

Are any other business possibilities likely to show promise for the coming era of space-based navigation? Miniature pocket-size receivers will probably experience healthy sales. So will specialized software routines and custom chips for the receivers. A typical multichannel military receiver contains five computer chips. Four of them perform 200,000 operations per second; the fifth performs 500,000. The software for that receiver consists of 60,000 computer instructions—about the same information content as a pocket-size dictionary. Some specialized civil receivers, depending on the application, will probably have about the same amount of software.

Extremely precise user sets using differential or interferometry-type solutions (to be discussed later) should also fare well in commercial competition. Inventors, rental marketeers, and computer programmers should find ready opportunities for advanced Navstar technologies. Of course, there will also be large numbers of commercial users of Navstar navigation: land-based surveying, offshore oil exploration, precise time synchronization, air traffic control, and a whole host of others—some of which have not yet been imagined. Even tomorrow's coal miners, as we shall see, may end up using the signals from the Navstar satellites.

NAVIGATION on the HIGH SEAS

Firms engaging in offshore oil exploration are anxiously awaiting the availability of the continuous navigation signals soon to be available from the Navstar satellites. Their exploration vessels send seismic pulses down into the water to construct maps of the subsurface geological features. However, useful images of the hidden layers can be constructed only if the ship's location is known when it triggers each seismic pulse. Shore-based transmitters can help pinpoint the ship's location when it is within sight of land. Unfortunately, many promising oil-bearing portions of the continental shelf are well beyond the horizon.

Researchers at Shelltech in Calgary, Canada, have already used the partial Navstar constellation to navigate oil-exploration ships 180 miles off the coast of Newfoundland. According to their published report, "Data collection efficiencies increased by 200 percent compared with missions using conventional methods of navigation." Officials at Shelltech were so pleased with the outcome of their oil-exploration experiments they are now using the system to guide the construction crews digging the Rogers Railway Tunnel near Calgary. With the help of Navstar positioning, they are expecting the two crews to meet in the middle within 6 or 8 inches!

DIFFERENTIAL NAVIGATION

Navstar navigation is quite a bit more accurate than most competing techniques, but the conventional Navstar system does not have enough precision for use aboard ships in constricted harbors and inland waterways. Fortunately, the U.S. Coast Guard and others are working on an improved concept called differential navigation to enhance its accuracy in these critical locations. A differential navigation system uses two receivers which continuously exchange navigation information, thus eliminating many of the errors common to the two solutions. Errors as small as 6 or 7 feet, or even smaller, can be achieved, depending on the distance between the two receivers and the sophistication of their computer-processing techniques.

To encourage the widespread adoption of differential navigation, Coast Guard researchers are developing standard signal formats for the data exchange. Private companies, including Dr. Peter MacDoran's ISTAC Corporation (Pasadena, California), are also developing differential-navigation hardware for profit-making purposes.

MacDoran masterminded his approach when he was working as a researcher at the Jet Propulsion Laboratory on the Topex oceanographic satellite, which is designed to measure the average heights of the world's oceans to an accuracy of a fraction of an inch. The Topex determines its position in space by picking up the signals transmitted by the Navstar satellites and processing them via special mathematical algorithms. Three-dimensional accuracies are expected to be about 4 inches—a fortyfold improvement over normal Navstar navigation. These impressive gains are achieved by using differential navigation coupled with special interferometry techniques adapted from astronomy.

Peter MacDoran does not intend to launch any satellites. His approach uses the signals from any available constellation, including the Glonass navigation satellites launched by the Soviet Union. Profits will come from the sales of his Bible-sized navigation receivers and from the services his company provides. So far, they have sold about twenty receivers for $57,000 each.

All necessary seed money for ISTAC has been raised from friends and associates who are supporting the closely held corporation. But if larger capitalization is ever required, MacDoran will probably have to solicit fresh supplies of money from venture capitalists and fellow entrepreneurs.

The study of coal-mine subsidence is one promising application of MacDoran's interferometry technique. After a large amount of coal is removed from a mine, the ground gradually sinks to fill in the gap. Interferometry-type Navstar receivers mounted on concrete "benchmarks" on the ground above the mines can be used to monitor the rates of subsidence. This promotes greater understanding of the rate and extent of surface-level subsidence under varying conditions to help the engineers decide where to locate future mines.

FLIGHT MONITORING and AIR TRAFFIC CONTROL

Guiding airplanes to and from America's 7,000 airfields is one of the most costly and labor-intensive navigation problems we face in today's technological world. America's commercial airlines operate only about 3,500 aircraft, but 250,000 smaller planes are also hurtling through the skies. Hundreds of ground-based

USING SATELLITES to TRACK ARCTIC ICEBERGS

In 1912 the "unsinkable" British luxury liner *Titanic* sank when it collided with an Arctic iceberg. This ship-ice encounter is well known to the general public but at least a dozen other less famous collisions have occurred in this century. During the five-month iceberg season, some shipping routes must be lengthened as much as 30 percent to skirt the worst concentrations of floating ice. This ties up valuable cargoes and cuts the productivity of shipborne crews.

To minimize the probability of damaging collisions, the International Ice Patrol, which is managed by the U.S. Coast Guard, gathers and disseminates daily information on iceberg sightings. Its ships and planes also crisscross Arctic waters in search of wandering icebergs. Radio stations manned by Ice Patrol personnel broadcast warnings to ships in the North Atlantic twice each day.

Researchers have attempted to destroy icebergs by bombing, torpedoing, shelling, and ramming, and by darkening their surface with lampblack to increase melting rates. In one test, twenty 1,000-pound bombs were dropped on a 250,000-ton iceberg. Unfortunately, only 20 percent of it was chipped away. Of course, icebergs are often much larger than 250,000 tons. Some are 50 miles long.

Because of their high degree of accuracy and their continuous availability, the Navstar satellites could provide an attractive method for tracking the 300 or so icebergs that pass below the 48th parallel in an average year. A Navstar receiver would be dropped onto the iceberg to broadcast its current position to any nearby vessels. Similar, but less capable, space-based tracking techniques have already been tested at least a dozen times. In one of the tests, researchers from Chevron parachuted an 80-pound transmitter down to the surface of an Arctic iceberg. It then relayed crude position coordinates to a NASA tracking station through Nimbus weather satellites.

Over a three-month interval, the iceberg ambled across 200 miles of open ocean. On the average, it traveled less than 5 miles per day, well below walking speed. About 20 percent of the time, it was stuck on the bottom or jammed against various islands. Unlike the Nimbus method of tracking icebergs with its time-consuming data relays and off-site computer processing, the Navstar approach could provide precise tracking with real-time warnings for any ships that might be in the vicinity of Arctic ice.

transmitters together with 11,000 professional air traffic controllers are assigned to help maintain safe separation distances.

Many experts are convinced that the Navstar satellites can help simplify airborne navigation and promote safer and cheaper flight operations. If the Navstar

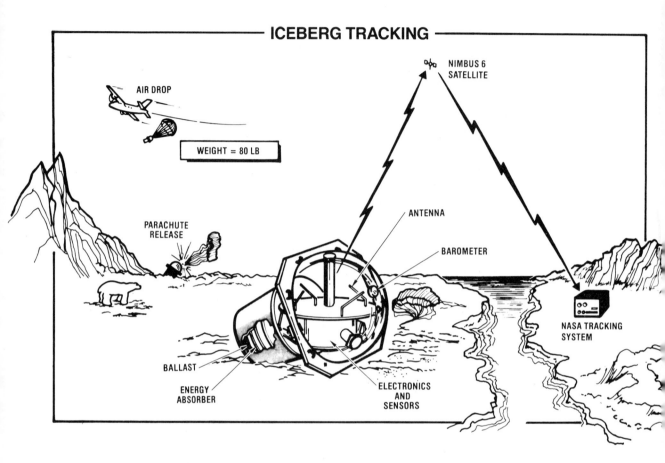

ICEBERG TRACKING

AIR DROP

WEIGHT = 80 LB

PARACHUTE RELEASE

NIMBUS 6 SATELLITE

ANTENNA

BAROMETER

NASA TRACKING SYSTEM

BALLAST

ENERGY ABSORBER

ELECTRONICS AND SENSORS

So far, American oceanographers have parachuted radio transmitters onto the surface of at least a dozen Arctic icebergs. Once in place, the transmitter relays radio signals through orbiting satellites to provide tracking pulses that can be used to reconstruct the convoluted trajectory of the iceberg to an accuracy of a few thousand feet. With Navstar tracking, accuracies can be improved and real-time warnings can be provided to any ships in the vicinity of the iceberg. This will enhance the safety of the crews and allow vessels plying the North Atlantic to reach their destinations sooner, more safely, and with less fuel consumption.

can crack this vast and expanding market, receiver prices will drop to much more affordable levels, thus encouraging deeper penetrations of other, larger markets such as trucking fleets, pleasure boats, and even private cars.

In July 1983, the Government Avionics Division of Rockwell International demonstrated some of the airborne capabilities of Navstar navigation by using two

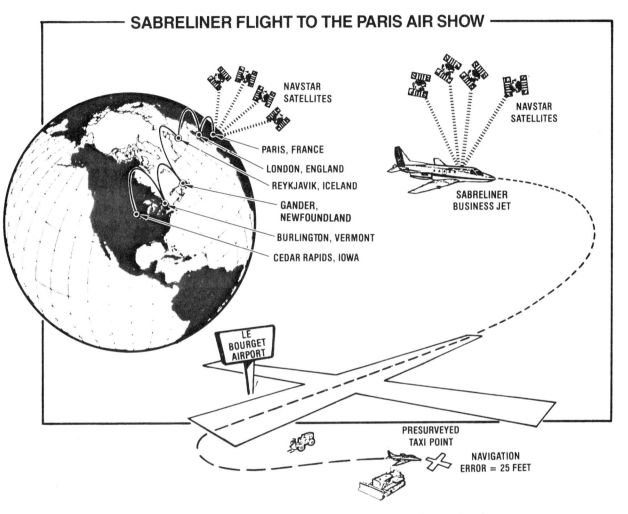

SABRELINER FLIGHT TO THE PARIS AIR SHOW

NAVSTAR SATELLITES

NAVSTAR SATELLITES

PARIS, FRANCE

LONDON, ENGLAND

REYKJAVIK, ICELAND

GANDER, NEWFOUNDLAND

BURLINGTON, VERMONT

CEDAR RAPIDS, IOWA

SABRELINER BUSINESS JET

LE BOURGET AIRPORT

PRESURVEYED TAXI POINT

NAVIGATION ERROR = 25 FEET

In July 1983, signals from the Navstar navigation satellites were used to guide a business jet from Cedar Rapids, Iowa, to the Paris Air Show. As these sketches illustrate, the flight was divided into five segments separated by waiting periods to allow the satellites to reappear above the horizon. When he landed at Le Bourget Field, the pilot taxied to a presurveyed spot in the apron of the runway, ending up within 25 feet of his intended destination.

receivers to guide a Sabreliner business jet from the Rockwell plant at Cedar Rapids, Iowa, across the Atlantic to the Paris Air Show. When the pilot landed at Le Bourget Field he made a blind taxi run to a presurveyed spot on the apron of the runway. After flying more than 3,000 miles, under constant direction from the Navstar signals, he ended up within 25 feet of his final destination.

Two months later, transoceanic navigation suddenly received renewed attention when Korean Airlines Flight 707 strayed off course and was destroyed by a Soviet air-to-air missile. Within days of this tragic incident, the United States Congress directed the Federal Aviation Administration to take a fresh look at satellite-based radio navigation.

For complete safety, the FAA is developing monitoring systems to ensure that unsuspecting pilots will never be led astray by a malfunctioning satellite. Signal monitoring may be accomplished onboard the satellites, from ground-based stations, or automatically by each aircraft. All three approaches are being investigated. But regardless of the outcome, the Navstar system will almost certainly be certified for use by tomorrow's airplanes, thus opening up vast new opportunities for sales of the receivers in mass-production quantities.

PRECISE TIME SYNCHRONIZATION

Unlike airborne navigation, which must await the launch of the full constellation of GPS satellites, precise time-synchronization receivers are already in widespread use. When a navigation receiver solves for position, its clock is automatically updated by the signals from the satellites. With the proper equipment, that same clock-correction signal can be used to synchronize atomic clocks anywhere in the world. In fact, time-synchronization receivers are cheaper and easier to produce than the ones being used for navigation. Typical accuracies are about 30 to 50 billionths of a second! (In 50 billionths of a second a supersonic transport screaming through the sky at 2,000 miles per hour moves forward a distance equal to one thin coat of paint.)

But why do we need to synchronize atomic clocks to such astounding precision? When you are meeting a friend for dinner, time accuracies that great are hardly ever required. You would never think of asking your friend, "Please meet me at 7.376125973 seconds after twelve." For ordinary social interactions, time accuracies measured in minutes or seconds will almost always suffice. But when machines interact with other machines, extreme accuracies may be required. Communication links, computer networks, surveillance systems, and military encryption devices all require extremely precise time. So do certain kinds of astronomical observations.

The Transit navigation satellites can provide us with time synchronization that is accurate enough for many scientific and industrial purposes. So can atomic clock trips in which portable atomic clocks are flown on commercial jetliners to distant locations to keep widely separated timing devices in proper synchronization. However, the timing pulses broadcast by the Navstar satellites are hundreds of times more accurate than those available from any other global system. The full constellation of eighteen satellites is not yet available, but most time-synchronization applications do not require access to four satellites. Clocks at known locations need the signal from only one satellite—a coverage that is provided by the present constellation at most locations sixteen to twenty hours each day.

Approximately one hundred time-synchronization receivers have already been sold, mostly to scientific laboratories and military users. Most of these sales have been made by Stanford Telecommunications of Palo Alto, California, which specializes in time-sync receivers.

NAVIGATING YOUR FAMILY CAR

Visitors at the 1982 World's Fair in New Orleans got an opportunity to see an unusually interesting exhibit. "Have you seen that fancy navigation display at the Chrysler Pavilion? It puts pretty maps right on your dashboard, with a little marker that shows where you are!"

"I saw it. And I loved it! But I hear they're not really selling it, at least not yet."

True, the dashboard-mounted device on display was not for sale. In fact, it wasn't even fully functional. Chrysler's engineers had fibbed a bit when they put their display together. But in the meantime, Ford, Chrysler, and General Motors have all demonstrated operational Navstar receivers for use on ordinary private cars.

Signals from the Navstar satellites fix the car's location, which is displayed against a background of freeways and streets on a television screen mounted in the dashboard. In one system your car's marker remains at the center of the screen and, as you drive, the electronic map turns and moves so the street ahead always points toward the top of the display.

Eventually, compact disks, similar to the ones that bring you the voice of Barbra Streisand with such vibrant realism, will store color maps of all fifty states. Touch a button and the map scale will change to any of seven different levels of magnification. The biggest scale displays the entire 41,000-mile Interstate Highway System. Zoom in for a close-up and all the streets in your neighborhood will come into view.

Digital maps for this and other applications are already becoming big business. Unlike the paper maps printed in an atlas or an encyclopedia, they can be updated, manipulated, and analyzed in a number of interesting ways. Navigation aside, digital maps are becoming enormously profitable. By one estimate they are, today, a $200 million yearly business, and they should reach $1 billion a year by the early 1990s. The digital maps of tomorrow will be computer-processed to determine optimal routes for trucking companies and delivery firms, thus cutting driving distances and travel times, and in the process saving substantial amounts of fuel.

Digital maps coupled with accurate electronic navigation can also simplify dispatching operations for taxi fleets, ambulances, and delivery vans. The position of each vehicle will be displayed in the cab of the vehicle. At the same time it will be transmitted to dispatching headquarters, where it will be displayed on a larger digital map that highlights the locations of all the other drivers on the company payroll. This and other relevant information will be computer-processed to optimize the drivers' routes, speed deliveries, help handle emergencies, and minimize the expensive "down time" of the vehicles in the fleet.

GEOSTAR'S PRIVATELY OWNED NAVIGATION SATELLITES

In the remainder of this century the government's Navstar navigation system will produce billions of dollars in revenues for private, profit-making companies, but other competing constellations of navigation satellites may also carve out a portion of the enormous profits to be made. The principal advantage of most competing systems is that they provide both reliable navigation and two-way communication.

The Geostar Corporation (Washington, D.C.) is a front-runner among the proposed satellite-based radio-navigation systems. Geostar officials have already raised at least $49 million from private investors, venture capitalists, and commercial institutions, and they are looking for tens of millions more. They have also collected deposits for more than 5,000 navigation receivers from government agencies, delivery services, and private trucking firms. These agreements call for a total receiver price of $2,900 plus a $35 monthly servicing fee. Geostar's officials plan to use this and other money in the early 1990s, to launch four privately owned navigation satellites into geosynchronous orbits aboard the French Ariane. They have already demonstrated their concept using both ground-based transmitters and a "piggyback" payload carried aboard a commercial communication satellite (GStar II), and they have obtained approval from the Federal Communications Commission for the frequency allocations and the orbital slots they need for their satellites.

The Geostar concept was developed in 1978 by Dr. Gerard O'Neill of Princeton University. His inspiration was born of tragedy when two airplanes slapped together above sunny Southern California. "In clear skies over San Diego, the nation witnessed a horrible air tragedy," wrote Rob Stoddard in *Space Communications*. "Despite good weather conditions and state-of-the-art communications, a small private plane collided in midair with a crowded 727 commercial jetliner, sending scores of people plunging to their deaths." O'Neill, himself a frequent air traveler, was shattered by the early descriptions of the incident even before he learned that a close friend was aboard the 727. "There had to be a way to avoid this type of tragedy in the future," he later told a reporter.

By funneling his grief into constructive channels and using his considerable scientific expertise, O'Neill developed the Geostar concept, a satellite-based radio-navigation system that provides precise position coordinates and allows users to exchange simple "telegram messages" anywhere in the United States. Three competing companies, MCAA American Radio Determination Corporation, McGaw Space Technologies, and Omninet Corporation, are also planning to develop systems that make use of satellites to provide positioning and simple message services to mobile users, but Geostar is by far the most advanced.

Unlike the Navstar receivers, which themselves perform the navigation solution, Geostar's receivers are more akin to simple two-way radios. When a Geostar receiver requests its position, interrogation pulses are automatically transmitted to all three of the geosynchronous satellites, which, in turn, relay the request to a centrally located computer on the ground. The ground-based computer then performs the navigation solution and sends the results back to the user through one of the three satellites. For a small fee, the same communication channels can be used to relay short "telegram messages" between two or more Geostar subscribers.

Geostar's communication links are more complicated than the ones that service the Navstar users. But the receivers are simpler, and for the mobile population O'Neill and his colleagues are planning to serve, real-time communications will probably turn out to be far more valuable than the navigation services they are planning to provide.

By December 1985, Geostar had received firm orders for at least 5,000 transceivers each secured by a 5 percent deposit against the full price of $2,900 each. According to *Aviation Week,* Sony and Ma/Comm are each under contract to deliver 10,000 Geostar receivers. In the early 1990s, when all three dedicated satellites are slated to be in operation, Geostar's officials are hoping to have more sophisticated "pocket-size" receivers in production at a cost of about $500 each.

Most of the orders received so far have come from transportation companies, including Mayflower, Leaseway Transportation, and W. R. Grace. Four government agencies also hold sizable options on Geostar receivers.

Several years ago, Geostar's researchers conducted a series of tests at a site in the Sierra Nevada to check the feasibility of the Geostar concept. Later a piggyback payload carried aboard a communication satellite, GStar II demonstrated that the hardware also worked in space. Two other piggyback payloads aboard GStar III and SpaceNet IIIR will provide message relay without navigation. Those users who need navigation can use the ground-based Loran C for crude positioning. In 1989, GStar IV will carry another transmitter into space to provide accurate positioning. After that, in the early 1990s, dedicated Geostar satellites will be boosted into space.

For proper operation the full Geostar system required fifty-one separate inventions. In November 1982 the first patent was developed, and by October 1986 the FCC cleared the way for the Geostar Corporation to launch the necessary

THE GEOSTAR NAVIGATION SYSTEM

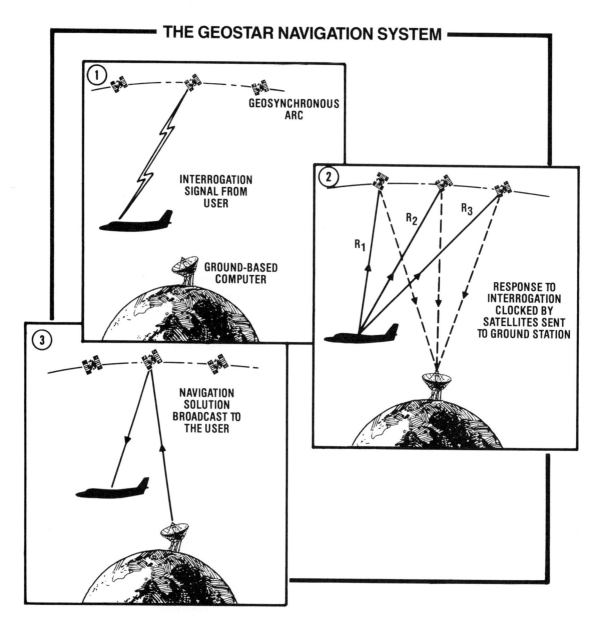

Unlike the Navstar Global Positioning System, Geostar will use a large ground-based computer to solve for each user's position whenever a request is received. Once the solution is complete, the position coordinates will be sent back to him through the satellites. This involves more complicated communication links and requires a costly mainframe computer at "Mission Control," but it simplifies the design of the receivers and provides the capability for two-way "telegram messages." The Geostar Corporation is a private, profit-making company that has already raised tens of millions of dollars for this space-age project. Investors include entrepreneurs, venture capitalists, and private banking institutions.

satellites. Over fifty individuals aired comments at the hearings, which included supporting testimony from the Association for American Railroads, the Bureau of the Census, several local police and fire departments, the Federal Drug Enforcement Administration, and two airlines, Western and United.

By the end of the third quarter of 1985, Geostar officials had raised $12.5 million from equity placements at $1.25 apiece. Incidentally, those purchased two years earlier (in 1983) had risen in value from $1.25 to $8 each. From January through July 1986, they raised an additional $21 million for a total capitalization of $39 million.

"It started off being individual investors," said Geostar's director of finances. "But in the meantime, it has evolved over time to being fairly significant institutional investors." However, despite impressive success in capital markets, Geostar has so far raised only a small fraction of the money it will need to launch the complete constellation of dedicated satellites. The documents submitted to the Federal Communications Commission forecast total on-orbit installation costs at just under $277 million. Overall expenditure and revenue projections further indicate that Geostar expects to raise $1.99 billion over a seven-year period, much of it from receiver sales and services to clients.

In their attempts to raise start-up capital, Geostar officials have been working with First Boston Corporation and Wheat First Securities in San Francisco. Martin Rothblatt, Geostar's chief operating officer, attributes their impressive success to these special ongoing relationships. But, of course, everything has not been easy at Geostar. "Danger may still lurk ahead," says Rob Stoddard of *Space Communications.* "A recent equipment failure combined with uncertainty over launch capabilities have dealt a one-two punch that has set back Geostar's start-up date by about one year."

The on-orbit failure occurred when a 45-pound piggyback payload for the Geostar was carried into orbit aboard GTE's GStar II satellite. The payload, which was built by the Astro-Electronics Division of RCA, operated successfully for about six weeks before it failed. Geostar officials have filed an insurance claim for its full value of $2.7 million, and an identical package is to be launched on the GStar III satellite—if the analysis team can isolate the difficulty in time to devise a fix.

The second setback occurred when the shuttle *Challenger* exploded and there were several later booster-rocket failures. Like many other companies with payloads waiting on the ground, Geostar is finding that reliable launch services are not easy to locate. Their officials have held exploratory talks with representatives from China and Japan, but they are still confident that the French Ariane will be able to carry their payloads to the geosynchronous altitude. In the meantime, despite a few setbacks, there has been "no loss of customer orders, no loss of financing, and no loss of vendor support," says Martin Rothblatt.

He failed to mention possible problems with competing navigation services. The FCC has, in fact, authorized two other firms to launch their own position-location satellites. And still another, Panar in Houston, Texas, is planning to provide similar navigation with its Starfix system, which will operate by using leased communication channels on four conventional communication satellites. Another privately owned navigation system, called "Starfind," is being masterminded by a small concern called Starfind, Inc., of Laguna Niguel, California. Already Starfind officials have contracted with Space Services, Inc., of Houston to handle the launches for their geosynchronous satellites. However, Geostar officials do not regard either Starfix or Starfind as a realistic competitor because they cannot provide the two-way navigation and communication services Geostar's experts are planning for their more sophisticated satellites.

Another form of competition may come from *mobile* communication satellites which can, at a considerably higher price, provide two-way voice communications for trucking fleets and other mobile users. However, industry observers contend that Geostar has an impressive lead over these more poorly capitalized competitors. In the long run, both Geostar and the mobile services will likely carve out large enough market niches to ensure their survival—and their profitability.

THE COMPETITION from ETAK

But even if it has no peers in space, Geostar still faces potentially formidable competition in the vehicular market from self-contained navigation systems whose hardware is located entirely on the ground. The most viable ground-based system is made by Etak of Palo Alto, California. The Etak system, which is already on the market, does not use radio-navigation transmitters of any kind. Instead, it relies upon "dead reckoning," a self-contained computer-based approach. An electronic compass and wheel-motion sensors are used to keep track of the movements of the vehicle as it travels along the highway. Computerized map-matching updates the car's position whenever it rounds a sharp corner or makes a right-angle turn. Etak officials claim that position accuracies of 50 feet are routinely achieved.

For the past two years, motorists in California have been buying the "affordable" model for $1,395 with a 4½-inch video screen and a larger 7½-inch version that costs $200 extra. Ordinary cassette tapes, which store the digital maps, retail for $35 each. Three tapes provide a complete set of maps covering San Francisco and its suburbs. With nationwide sales just beginning, Etak is projecting annual revenues in the $10 to $20 million range.

Future products from Etak will probably feature computer-optimized routing, dispatcher services, information on hotels and restaurants, full-color graphics, and perhaps even a flat-panel display that attaches to the sun visor of your car. If Etak

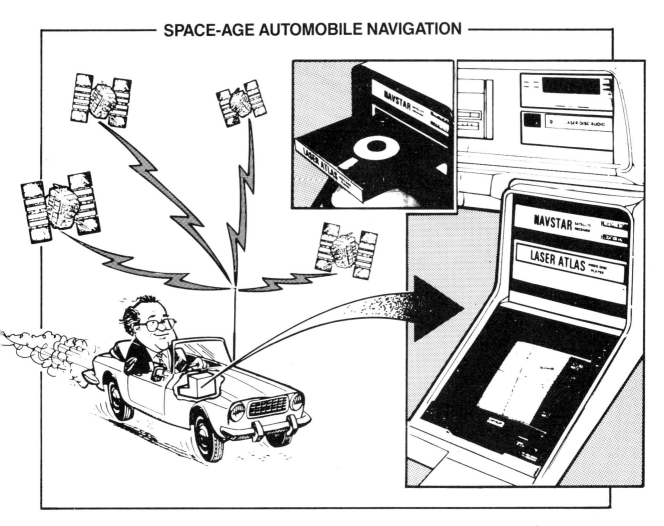

SPACE-AGE AUTOMOBILE NAVIGATION

This simple, but sophisticated, method for future navigation uses both dead-reckoning techniques and signals from the Navstar navigation satellites to fix the position of ordinary private cars. A cursor representing your car's location is superimposed on a full-color map of the surrounding streets and highways. As you travel along the road, the electronic map twists and turns so your car's cursor always remains at the center and the road ahead points toward the top of the screen. Another cursor marks your destination. At the touch of a button, you will be able to shrink or enlarge the full-color maps, choosing any of seven different levels of magnification.

eventually switches to compact laser disks, they would have enough extra storage capacity to provide electronic travel guides including pictures of tourist attractions and commercials aimed at vacationers and business travelers.

Etak is a closely held corporation, but General Motors has obtained warrants allowing it to buy 10 percent of the company's stock and is in the process of arranging joint production deals. General Motors officials have also announced that by the late 1980s, factory-installed versions should be available on at least a few GM cars.

TOMORROW'S HYBRID APPROACH to NAVIGATION

Although today's automotive navigation systems usually rely upon radio beacons or stand-alone navigation systems such as the one developed by Etak, navigation expert Robert L. French of Fort Worth, Texas, emphasizes the advantages of hybrid navigation systems for vehicles, ones that combine space-based radio navigation with dead-reckoning techniques. Initial positioning information for your car would be obtained from the satellites, but then if their signals are ever temporarily blocked by tall buildings or other obstructions, dead reckoning would ensure reasonably accurate navigation. On the other hand, if you veer off the highway for a quick trip through the woods, satellite navigation would keep your car from losing track of its position. A large fraction of the total cost of any convenient auto navigation system will be in the video display and the software to make it run properly. Consequently, a hybrid system of the type Robert L. French envisions would probably cost little more than a stand-alone version using either of the two different techniques.

Commerce should fall into four broad categories: telecommunications, remote sensing, materials processing, and launch services. And, in addition, there are things we cannot yet imagine. As Tom Brosz, editor of Commercial Space Report, *puts it, "In the Fortune 500 of space four hundred of them will be in things we don't yet know are worthwhile."*

"What They're After: Pennies from Heaven"
Esquire, May 1984

8

PRIVATELY OWNED BOOSTER ROCKETS

It is happening on a tiny island off the southern coast of Texas, an island populated by cattle and beefalo grazing contentedly on thick, mosquito-infested pastures. In hard hats and swimming trunks, they stride by in animated groups: young, dedicated engineers—with dreams as big as Texas ranch country—ready, willing, able to launch America's first privately financed booster upward toward the space frontier.

They gaze out across the grass at their strange space-age contraption from their bargain-basement "mission control," an olive-drab metal shed set behind a wall of sandbags. It sits all alone on a foot-thick slab of concrete, a 36-foot needle-nosed cylinder similar to the Redstone that, twenty years earlier, lifted Alan Shepard into space. Like Redstone and Thor, most reliable of the space-age boosters, it burns liquid oxygen and kerosene.

They call it their Percheron, because, like that sturdy French workhorse, its strength and dependability will weigh heavily on the minds of well-heeled investors who must join them if they are to make a business of launching payloads into space.

"Everyone laughed when I first told them about launching a rocket," says chief financier David Hannah, Jr. "Now I think people are starting to believe this dream can come true." Their futuristic dream of ferrying payloads into space is definitely no joke. It is financed by serious capital, $1.2 million of it in past profits from Texas "black gold" and sunbelt real estate. "Within ten years we could make $100 million to $120 million a year from twelve or so launches," Hannah observes with a broad Texas grin. His dream is embodied in Space Services, Inc., a Houston-based firm he founded in 1979.

Hopes are high that day on Matagorda Island, and everyone sweating with them in the burning Texas sun is on their side, even the hardnosed press reporters. But this day's launch is not to be. A glitch in the ignition system forces a postponement, so the big, disappointed bird must sit on its pad for another week. Once that difficulty has been ironed out, another countdown can begin. This time, when a tense finger presses the "launch" button, the Percheron blows up. However, the following year after fresh infusions of capital—$6 million from fifty-seven investors—another try. And finally Percheron does fly!

For launches into earth orbit the inexpensive Percherons were designed to be used in tandem. As *Newsweek* put it, "Seven rockets linked like a bundle of asparagus stalks would be needed to lift a satellite into a geosynchronous orbit 22,300 miles high." For that service, the fledgling company plans to charge $15 million—$7 million less than NASA's lowest rate. How have NASA's harried bureaucrats reacted to its menacing new competitor? "God love 'em. I hope they do it," said the space agency's administrator, James Beggs. "I'm a free-enterprise man."

After their first successful flight in September 1982, the designers at Space Services graduated to the Conestoga II, a multistage solid rocket capable of hurling a 950-pound satellite into a 500-mile polar orbit. Their price, about $10 million per flight, is comparable to the cost of the government's Scout, which has only about one-third the payload-carrying capability.

Space Services, Inc., is headed by former astronaut Donald (Deke) Slayton, who, together with Houston real-estate developer David Hannah, is trying to market the Conestoga for a variety of missions: remote sensing, search and rescue, low-altitude communications, and zero-g materials processing. Of course, materials processing is sensible only if the samples can be returned to earth. In one novel concept the Conestoga would orbit a small materials-processing satellite. Then, once its processing operations were complete, it would be plucked from orbit by the space shuttle.

The logo of Space Services, Inc., is filled with romance and patriotism. Within a dark circle, a covered wagon is pulled by two horses above a blue-green earth. On the left is an American flag, on the right the banner of the state of Texas. "We're here to stay," says David Hannah. "We have a key staff of about eight people. There are twenty of us working together in concert, but a lot of those have other sources of income." How will they attract sustaining business to keep up day-to-day operations? "The Landsat market is going to expand," explains Hannah. "We are going to play a part one way or the other."

In addition, a study by Battelle's Columbus Laboratories revealed "a market for at least ninety-six launches of Conestoga-class payloads over the next ten to fifteen years." That study was completed when the shuttle *Challenger* was still flying, and before the failure of several other rockets, including the French Ariane; today's business prospects should be considerably better. Those failures have left 150 payloads stranded on the ground with their sponsors scouring the world for the few available rockets. The Ariane, which can handle only ten launches per year from its pads in the jungles of French Guiana, is booked through 1989. Despite a

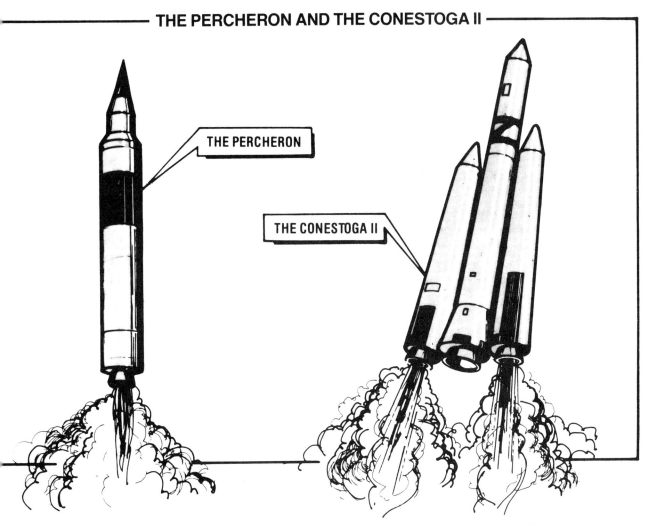

THE PERCHERON

THE CONESTOGA II

The Percheron rocket was developed by a courageous fraternity of Texas entrepreneurs. It blew up on its first launch, scattering debris across a small island off the south coast of Texas. But its developers were not deterred. A second try was successful, and their new booster, the Conestoga II, stands ready to carry thumb-size capsules containing cremated human remains into long-term orbits among the twinkling stars on the celestial sphere.

price hike from $30 million to $50 million per launch, the French signed eighteen new contracts in 1986, compared with eleven the previous year.

Moreover, Conestoga's sponsors have uncovered another surprising, almost eerie, source of business. This is how *Aviation Week* described it in January 1985: "The first commercial space satellite contracted for launch on a privately developed U.S. space booster will carry into orbit a payload of several thousand cremated humans on a space burial mission, initiating a new commercial space venture that would memorialize deceased individuals."

A SHORT HISTORY of ROCKETS

The ancient Chinese built the first rockets: slender tubes stuffed with black gunpowder fastened to long flat sticks that jutted out behind the rocket to promote stable flight. These early solid-fueled rockets, called Chinese fire arrows, were used in quantity on the outskirts of Peking in 1232 by special Chinese rocket brigades to push back Mongol cavalrymen, and in 1249 by the Moors in their successful campaign along the Iberian Peninsula.

Near the beginning of the nineteenth century, Englishman William Congreve concocted superior powder blends and moved the stabilizing stick to the center of the rocket for improved accuracy. In 1807 the British blasted Copenhagen with 25,000 Congreve rockets, and in 1814 they bombarded Fort McHenry, inadvertently providing the inspiration for our national anthem.

In 1903 a lonely Russian schoolteacher, Konstantin Tsiolkovsky, correctly concluded that rockets fueled with liquid hydrogen and liquid oxygen would be considerably more efficient than the simpler solid-fueled rockets then in use. He also devised a concept for stacking rockets one atop the other to give the desired speeds for interplanetary travel.

Twenty-three years later, Dr. Robert Goddard knelt on the frozen soil in his Aunt Effie's cabbage patch in Auburn, Massachusetts, and casually used a blowtorch to ignite the world's first liquid-fueled rocket. Goddard is revered today, but his contemporaries criticized him mercilessly because he had once mentioned the possibility of launching a payload to the moon. Years later when one of his rockets reached its design altitude of 2,000 feet, a banner headline wryly commented: "Moon Rocket Misses Target by 237,799½ Miles!"

The rockets built by Goddard and his team were all handcrafted, but Germany's rocketeers, working under the direction of Werner von Braun, constructed liquid-fueled rockets in mass-production quantities. When World War II ended, many of the German scientists came to Los Alamos to help in the American military and space efforts.

In 1961, when President Kennedy boldly anounced that the United States would conquer the moon, we had not yet orbited a single astronaut. The Saturn V, as ultimately developed for the mission, was the pinnacle of the rocket maker's art. But it was expendable. NASA's space shuttle is a *reusable* booster. It delivers payloads weighing as much as 65,000 pounds and brings others back to earth for refurbishment and repair, gently landing, as TV newsman Edwin Newman once noted, "like a butterfly with sore feet."

The burial missions will place the first orbiting mausoleum 1,900 miles above the earth, where it is expected to remain for at least 63 million years. On clear nights, the highly reflective spacecraft can be seen shimmering against a background of twinkling stars by friends and relatives back on earth. Japanese-Americans, who have long, reverent traditions favoring cremation, are expected to be heavy users of these unique burial services.

A consortium of Florida morticians and former Kennedy Space Center contractors, called the Celestis Group, has already signed an agreement with Space Services for the necessary Conestoga boosters. The cost, which has been set at about $2,500 to $3,000 per burial, is competitive with either cremation or conventional interments on earth. An additional fee of $500 will be collected for the special cremation, which produces only enough ashes to fill a thumb-sized aluminum capsule tastefully engraved with religious symbols and memorial messages.

About 6,000 such capsules will be carried into orbit on each Conestoga flight. Marketing surveys indicate a demand for as many as ten missions a year by the mid-1990s. At that level, Space Services should make a profit of about $30 million a year.

One small glitch: the state of Florida has charged that the Celestis Group is operating an "unlicensed cemetery," not merely a "transportation service" as Celestis maintains. According to Florida law, a cemetery must "include at least 15 acres of land and a road that leads to a highway." If the Florida courts do outlaw this promising enterprise, other alternatives are readily available. Celestis may, for instance, move its operations to Virginia, Hawaii, or Mississippi. The Mississippi state government has suggested Cat Island off the coast of Gulfport as an ideal launch site. Deke Slayton, however, prefers the southernmost point on the island of Hawaii.

THE SMALL-BOOSTER COMPETITION

In late February 1987, a local power company, Houston Industries, Inc., formed a venture-capital subsidiary to invest in the rockets being built by Space Services, Inc. Company officials did not specify the amount of money involved, but *Aviation Week* quoted one analyst as saying that he expected as much as $30 million to change hands. This fresh source of capital will allow Space Services to develop the Conestoga launch vehicle considerably faster than most industry observers had anticipated. It will also help the company battle for the small booster market against its main competitor, the American Rocket Company, AMROC, of Palo Alto, California, which recently found a big backer of its own—the Canadian investment banking firm McLeod Young Weir, Inc.

Both companies are hoping to capture the market for relatively small payloads, those weighing less than 3,000 pounds. According to *Aviation Week,* there may be a surprisingly large number of them available to fly in the next few years, with "demand coming from the Strategic Defense Initiative, the oil and earth resources industries and news organizations that hope to orbit reconnaissance satellites." Other possible users are "the Air Force Space Technologies Center, NASA, and intelligence agencies, which recently have shown increased interest in using small launchers to orbit small surveillance satellites." Moreover, in May 1987 the National Oceanic and Atmospheric Administration announced that for the first time it is seeking commercial launch services. Beginning in late 1989, five geo-synchronous weather satellites are to be carried into space by privately owned boosters.

AMROC has been testing its new hybrid engine (in which a liquid oxydizer is sprayed over a solid fuel), but has not yet flown a mission into space. However, a suborbital launch is being planned, to be followed by a flight into orbit with a Defense Department payload onboard.

George Koopman, president of AMROC, says that his company "has raised more than $1 million in private financing to date and needs to raise a total of $10 million before the development program is complete." Although Space Services is comfortably ahead of its main competitor so far, AMROC officials claim they can eventually orbit payloads for half the $15 million Space Services is quoting.

BUSINESS PROJECTIONS for PRIVATE LAUNCH SERVICES

In his 1983 State of the Union Address, President Reagan vowed to "help an expendable-launch services industry get off the ground." This was before the shuttle tragedy, which, according to some authorities, backed up shuttle payloads until at least 1995.

A solid business for privately owned boosters will surely materialize, but exactly how big will that business turn out to be? Arianspace, parent company of the Ariane booster, for instance, believes that at least 180 commercial satellites will need rides into space by 1991. Even with a conservative estimate of $30 million each, that adds up to $5.4 billion in launch costs alone. William F. Rector, vice-president of space programs for General Dynamics, estimates that 245 commercial satellites will be launched between 1986 and 1995 with launch costs totaling about $10 billion.

If improved technology pulls prices down, or if today's disabled boosters take longer to repair than anticipated, business could be even more brisk. Moreover, commercial launches are not the only source of new business. Private, profit-making companies will capture some of the launches formerly handled by government-sponsored rockets. There are even proposals to open up space-station supply to competitive bidding.

Dr. Peter M. Banks of Stanford University, writing in *Aerospace America*, argues for a "more equitable market," with agreements that would resemble America's early air-mail contracts, which provided hefty subsidies for many of our early commercial airlines. "It would seem reasonable to suggest that transport and delivery of materials to erect and operate the space station be done competitively by private enterprise," Banks argues. "Delivery payments by the government for such transport should match the true costs of space shuttle operations already planned to be borne by NASA."

How much money is Dr. Banks talking about? Even if the transportation services were offered at half the cost of shuttle delivery, over $750 million per year would pass to private-sector companies. To ensure that the new business is fully competitive, he believes that "no funds should be expended to support the design of private systems." In his opinion, those who pursue this launch-vehicle bonanza should supply all necessary research and development monies, but they would be paid promptly, and handsomely, for the goods they deliver into space. Another promising approach toward privatization of space transportation would be to sell or lease the shuttle itself to private, profit-making companies.

PRIVATELY OWNED SPACE SHUTTLES

In 1984, Astrotech of Pittsburgh, Pennsylvania, offered to buy one of the existing shuttles from NASA and to commission the construction of another one to be operated at a profit. Estimated cost? About $3 billion, $2 billion of which would have been paid by year's end. Astrotech is headed by Al Rockwell, seventy-three-year-old ex-chairman of Rockwell International, who was quite serious about the transaction. But could the shuttle be run effectively as a profit-making business? The experiences of the French Ariane seem to suggest that the private sector can handle space operations.

Another approach toward privatizing a portion of the shuttle has been pursued by Commercial Cargo Spacelines of New York City. In 1984 their representatives signed a memorandum of understanding with NASA in which they agreed to charter complete shuttle cargo bays.

How could they hope to compete with NASA in booking payloads on the shuttle? "Marketing has never been a part of their charter," explained one company executive. In search of new, previously untapped business, representatives from Commercial Cargo Spacelines have touched base with potential customers in such unlikely places as Thailand, Colombia, Nigeria, South Korea, and Peru—places that are hardly on the normal travel itineraries of NASA bureaucrats. In addition, their organization is structured to provide broad-ranging services to potential customers, services such as upper-stage motor selection, payload integration, and postlaunch analyses, which are unavailable from NASA or tend to be of daunting complexity.

The *Challenger* explosion created major disruptions in the business plans of Commercial Cargo Spacelines. But before that happened, company executives had arranged for millions of dollars in venture capital and other forms of financial backing based on projections for around $200 million in annual revenues.

THE MEDIUM LAUNCH VEHICLE

After an orgy of haggling in political corridors, Washington's power brokers finally decided to replace the space shuttle *Challenger* with another shuttle, at a cost of about $2.7 billion. However, because the new swept-wing craft cannot be hammered together for several years, and because the three remaining shuttles will be grounded for about two years, 150 or so expensive satellites are sitting on the ground—gold and silver birds with clipped wings. In the meantime, the government is seeking any available boosters and cranking up old assembly lines to build more expendable rockets from existing blueprints.

Specifically, Representative Bill Nelson of Florida has introduced legislation authorizing NASA to purchase fifteen expendable boosters each capable of carrying 2,800 pounds to the geosynchronous altitude. And the U.S. Air Force will be purchasing expendable boosters with various performance capabilities for its own use.

Since these new boosters are needed as soon as possible, they must be produced with existing facilities. Leading candidates include the Atlas from Convair in San Diego, the Thor-Delta from McDonnell Douglas in Huntington Beach, California, and the Titan from Martin in Denver, Colorado.

In January 1987, the Air Force signed a contract with McDonnell Douglas for a fleet of twenty expendable boosters to lift its military payloads into space. Total value: $734 million. This contract is important in its own right, but it also means that the company will not have to spend its own money developing a rocket that can compete with the Ariane, which lately has had a virtual monopoly on the space transportation market.

In addition, Hughes and Boeing Aerospace have formed a team to develop the Jarvis, a new booster. Their Jarvis rocket, which is named after the Hughes technician killed in the *Challenger* explosion, will be assembled from existing shuttle and Saturn hardware. Far more capable than the other three proposed boosters, the Jarvis will carry a payload of 85,000 pounds—20,000 pounds more than the planned maximum for the space shuttle! It will also be able to deliver 17,500 pounds to the geosynchronous altitude.

Although the new Hughes/Boeing vehicle would chew up $1 billion in research and development funds, it would, as Anthony J. Iorillo of Hughes has testified, "give our country a world-class launch vehicle that could compete with new foreign launchers in the 1990s."

LEN CORMIER and HIS REUSABLE SPACE VAN

"The private sector needs a railroad, but the launch-vehicle industry is providing painted wagons." The speaker is Len Cormier, pioneer designer of Rockwell International's space shuttle, who has formed a company of his own called the Third Millennium (MMI) to do something about the problem. His principal objective is to build a smaller, more efficient, flying machine to be owned and operated by private enterprise. Cormier is convinced that, by the year 2001 (Roman numeral MMI), space commercialization will fill the void around earth, making it in effect a heavily traveled freeway.

How is the new company planning to build Cormier's dream machine? First by raising a large heap of money, $750 million to be exact, then using it to construct a "space van," designed to spring from the back of a 747 and carry a 6,600-pound payload into space. "Air launch will provide a significant fraction of the energy required to get to orbit," says Cormier. "The 747's energy contribution is comparable to the solid boosters on the shuttle."

Just before it separates from the mother craft, the space van's eight Pratt & Whitney engines, burning a mixture of liquid hydrogen and liquid oxygen, will be ignited. A few minutes later, it will edge into a 210-mile-high orbit, where its lone pilot will drop off his payload before returning to earth.

Flown in a different mode, the van will act as a second stage, climbing to a height of 46 miles before releasing a larger self-propelled payload bound for a low-altitude orbit, or beyond. The stubby craft, which is about half the length of the shuttle orbiter, will be based in American Samoa just south of the equator. The equator is the ideal location for a launch site because the earth's rotation will help sling the payload into space.

On many missions the space van will deliver fuel and oxidizer to an orbiting depot for use in later journeys to other locations in space. Cormier envisions a fleet of three fully reusable space vans, each of which will make one flight a week. When no other assignments are available, they will carry propellants to the depot in preparation for future needs. "We'll have incredible access to the depot," says Cormier, "and we'll be capable of flying up to it every couple of days."

The depot will be equipped with robots and manipulator arms operated from the ground by remote control. Most of the time, these teleoperator devices will be left in space, thus further reducing the demands on the space van. Why should they stay in space? "You don't carry the ramps that let you off the airplane on the airplane itself. You leave those at the airport," Cormier explains. It may seem obvious that we should do the same with space vehicles, "but it's often hard to prove the obvious."

What makes the space van so incredibly economical? It is reusable. It uses an airplane for its initial boost. It uses wings to generate lift on its ascent trajectory

THE THIRD MILLENNIUM'S RESABLE SPACE VAN

TOP VIEW

SIDE VIEW

BACK VIEW

Len Cormier's space van, a reusable hydrogen-fueled shuttle craft, is ready to spring from the back of a Boeing 747 for a round-trip journey into space. The little piloted vehicle is designed to carry a 6,600-pound payload, then return to its airfield on American Samoa. Although its payload-carrying capability is only about 10 percent that of the space shuttle, Cormier and his colleagues claim that with enough business, their space van could take payloads into orbit for 5 percent of the lowest commercial rate charged by the shuttle.

and for the return to earth. And it uses a propellant depot with extra fuel and heavy equipment being left in space.

The wings and the other design efficiencies allow the van to get by with the minimum possible number of engines. Engine maintenance has always been one of the most costly items in operating a rocket. The wings also allow the craft to reenter the atmosphere along a more gentle glide slope than the shuttle; consequently, it comes in 500 degrees cooler. Thus it can use an inexpensive, easily maintained heat shield instead of the insulating tiles that caused so many headaches for the designers of the space shuttle.

Even at low launch rates, Cormier's space van is surprisingly economical. It can deliver a 6,600-pound payload into a low-altitude orbit for about $10 million. At a higher launch rate—one or two flights per week—the cost drops to about $2.5 million a flight, or about $300 per pound of payload delivered into space. This is roughly one-tenth the true cost of today's shuttle-delivered payloads.

Lately, Cormier has been toying with a new launch procedure that would use a floating barge instead of a 747. What is motivating this new approach? Tourist flights! Tourists, he fears, may regard his airborne launch scheme as too risky for routine trips into space.

GETAWAY SPECIALS and HITCHHIKER PAYLOADS

NASA normally charges about $1,400 per pound to carry large payloads into space aboard the shuttle. But if you have a smaller load—60 to 200 pounds—they may be willing to deliver it for only $50 per pound— $3,000 for a 60-pound load. You may even be able to get the astronauts to release your package into space, so you can have your own orbiting satellite!

In order to take advantage of the average 25 percent of the shuttle cargo bay that goes unused on a typical flight, NASA in 1976 set up the "Getaway Special" program for small, noncommercial payloads. Industrial giants such as General Motors and 3M have sponsored some of them; others have been delivered for academic experts, the U.S. government, and ordinary private citizens.

Large military and industrial payloads struggle for their place on the payload manifest, but Getaway Specials are assigned on a first-come, first-served basis. A $500 deposit reserves your spot in line. Within eighteen months, however, you will have to make the final payment. Dozens of Getaway Specials have already flown in space and over 500 more berths have been reserved, many by high school and college students. Useful experiments performed so far have included seed germination, electrophoresis separation, microorganism growth, fluid dynamics, and metal solidification.

Despite the small size of the Getaway Special canisters (the smaller ones contain only 2.5 cubic feet of usable space), their sponsors have managed to perform

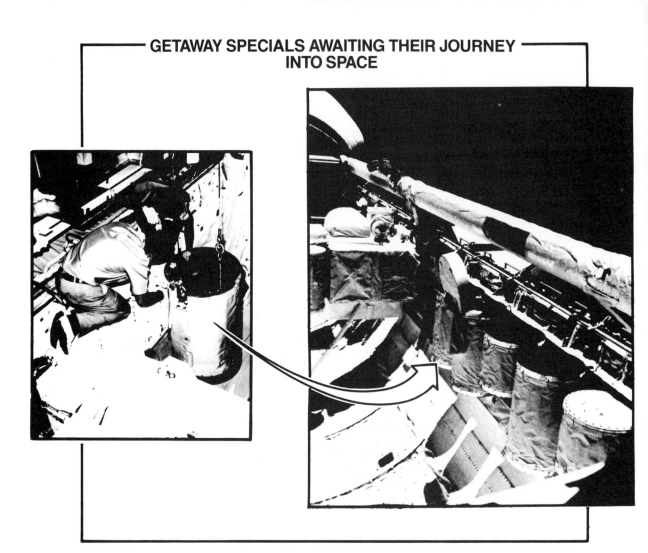

Six Getaway Special canisters slung beneath Canada's remote manipulator arm are awaiting their turn in space. To fill empty spaces in the shuttle cargo bay, NASA takes these little payloads aloft for $50 a pound—about 3 percent of the rate it charges regular spacebound customers. The second payload from the left was the first Getaway Special with a lid that swung open to expose the equipment inside to the environment of space. Future versions will be rigged with springs to eject small satellites into orbit.

some surprisingly clever and sophisticated experiments. In 1984, for instance, the Naval Research Laboratory developed an experiment to measure the radiation fields in the earth's upper atmosphere. This experiment featured the first canister equipped with a lid that could swing open to expose the payload inside to the environment of space. Student experimenters from the U.S. Air Force Academy in Colorado performed another impressive task, a metal-beam-joining experiment, that was considered a complete success.

Ivan Vera, a Venezuelan graduate student from the University of Pennsylvania, developed an experiment funded by the National Electric Company of Venezuela. His unit was designed to produce semipermeable membranes in space, membranes that are important to a number of advanced technologies, including kidney dialysis and desalinization of seawater. According to one industry observer, Vera's experiment may have been the first from any Latin American country intended to demonstrate the commercial potential of space.

Normally the equipment remains in the shuttle cargo bay, but a research team at Utah State University is developing a method for launching a small satellite from a Getaway Special canister. It is rigged with a lid that swings open and a simple spring mechanism to eject the payload into space.

Several private firms are available to help you if you want to develop a Getaway Special payload for a flight on the shuttle. Examples include Instrumentation Technology Associates of Spring House, Pennsylvania, Getaway Special Services of Bellevue, Washington, and Quartic Systems, Inc., of Salt Lake City, Utah. These specialized companies provide integration services, advice on experiment selection, racks for mounting the equipment, and various types of supporting hardware such as batteries, data recorders, pressure transducers, and accelerometers.

"We're set up to service any kind of customer—from the aerospace company that doesn't want to put a package together to the first-time user," says John Cassanto, president of Instrumentation Technology Associates. He and his competitors will also help with the larger, more sophisticated, "Hitchhiker Payloads" now being masterminded by NASA to fill larger nooks and crannies in the shuttle cargo bay.

A Hitchhiker Payload can weigh as much as 1,200 pounds and, unlike the smaller Getaway Specials, can be connected to the shuttle's support systems to obtain electrical power and data communications. Thus customers on the ground will be able to send control commands and interrogation signals directly to their Hitchhiker Payloads. Real-time data and status reports from their experiments will be available on demand, and in some cases, the shuttle astronauts will provide simple services for the Hitchhiker Payloads.

THE AEROSPACE PLANE and the "ORIENT EXPRESS"

In his February State of the Union Address in 1986, President Reagan unveiled the plans for a hypersonic jet that could, in just two hours, hurl itself from Washington, D.C., to Tokyo, Japan. "Skeptics might have thought he was dreaming," commented Barbara Rudolph of *Time* magazine. "But, in fact, the Pentagon and U.S. aerospace companies have been working for several years toward making that vision a reality."

A week later the President shared a model of his impressive plane—if one can call it that—with students at Thomas Jefferson High School in Annandale, Virginia. They were much impressed with the new machine, particularly when he explained that with modifications, it could carry both paying passengers on earth and satellites into space.

The aerospace plane is based on an old concept, one that has been kicking around the aerospace industry for several years: a single-stage vehicle using both air-breathing engines and rockets to reach orbital speeds. Supporters are convinced that this imaginative approach can reduce the cost of orbiting satellites by a factor of ten, or more, to less than $200 per pound. Some even claim that more advanced versions could drive costs down to $20 per pound—if demand is sufficiently brisk.

Space-age engineers have long looked with envy at the jet engine, which is far more efficient than the rockets they are forced to use to carry payloads into space. A turbojet is so much more efficient than a rocket because it sucks its oxygen from the air, and it ejects air molecules in addition to its combustion by-products to hurt itself forward. This gives it an efficiency edge of about ten to one over a rocket using the same fuel.

Former test pilot Scott Crossfield, who once flew the X-15 at Edwards Air Force Base, argues that rockets, including the shuttle, are inherently uneconomic. "Seventy-eight percent of the fuel it carries at such high cost is oxygen. That's ridiculous. Twenty percent of the atmosphere is oxygen and you can get that for free."

The space shuttle does, in fact, carry 666 tons of oxygen, or twenty-eight times its maximum payload capacity, and, ironically, it expends half its fuel (and oxidizer) in reaching Mach 6 (six times the speed of sound) during a time when there is freely abundant oxygen all around it in the atmosphere. Why not breathe that air—as human beings do—rather than carrying it along in a separate tank? Performance gains can, indeed, be made in this way, but they are not as large as you might assume from Scott Crossfield's seemingly compelling argument.

Aerospace expert Dr. Tom Heppenheimer explains the other side of the coin: "A rocket's structure is simple—it is a cylinder that bears weight predominantly along its length as it lifts off and accelerates. A conventional air-breathing craft, by contrast, gains its lift from the fuselage and wings, which weigh considerably more than a rocket's simple cylinder."

Nevertheless, despite this careful scientific qualification, burning the surrounding air does hold promise for an efficient "Orient Express" that could revolutionize both air travel and space transportation, especially when this advanced concept is combined with new materials technologies, new thermal protection concepts, and new computer simulation techniques.

In 1986 the U.S. Air Force commissioned General Electric and Pratt & Whitney

ROCKET PROPULSION FUNDAMENTALS

White-hot combustion by-products blasted rearward with blinding speed generate the reactive force that hurls a rocket skyward. Pressure inside the rocket combustion chamber pushes in all directions to form balanced pairs of opposing forces which nullify each other except where the hole for the exhaust nozzle is placed. Here the pressure escapes, causing an unbalanced force at the opposite side of the combustion chamber that pushes the rocket forward.

Both rockets and jets are based on the same principle that causes a toy balloon, carelessly released, to swing in kamikaze spirals around the dining room. A jet sucks its oxygen from the surrounding air, but a rocket carries its own oxidizer. The oxidizer can be held in a separate tank, mixed with the fuel, or embedded in oxygen-rich compounds.

A *liquid* rocket usually has two separate tanks, one for the fuel and the other for the oxidizer. The two fluids are pumped or pushed under pressure into a small chamber above the exhaust nozzle, where they are burned.

A *solid* rocket is like a slender tube full of gunpowder; the fuel and oxidizer are mixed together in a rubbery cylindrical slug called the grain. Solid propellants are not pumped into a separate combustion chamber. Instead, burning takes place along the entire length of the cylinder. Consequently, the tank walls must be strong enough to withstand the combustion pressure.

Rocket design decisions are dominated by the desire to produce the maximum possible velocity when the propellants are burned. A rocket's velocity can be increased in two principal ways: by using propellants with a high efficiency and by making the rocket casing and its engines as light as possible.

Unfortunately, efficient propellants tend to have undesirable physical and chemical properties. Liquid oxygen is a good oxidizer, but it will freeze all lubricants and crack most seals. Hydrogen is a good fuel, but it can spark devastating explosions. Fluorine is even better, but it is so reactive it can actually cause metals to burn.

Miniaturized components, special fabrication techniques, and high-strength alloys can all be used to shave excess weight. But as one early designer wryly remarked, "you can add only so much lightness." The solution is to use a "staging" technique in which a series of progressively smaller rockets are stacked one atop the other. Such a multistage rocket cuts down its own weight as it flies along by discarding empty tanks and heavy engines. However, orbiting even a small payload with a multistage rocket requires an enormous booster. The Saturn V, for example, outweighed its Apollo payload sixty to one.

to work on the engines for the aerospace plane. They also signed separate $7 million agreements with five leading airframe contractors: Boeing, General Dynamics, Lockheed, Rockwell International, and McDonnell Douglas. The resulting "aerospace chameleon," which is also called the X-30, will be designed in a $700 million follow-on study.

At low speeds the hydrogen-fueled engines of the X-30 will use compressors similar to the ones on ordinary turbo jets to compress the incoming air. But at higher speeds the air will be shunted around the compressors, because it will be compressed by the ram effect. Computers will control the dimensions of the engine's inlet ducts and the exhaust nozzle for the different flight regimes. Space-bound versions of the X-30 will carry rockets to maneuver in space, where there is no air for the engines to breathe. Cooling of critical areas such as the engines and leading edges of the wings will be aided by circulating liquid hydrogen fuel under the skin just as circulating water cools the block of an automobile engine.

The military's enthusiasm for the aerospace plane stems from its cost effectiveness, versatility, and responsiveness. On short notice, it can inspect and destroy enemy spacecraft, deploy observation and surveillance satellites, and swoop into orbit with large laser battle stations on its back—battle stations that will be needed for tomorrow's "Star Wars" ballistic missile defense. This is how the *Orange County Register* described the military lure of the X-30 aerospace plane: "If successful, the project could lead to twenty-first-century military and civil runway-to-orbit space planes capable of rapid access to space, airplane-like flexibility, and dramatically lower costs for delivering payloads to orbit. The same technology could give birth to nonorbiting vehicles like long-range military interceptors or civil passenger or cargo transports that could travel above 100,000 feet at speeds as high as 8,000 miles per hour."

NASA would also benefit from the new technology because the plane could be "a successor to the space shuttle and could be used to deliver science and other payloads to orbit, to service and repair satellites and to ferry people and supplies between earth and the permanent space station the agency plans to build in orbit in the 1990s."

Fully loaded, the aerospace plane will probably weigh a million pounds, about the same as the military's giant C-5 aircraft. Its payloads will weigh up to 20,000 pounds. Delivery costs to low-altitude orbits will be a few hundred dollars per pound or less, assuming frequent journeys into space. Turnaround times will be measured in hours and minutes rather than weeks and days. Some studies call for a sortie every twelve hours, on average.

According to the research staff at McDonnell Douglas, commercial flights of their "Orient Express" could begin early in the twenty-first century for about the same ticket prices as today's jumbo jets. Each plane would make four trips a day at Mach 5.5, crossing the Pacific in two hours with 300 passengers. A spacebound

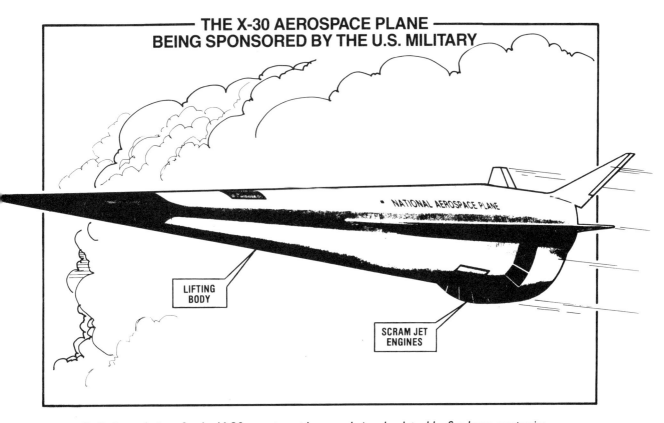

Preliminary designs for the X-30 aerospace plane are being developed by five large companies for U.S. military forces. Air-breathing engines will drive the hydrogen-fueled single-stage booster to Mach 5 or beyond, but rockets will take over at the fringes of space. The aerospace plane, which features flexible, low-cost operations, could be modified to carry planeloads of paying passengers continent-to-continent in two hours or less.

version carrying tourists to orbiting motels could begin making regularly scheduled flights a few years later.

Wolfgang Demish, an aerospace analyst at First Boston Corporation in New York City, is convinced that the aerospace plane will receive an enthusiastic reception from both industry professionals and the traveling public, a public that, in his opinion, has grown weary of watching small-screen double features while ambling along 7 miles above the Pacific. As he puts it: "Anything that transforms the Pacific trip from a prison in which you're nailed to a chair for sixteen hours will be extremely well received."

THE FOREIGN COMPETITION

The United States is not alone in exploring new possibilities for an aerospace plane. In 1986 the British government officials announced that they would pour

$4.2 million into the design of their HOTOL (horizontal takeoff and landing) booster. Like America's version, it will be driven by air-breathing engines initially (to Mach 5), but then it will transition to rockets for the final boost into orbit. On takeoff it will be mounted on a rapidly moving trolley that releases it at a speed of about 300 miles per hour. Once airborne, its air-breathing hydrogen-fueled engines will provide the necessary thrust.

The plane, which the British estimate will consume $7 billion in research and development funds, is to be designed and built by an eleven-member consortium of European nations, provided equitable agreements can be reached.

Propulsion-system details have not yet been released. But savvy experts are speculating that the British are probably planning to use "cryojet" engines in which hydrogen fuel would be used to cool the onrushing air to about the same temperature as the natural atmosphere surrounding the craft. The desire for large savings in delivery expenses has been the main driver in the HOTOL design. "We are not interested in minor cost reductions or evolutionary cost cutting. We are going for the jugular," says Peter Conchie, director of business development at British Aerospace.

No pilot will be on board to fly the HOTOL. Instead, its flight path will be computer-controlled and directed from the ground. "We will have to use expert systems in the ground control system, because the decision time will be so short, we think we can get away from using humans at all," Conchie told a reporter from *Commercial Space.*

This does not mean, however, that the vehicle will be incapable of carrying passengers. A passenger module is already under development to take mission specialists into space. For earthbound destinations, the craft will be fitted with a cabin holding sixty passengers for a seventy-minute trip from Europe to Australia.

If the HOTOL design proves feasible, West Germany is prepared to participate. But in the meantime, West German scientists are working on a similar vehicle using a more conservative approach: a two-stage, air-breathing hypersonic aircraft that carries a smaller winged orbital vehicle. They call it the Sanger. The lower stage returns to earth immediately, while the smaller orbital vehicle carries a crew of two plus ten passengers and a 4-ton cargo directly into orbit. An earthbound version stuffed with 200 passengers would span continents on 8,000-mile journeys, making it a serious competitor to America's "Orient Express."

Germany's aerospace experts are proposing the Sanger because they have lingering doubts about the feasibility and practicality of the British HOTOL concept. "The HOTOL engine would be superior to all other concepts, including Sanger, if it works," said Ernst Hoegenauer, one of the masterminds of the Sanger design. "But the HOTOL engine is still a paper tiger. Its design is not impossible, but it still has a long way to go."

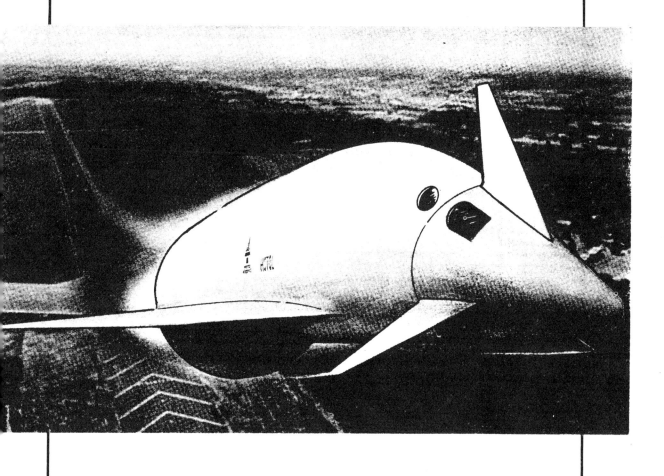

The British HOTOL (horizontal takeoff and landing) aerospace plane, with its strange, wormlike shape, will fly into space, drop off its payload, then return to its landing field completely under the control of computers and ground personnel. The pilotless hydrogen-fueled spaceship, which will spring off the ground at 300 miles an hour from a moving trolley, will burn liquid hydrogen mixed with the ambient air until it reaches Mach 5.5. Rockets will then take over for the final push into orbit. Proponents claim that the HOTOL will carry payloads for one-twentieth the true cost of space-shuttle delivery.

West German officials believe the Sanger will be able to carry hefty cargos into orbit for about $900 a pound, including development costs. This is about one-fifth the cost for the American space shuttle or the French Ariane, but it is still about four times the cost of the British HOTOL—if the HOTOL works as advertised.

Other fancy foreign boosters are also in the works. The Russians, for instance, are almost ready to fly their version of the space shuttle, and the French are designing the Hermes, a winged craft that will ride into orbit atop an uprated version of the Ariane.* The Japanese have also announced plans for a reusable booster to be active near the turn of the century. The space shuttle itself may also be upgraded. Plans are on the drawing boards to raise its payload-carrying capability to 170,000 pounds.

Of course, expendable boosters have not dropped out of the race. The Ariane continues to capture big chunks of business, and the Chinese have attracted a few foreign customers, including some Americans, for a ride on their "Long March" rocket. The Russians are, in addition, advertising for commercial customers for their Proton booster, and in May 1987 they flight-tested their massive new Energia rocket, a hydrogen-fueled mammoth capable of carrying a 200,000-pound payload into space.

LASER-POWERED ROCKETS

The aerospace plane and the HOTOL booster will employ extremely advanced technologies to drive launch costs down to more affordable levels. But an even more daring launch technique is also in the works: a rocket propelled by a powerful laser beam. The use of a laser may not, in itself, sound particularly futuristic. These days common, everyday machines such as audio compact disks and supermarket scanners are operated by laser. But the laser will not be aboard the rocket, it will be on the ground; and it will beam its energy hundreds of miles to the rocket flying overhead. The concept has attracted several aerospace companies and engineering firms into a $2 million program being run by the Strategic Defense Initiative Organization (SDIO).

Laser-driven rockets will be powered by free-electron lasers, a new design developed in conjunction with the "Star Wars" program. Most lasers are only about 5 percent efficient, but according to researchers at California's Lawrence Livermore National Laboratory, the free-electron laser may approach an efficiency of 40 percent. As the rocket flies vertically upward, the laser will vaporize material from its lower edge to impart thrust. Various materials have been suggested, including ice, plastics, and even coal. The trick is to pick a compound that is rich in hydrogen, because the light atoms of hydrogen make ideal rocket propellants.

In one scheme proposed by Avco-Texron engineer Dennis Reilly, the laser pulses would come in closely spaced pairs. The first would vaporize a thin film of material on the bottom of the block; the second, more powerful pulse would then

*In its initial flights, the French Hermes may fly into orbit on the Soviet Union's expendable Proton booster.

impart a sharp spike of energy to cause the film to expand rapidly. Computer simulations indicate that a laser-propelled rocket may be able to deliver 15 percent of its liftoff weight into orbit. This compares with only 1.5 percent for the space shuttle and 2 percent for America's version of the aerospace plane.

Two study groups are concentrating on laser-powered rockets. One of them is headed by TRW in Redondo Beach, California, and the other by Boeing in Seattle, Washington. Their engineers are trying to find the best techniques for imparting thrust to the solid blocks, and they are studying a number of methods for controlling its flight path as it travels into space. According to Dr. Tom Heppenheimer, contributing editor for *High Technology,* "Ground controllers might tilt the rocket by moving the laser beam off-center. Another control mechanism is to aim the laser at the block at an angle, rather than from directly below; the orientation of the block will thus determine the direction of the exhaust and its thrust."

Launch costs have been estimated as low as $8 per pound of payload delivered into orbit. Amortizing the R&D costs for the laser would raise that to about $45 per pound, compared with some $4,000 per pound for shuttle launches. The laser could propel only small, compact payloads, but if it operated more or less continuously, it could orbit 64,000 tons each year of its operation. Initial test flights of small, tethered craft are scheduled for 1991 or 1992.

This competition to develop cheap and reliable space-age transportation is an encouraging sign for the future industrialization of space. Indeed, large numbers of profitable space facilities would likely be in orbit already if rockets bound for the "high frontier" were not today so outlandishly expensive.

The advent of the space station focuses our attention upon a basic question: Why do we have a civil space program? Why do we concern ourselves with rockets and satellites? My own view is that we have a space program not because of the excitement the program engenders and certainly not because the Russians have one. We have a space program because there are things we can do in space that we can't do on the ground. What things? Astronomy, materials research, navigation, communications, earth observations are all activities that lend themselves to space. And there are others. Space has become simply a place where we do useful things.

Bob Traxler, Congressman (Michigan)

9

TOMORROW'S MANNED SPACE STATIONS

It is an international project combining the best efforts of aerospace professionals throughout the Western world. When it is completed in the mid-1990s there will never again be a time when all of America's citizens will be living on the planet earth. From that day forward, at least six or eight of them—men and women—will be enclosed within its aluminum walls, a snug home in space constructed by silver-suited astronauts just above the wispy fringes of the atmosphere. It is America's manned space station, a multibillion-dollar undertaking that will form the focus of space commercialization into the next century and beyond.

"Silently drifting across the sky, it will resemble nothing as much as the imaginative creation of an inventive youngster with an Erector set," says *Time* reporter Frederick Golden. "It will consist of sleek metal cylinders, winglike panels, sinewy aluminum beams and long, cranelike arms." NASA's sloganeers are calling it "the next logical step in space," a gangling complex of stiff girders holding a cluster of trailer-sized modules interlinked like fat sausages.

Like a Swiss Army knife, it is being designed to serve a host of users: commercial, governmental, military, and international. These are some of the many things NASA believes it will be:

- A *zero-g scientific laboratory* where trained scientists can study the earth, the sky, and the vast regions in between to learn more about the fundamental processes of chemistry, biology, electronics, metallurgy, life sciences, and agriculture.
- An *assembly base* where astronauts can put together large space structures

such as solar arrays and communication antennas for later transportation to other, more favorable locations in space.

- A *servicing and repair facility* where commercially important satellites can be repaired and upgraded and their attitude-control propellants replenished.
- A *manufacturing center* where valuable space-age products such as computer chips and pharmaceuticals can be made for sale to the people on earth.
- A *transportation base* where rockets and their payloads can be assembled and refueled in preparation for ambitious trips to the moon, Mars, Jupiter, and other distant destinations.
- A *storage depot* where tools, equipment, spare parts, and possibly even complete, functioning satellites can be stored for ready availability against future needs.
- An *observation post* high above the haze of the earth's atmosphere where scientists and their instruments can study the earth, its planets, and the most distant corners of the universe.

If its designers have their way, it will be all seven of these things and more, and it will also be a comfortable place to live. "NASA wants us to make the space station as earthlike as possible," says Mahmud Yakut, program manager for advanced hardware systems at McDonnell Douglas. "They want to get away from the camping food—the stuff in tubes and freeze-dried packages—we've had up to now." Meals will be varied and tasty, with fresh supplies arriving from earth every ninety days.*

The station will have a modern decor featuring tasteful blues and whites.** Its kitchen will be equipped with such cushy spaceborne luxuries as a microwave oven, a trash compactor, and an electric dishwasher. However, it will not be equipment such as you could buy at your local appliance store. All of the devices on board will have to be specifically designed to function in the weightlessness of space. A conventional dishwasher, for instance, would spray the cups with water, but once there, it might just hang inside—even if the cups were upside down!

---

*The Soviet space station designers are also upgrading the meals for their space crews. According to the English newspaper, the *Guardian,* the cosmonauts are no longer satisfied with "borsch, bean stew and black bread." Instead, their new menus are being put together by two top French chefs. Among other things, Russians aloft will, in the future, be dining on "canard a la cuillers aux artichauts (duck in artichokes), compote de Pigeon aux dattes (pigeon with dates) and compote de lapin aux pruneaux (rabbit with prunes)."

**No earth tones will decorate the space-station walls. Skylab's astronauts complained that browns and yellows made them sick.

SYNERGISM and the U.S. SPACE STATION

synergism (medicine) the mutually cooperating action of separate substances which taken together produce an effect greater than any component taken alone.

Like the dams of the Tennessee Valley Authority, the U.S. space station will depend on the almost magical effects of synergistic interactions. Before the TVA project began in 1933, high waters periodically inundated the flood plains of the Tennessee Valley, sweeping away in destructive fury buildings, houses, human beings.

During the Roosevelt administration, large concrete dams thrown up along the rivers halted the swirling water in its path. But flood control was just one of the many benefits brought by the TVA. Those same dams provided abundant electricity, navigable waterways, and irrigation water released in carefully controlled amounts. The power was used to produce inexpensive phosphate fertilizers, thus making the land productive enough to warrant irrigation. Good farming practices brought renewed prosperity, so the lakes created by the dams became recreational areas for the local residents, who now had more money to spend. These and other beneficial synergisms worked minor miracles in the valleys of Tennessee and five surrounding states.

Beneficial synergisms on a grand scale often require the resources of big government. But private enterprise benefits too. Witness the westward expansion of the railroads, financed largely by land grants to private entrepreneurs who used rail transportation to sell the land.

NASA's masterminds are working toward beneficial synergisms 250 miles above the earth. Manufacturing in space will be stimulated by the permanent presence of the astronauts living aboard the station. So will the regularly scheduled shuttle flights that bring fresh supplies and take away useful products made in the space-borne factories. Some of the products—large space structures and communication antennas—will be used in space. Others will be sold at a handsome profit to consumers on earth.

Substantial savings can be achieved because less redundancy will be required. After all, the space station's astronauts and their remotely controlled robots will be available to repair or replace any component that happens to malfunction. The astronauts can also help in refueling operations, satellite retrieval and repair, and the assembly of large space vehicles leaving for destinations deeper in space.

WHAT WILL IT BE LIKE to LIVE and WORK in SPACE?

Each astronaut will have his own private bedroom—a small cubical including bookshelf, bulletin board, and a space for a videocassette recorder. In their off hours, the astronauts will be able to watch network television shows beamed to them from other orbiting satellites. Chats with their friends on earth will also be possible, using picturephone transmissions.

If you are chosen as one of the space-station astronauts, you will live in a comfortable shirt-sleeve environment much like the passenger cabin of a commercial airliner. During your three-month tour of duty, you will have regular chores, involving science and astronomy, manufacturing in space, and, perhaps, tending the monkeys and other experimental animals on board—with ample help from the robots and computers. Occasionally, you may be assigned to leave the station propelled by a jet-powered backpack to retrieve a malfunctioning satellite, or to help nudge new space-station modules into place along the station's open framework.

In your idle hours you can play cassette tapes, browse through the library, chat with your fellow crewmates, and pedal the stationary bicycle brought along to help keep you in shape. Music and sounds from earth—bird calls, crashing waves, train whistles, the pitter-patter of falling rain—will be heard in the station during working hours. Russian experiments have shown that morale and productivity are improved when those on board can hear popular music and familiar sounds. Of course, you will also have headphones so you can listen to your own favorite selections without disturbing the other astronauts.

Your first few trips back to earth may be emotional events, but by the turn of the century, when you tell your girlfriend you have just returned from space, her reaction will be about the same as if you had come back from Indianapolis or Kansas City. According to one NASA representative, "By the late 1990s, orbiter trips to and from the space station will become commonplace, no more noteworthy than the departure and arrival today of ships and trains."

THE SPACE STATION and ITS ECONOMIC BENEFITS

Many experts see the manned space station as the key to large-scale commercial operations in space. One of its advantages is obvious: it allows the astronauts to stay in space for extended intervals to take advantage of their early learning experiences. But in addition it can help drive transportation costs down to much more affordable levels. One NASA official uses a clever analogy to explain: "Without the space station the shuttle astronauts are in somewhat the same situation as the office worker compelled to carry a desk and chair home each afternoon and then to return them to the office the next morning. At present nearly everything . . .

must be carried into orbit on each flight and brought back again, only to be launched all over again if needed on another flight."

The space station will also serve as an efficient springboard to other parts of our solar system, and beyond. If we could shrink the earth down to the size of a basketball with all the planets and their moons scaled down proportionately, the space station would be a tiny gnat less than half an inch away from our basketball-sized earth. The moon would be a softball 30 feet away from the gnat-encircled basketball earth. However, in terms of the energy required to get there, the space-station gnat would be almost exactly halfway between earth and moon.

This paradox is best explained by representing the gravitational fields of the earth and the moon and the other massive bodies in space by whirlpool-shaped contours called "gravity wells." The gravity well representing the earth is about twenty times as deep as the gravity well for the moon, because the earth's gravity is so much stronger. When the Saturn V rocket carried the Apollo capsule from the earth to the moon, it had to expend the same amount of energy that would be required to lift it upward 4,000 miles against the pull of a 1-g gravitational field. The space station barely skims over the atmosphere a thousandth of the way to the moon. But propelling the Apollo capsule up to the space station's orbit would require the same energy as carrying it vertically upward 2,000 miles in a constant 1-g gravitational field. In other words, in terms of energy, the space station is halfway to the moon!

A deep-space probe could be launched from the space station much more efficiently than from earth, because the probe would not have to be designed to withstand the punishing trip through the atmosphere. We could bring it up from the earth piecemeal inside the shuttle cargo bay, where it would be largely shrouded from punishing loads. Then, once we had it there, we could fashion it into a light but delicate spacecraft that would fall apart if it had to withstand drag with the atmosphere. Thus the space station will serve as an efficient staging area when we fly missions to other, more distant points in the solar system.

Just as the transcontinental railroads of the 1860s opened up a vast western frontier for exploitation by American pioneers, the space station will serve as a gateway to an even closer frontier seven or eight generations later. As it curls along its orbit 250 miles high, it will help make space accessible and affordable, thus providing important new opportunities for profitable spaceborne operations. The major stock exchanges do not yet trade in Galaxy Manpower, Heavenly Food Supply, Ace Satellite Repair, or Zero-G Light and Power, but new companies of this type could eventually emerge as the darlings of savvy investors, now that the space station is about to make space more economically viable.

Jim Rose, manager of the McDonnell Douglas electrophoresis program, believes the space station will help his company produce pharmaceuticals in space: "Work-

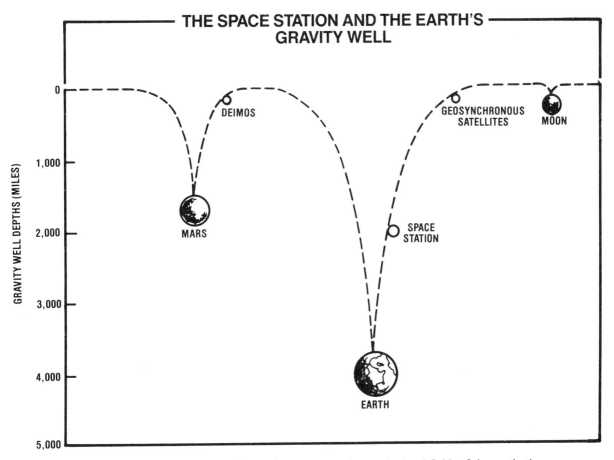

THE SPACE STATION AND THE EARTH'S GRAVITY WELL

Whirlpool-shaped contours can be used to represent the gravitational fields of the earth, the moon, and all other massive bodies in space. The depth of each gravity well and the slopes of its curving walls are proportional to the amount of energy required to orbit or escape that particular body at various altitudes above its surface. Notice that the earth's gravity well is twenty times deeper than the gravity well of the moon. This is true because it takes twenty times as much energy to escape the earth. Notice also that in energy terms, the space station is almost exactly halfway between earth and moon. Because of its prime location in the earth's gravity well, the space station is an efficient staging point, assembly station, and refueling depot for subsequent journeys to the moon, the planets, and other distant points in space.

ing in the space-station environment, we could perhaps bring as many as fifteen new products to the marketplace in a ten-year span." By contrast, in his estimation, "We could develop only three new products in the same time frame if we were confined to work aboard the shorter space-shuttle flights."

Former NASA administrator James M. Beggs, one of those best qualified to venture an opinion, sees cumulative revenues from space-age products and services in the hundreds of billions of dollars by the year 2001. President Reagan shares his enthusiasm for the economic potential of space. "We can follow our dreams to the distant stars, living and working in space for peaceful economic and scientific gain," he said in his 1984 State of the Union address. Having so cogently summarized the economic attraction of the space frontier, he then went on to issue an order directing NASA to "develop a permanently manned space station and to do it within a decade."

FINANCING the SPACE STATION

In 1985 and 1986, a combined total of $385 million was expended for space-station design and development. Budget requests rose to $767 million the following year. All together, government planners initially expected to spend $8 billion or more between now and 1994—when the station will house six or eight astronauts on a continuous basis. These hefty expenditures are to be supplemented by another $2 to $5 billion in contributions from other interested countries, including Japan, Canada, England, and West Germany.*

NASA's space-station experts are also soliciting services, technical expertise, and hardware modules from private, profit-making companies large and small. If you have an imaginative idea and can deliver it in usable form, the space station may provide you with an extraordinary opportunity for entering the business of space. A NASA pamphlet, "The Next Logical Step," calls the space station "a spawning ground for innovation—a nurturing place for new technologies."

SPACE-STATION ARCHITECTURE

The completed space station will be about the size of a small football stadium. Skilled astronauts will assemble it in space, using cranes and robots to help them attach spidery girders and large sausage-shaped cylinders ferried into orbit by the shuttle.

The biggest and most complicated elements of the space-station complex will be launched into a 290-mile assembly orbit tipped 28.5 degrees with respect to the equator. Eventually, after many shuttle flights, its girders and other modules will weigh 200,000 pounds, with another 200,000 pounds of equipment, astronauts, and supplies packaged inside its cylindrical modules and attached to its spindly framework. In addition, the astronauts and robots aboard will service several detached "free-flying" modules. Some will fly in formation with the space station; others will be carried to different locations, including sharply intersecting

---

*The latest estimates for space-station construction are higher than these figures. Some of them range as high as $16 billion. As a result, the initial operational structure may be scaled down somewhat.

orbits that pass over the poles. In the long run, spaceborne tugs may deliver derivative versions into geosynchronous orbits or to a staging point midway between earth and moon.

Most early concepts for manned space stations—those proposed by Russia's Konstantin Tsiolkovsky, Germany's Werner von Braun, and England's Arthur C. Clarke—were shaped like big Ferris wheels ponderously rotating at about one revolution per minute to create artificial gravity for the astronauts living inside.

In the meantime, however, we have learned that space travelers can function effectively in the natural weightlessness of space and that zero gravity is a valuable resource for space manufacturing. Consequently, the space-station astronauts will live and work in a microgravity environment on a nonrotating station. Actually, NASA's baseline design does rotate very slowly—three-quarters of a revolution every hour. This maintains its lower end in a permanent earth-pointing orientation as it travels around its orbit. It uses gravity-gradient stabilization, which does not require any propellants. If the station begins to depart from the vertical, the slightly stronger pull of gravity on its lower end snaps it back into a vertical orientation. This clever method of attitude control is simple and efficient, but it does create tiny g-forces near the station's upper and lower ends. Near its center of rotation, however, astronauts and experimental modules will experience, at most, only a few millionths of a g.

Until 1985, NASA's baseline space-station design, the so-called Power Tower, featured a single long, slender mast sticking vertically upward away from the earth. At first the Power Tower seemed like a reasonable compromise design that took into account several conflicting demands, but then potential users began to raise a number of practical objections. Companies interested in manufacturing in space, for instance, complained that there were not enough mounting points for new equipment, and that the proposed configuration did not provide attractive levels of microgravity. The sausage-shaped modules that were to house zero-g manufacturing were situated well away from the center of rotation, so as the station tipped and turned to maintain its earth-seeking orientation, artificial gravity forces amounting to about 10 millionths of a g were automatically produced.

A safety-related complaint came from the astronauts, who did not like the way the trailer-sized habitability and experiment modules were attached together to form a closed loop in "racetrack" fashion. If one of the modules was suddenly punctured by a meteoroid or a stray fragment of space debris, or if something inside caught fire, the astronauts could not easily isolate that module from the others in the loop. If they did, some of the other modules would be considerably less accessible.

In the past, NASA's talented leaders have often been criticized for ignoring outside opinions, but in this case their reactions were surprisingly swift and responsive. After listening to the arguments of their critics and toying with various alternatives, they scrapped the Power Tower design, substituting in its place the Dual Keel, a novel configuration in which the space station's girders are arranged in a flat figure-8 pattern. In the new design, two long towers run straight up to form a double backbone braced by three long crossbeams. The sausage-shaped aluminum modules are then mounted horizontally near the center of the Dual Keel.

The Dual Keel involves three major advantages: it provides large numbers of mounting points for extra equipment, it places the factory modules closer to the center of rotation for lower gravity manufacturing, and it eliminates the hazardous "racetrack" architecture of the habitability modules in favor of a new "cross-strapping" method of interconnection to allow any one of the modules to be isolated without seriously affecting the accessibility of the others.

Warren Reade of the European Space Agency admires NASA's intuitive skill and flexibility in developing the new configuration. "The Dual Keel is an ingenious concept because it will let NASA build a virtual city in the sky," he says. "Having the structure built on the twin-keel principle means we'll be able to have better balance in the center of the space station and run more industrial operations."

The astronauts in the space station will breathe the same mixture of gases as we do on earth—a 20 percent oxygen atmosphere at 14.7 pounds of pressure per square inch. This selection allows the use of inexpensive off-the-shelf equipment for scientific and commercial activities, and it helps the scientists correlate their experimental findings in space with their earth-based research. It also minimizes fire hazards.

In the early phases of construction, space-suited astronauts will deploy two flat solar arrays covered with thousands of thumbnail-size solar cells to power the assembly and to provide for the early operation of the station. As construction progresses, they will add extra solar arrays to provide more electricity. Eventually, these solar cells will cover a third of an acre to produce 75,000 watts of electrical power. This is about five times as much power as the shuttle's fuel cells provide during a typical mission, but it is still not enough. In the long run, 300,000 watts or more will be needed to drive all the space station's systems and to keep the astronauts alive and comfortable. Theoretically, extra solar arrays could be added to produce any amount of power desired, but an acre or more of flat panels would create excessive drag with the atmosphere.

Consequently, their power will be supplemented with a "dynamic" system that uses the sun to heat a fluid that will turn electric turbines. Flat hexagonal mirrors fastened together to form a parabolic reflector will concentrate the rays of the sun on the working fluid. The generators will spin at 50,000 to 60,000 rpms—about twenty times the rate at which the engine in a typical automobile revolves.

Either batteries or regenerative fuel cells—which convert hydrogen and oxygen into water to produce electricity—will supply power when the station is

The "Dual Keel" design for the manned space station features a flat figure-8 configuration with two vertical aluminum girders braced by three long crossbeams: two running across the top and bottom of the two vertical beams and a third cutting through their midsection. Spherical and sausage-shaped modules devoted to manufacturing, earth observations, equipment storage, and crew support are cradled under the central crossbeam near its center of gravity. The Dual Keel design, which replaced the earlier "Power Tower" configuration, provides large numbers of mounting points for experiments and commercial operations, and it reduces the gravity loads they experience by nearly a factor of ten. When it is completed in the 1990s the complex will span an area about the size of a small football stadium.

shielded from the rays of the sun. When it again flies into sunlight, the batteries will be recharged.

THE SPACE STATION'S ROBOTS

When everything is figured in, it costs something like $80,000 to keep an astronaut working in space for one hour. Consequently, anything that can reduce his workload—robots, computers, artificial intelligence, special tools—can be used to economical benefit on the manned space station. After studying the costs and benefits of station operations, a special Automation and Robotics Panel at NASA Headquarters recommended surprisingly widespread, sophisticated, and costly uses of automation: "The desired level of funding for automation and robotics research is 13 percent of the total space station cost," they noted in their report; ". . . a minimum acceptable level is 7 percent."

If these forceful recommendations are followed in the space station's ultimate design, the robots and computers on board will cost over $1 billion. Specific proposals have not been widely solicited from private business, but this may be a marvelous opportunity for bright young entrepreneurs to develop marketable concepts for artificial intelligence routines and robotics devices for use on the station and to support its operations here on earth.

In a separate but related action, the U.S. Senate Appropriations Committee produced a NASA budget bill that set aside 10 percent of the total space-station budget for the development of automation and robotics. They also expressed the opinion that by taking full advantage of artificial intelligence and expert systems (computer programs that mimic the "thought" processes of human experts), NASA could effectively devote 13 percent of the budget to various forms of space-age automation.

In their view, the space station should be used as a "test bed" for new ideas in automation. They recommended about a dozen specific long-term concepts for detailed study. Here are three samples:

- *Habitability intelligent controllers* to provide speech synthesis, automated medical decisions, physiological monitoring, and health maintenance.

- *Propulsion intelligent controllers* to manage fuel distribution, detect leaks, and evaluate problems.

- *Orbiting-platform intelligent controllers* to manage the station's manufacturing processes and provide automatic maintenance for the station itself and its detached free-flying modules.

The committee also expressed the opinion that in the mature stage of the space-station program, around 2010—shades of "Star Trek"!—data management systems could be developed to allow the astronauts to speak to their computers in "natural languages."

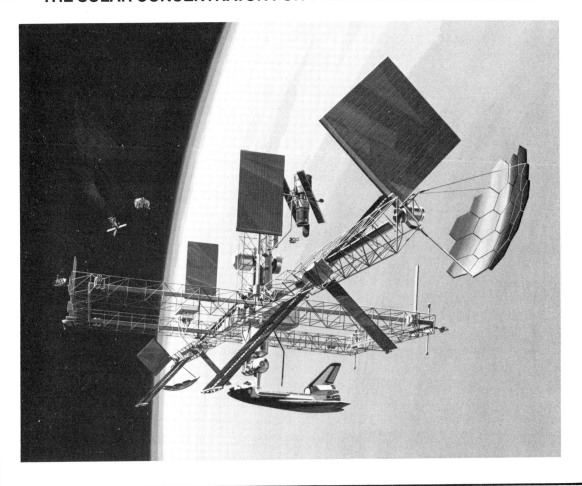

Part of the electricity for the manned space station will come from solar cells; part will come from generators spinning at 1,000 revolutions per second. These generators, which are similar to the ones used on earth to turn burning coal or falling water into electricity, will be powered by a boiling fluid heated by the sun. The segmented parabolic reflector on the right-hand side of this painting will concentrate the sun's rays onto the boiler. This hybrid approach to power production is necessary because larger flat-panel solar arrays would create too much drag as the manned complex moves through the upper atmosphere at 5 miles per second.

GETTING into the SPACE-STATION BUSINESS

When Congress passed the Gramm-Rudman-Hollings Act mandating a balanced budget by 1991, it imposed severe constraints on federal discretionary spending that could, within a few years, severely crimp space-station funding. This may slow progress, but it will also open up many of the enterprises associated with the station to financing by private, profit-making companies, many of which do not yet exist. Several creative methods for raising the necessary funds have already been proposed.

An excellent example of how alternative financing might work is provided by the dexterous robot arm to be manipulated remotely by the crew of the space station. Despite its name, it is actually several arms, together with their tools, cameras, power supplies, and computerized control routines. Spiderlike in appearance, the robot arm will help the astronauts during their extravehicular activities when they are assembling and servicing the space station.

In June 1986, NASA's experts strongly hinted that the telepresence robot might be developed by a private, profit-making firm. In the concept they proposed, the robot arm would be regarded as a "utility" for the space station that would be purchased for cash or in exchange for other valuable services. NASA's engineers would be willing to help the company develop the robot—even providing artificial intelligence routines for incorporation into its "brain"—and they would guarantee a certain number of paid uses per year. In addition, they would encourage the developer to retain ownership of the spindly-legged robot and to market its services to other customers, including the military, NASA contractors, and other private companies. Chrysler and Western Marine expressed interest in the concept, but so far no deals have been made.

Over the next few years, modules for the space station, its services, and its supporting hardware will probably be financed in similarly creative ways. In fact, NASA officials have already announced their intention to fund two other large projects under a similar philosophy: a second source for the solid rocket motors for the space shuttle, and a privately financed replacement for the shuttle *Challenger*. Today it does not appear that either of these two major projects will actually materialize, but other similar opportunities probably will as the space-station design matures and as its operations become more costly and more routine.

Donn C. Walklet, president of the space consulting firm Tera-Mar of Mountain View, California, thinks that the U.S. government may ultimately come to regard the space station itself as just another facility to be purchased or leased. After all, as he explains, the government owns many of the buildings it occupies, but "it also leases a considerable number from private owners and real estate developers." By analogy, the space station could be viewed as "nothing more than an industrial park in space—in essence, orbiting real estate." In his view NASA should probably conduct a "lease or buy" analysis for the space station to determine if private financing might in some instances be a more economical approach.

However, this issue need not be settled cleanly in terms of lease or buy. There is a middle ground in which NASA and private industry could share both the risks and the rewards. According to Walklet, "The government, through NASA, could finance the core facilities—the solar panels, docking ports, cooling and radiation devices, and telemetry facilities—while the private sector could own and finance the manufacturing and processing modules."

But why should the government be involved in the space station at all? If it is a reasonable, cost-effective investment, why not let private industry finance the entire facility? Actually, ample precedents exist for government involvement in businesses that eventually become self-supporting. Some are, today, among our country's biggest employers. Examples include the U.S. Postal Service, the Merchant Marines, the national railway system, and some of the major airlines (which were subsidized indirectly with fat airmail contracts).

Support services for the space station will constitute a large, "ready-made" commercial space industry. Major aerospace firms are going after some of the new business, but small entrepreneurs are probably at this moment meeting in someone's living room or garage in the Great Smoky Mountains or on a side street in Silicon Valley to map out their strategies too. Today's sophisticated entrepreneurs have the knowledge and enthusiasm to design, finance, and construct many of the necessary vehicles, modules, pallets, and free-flyers and to design the storage units and power facilities to support the space-station project in other important ways that could generate attractive profits.

How much interest does ordinary private industry have in building hardware for the space station or performing potentially useful private services? To answer this question, NASA asked Coopers & Lybrand, a space-oriented consulting group, to help determine the conditions under which businesses would be willing to make direct space-station investments. Altogether, officials from twenty American companies were interviewed, most of them in no way connected with the aerospace industry. The companies Coopers & Lybrand selected specialized in a variety of fields, including terrestrial communications, data management, banking, hospitality, power, construction, and waste management.

Basically, the survey showed that U.S. businesses are quite willing to pursue space-related ventures provided the government can assure them of a market for their services and a reasonable return on investment. Ground-to-space communications, waste disposal, and extravehicular activities were mentioned as activities of specific interest to the survey participants. So were data management and the development of a miniature warehouse for the space station. Most of the participants would require franchise-type protection to shield them from early competition—a reasonable request in view of the limited potential of the market and the small number of customers involved.

In response to one of the items in the questionnaire, which asked the respondents to evaluate "the minimum amount of risk protection your company would require from the government in such a venture," one executive penned this reply: "The technology risk can be managed—its been done before . . . the business risk is high because the market is unknown." Another responded to the same questions as follows: "If the government is willing to enter into binding contracts to use the services provided, we see this as a very attractive opportunity."

The results were rather revealing and surprising even to the financial experts at Coopers & Lybrand. Apparently, many companies would embrace an opportunity to compete in space. "U.S. companies are interested in establishing viable businesses in the space station," said John J. Egan, who headed the study team. And then he added, with a note of surprise: "They do not believe that their commercial involvement in the space station will require business practices that are out of the ordinary."

NASA officials will be glad to help fledgling companies find their way into the marketplace. One of their more popular space-station pamphlets includes this enthusiastic description of some of today's winners in space: "A sizable commercial enterprise has blossomed in the vacuum of space. It provides services of high quality at reasonable prices for the public, highly paid skilled jobs for workers, and dividends for investors."

NASA sees nothing new or unreasonable in purposeful business subsidies; such subsidies have existed in America since early frontier days. "The infrastructure we will build will be no different than those we established to meet the great goals of earlier days. We established public-funded programs to support development of our highways, airports, and railroads," explained NASA administrator James M. Beggs in a briefing at the White House. "The proposal to do the same for space will enable the commercial sector to work in partnership with government to open the realm of space to any number of promising enterprises."

INTERNATIONAL PARTICIPATION

Ticklish negotiations are now under way between NASA and several international partners vying to satisfy their own peculiar needs while at the same time developing just the right modules to complement and expand the space station's capabilities. Dozens, perhaps hundreds, of foreign nations and international companies will participate; however, only a limited number of *partners* will be welcomed into the project.

So far, Japan, Canada, and the European Space Agency (a consortium of ten European countries) are all negotiating for roles in space-station construction. European representatives have already held lively discussions on their continent's future in the business of space in several major European capitals, including Stockholm, London, and Bonn. Some of the participants talked bravely about developing their own autonomous space station. A few even wanted to shun any participation in the American program, but Roy Gibson, former European Space Agency director-general, is not impressed with Europe's prospects for autonomy, especially in view of the fact that their version of the space station exists only as a colorful wood-and-metal mockup at the Aeritalia facilities in Turin, Italy. "It's all very well to talk of autonomy twenty-five years from now," he cautions his fellow Europeans, "but you're biting the hand that feeds you if you don't exploit the U.S. opportunity over the next five to ten years."

In early discussions with NASA, representatives from the European Space Agency expressed a desire to provide a pressurized module linked with the space station but with the capability of detaching itself and operating autonomously. This approach would allow the Europeans to develop a sort of "mini space station" of great benefit to their long-term concept for developing their own independent capabilities in space. Unfortunately, NASA's response was decidedly chilly. The Europeans must have felt that their clever idea had run into an ideological or political deep freeze, but some American experts argue that detaching and later reattaching a 40-foot-long module would break too many interfaces.

European Space Agency officials are willing to keep their unit attached to the station, at first, but they want to maintain the *option* of detaching it at some future, undefined time. They have difficulty understanding NASA's unresponsive attitude. Further compromises are under negotiation; in fact, one compromise has already been made. Initially, the Europeans were talking about a detached module that would fly in formation with the space station. It was never to be connected to it at all!

While the Europeans and the Americans are engaging in technical and political squabbles, the Japanese and the Canadians are much closer to making firm commitments. The Japanese in particular are planning to develop one of the trailer-sized pressurized modules. It will be designed to handle a variety of operations ranging from life-sciences experiments to microgravity materials-processing. Their relations with NASA are generally cordial, but there are two points of contention. The Japanese want their module to be operated mostly by their own astronauts, and they want to protect any proprietary information gathered from their experiments. They could protect their results by encrypting the transmissions to earth or by recording sensitive data on portable memory disks for shipment in the shuttle. Later, they are hoping to design and build a small version of the shuttle of their own to further protect their commercial interests.

Like their European counterparts, Japan's businessmen are afraid the Americans will leave them behind in the race for the commercial development of space. Their contributions are expected to range between $3 and $3.6 billion by the time the station becomes operational about 1994. In an ambitious attempt to close the gap with the Americans, Japan has begun an accelerated program to develop innovative ideas for space commercialization. Recently forty-one of Japan's leading business firms formed a group called the Space Environment Utilization Center, armed with a charter to study and accelerate the commercial utilization of the space station and the space shuttle. The group includes firms involved in construction, chemicals, international trade, metals, and minerals.

The Canadians have an even more clearly focused idea on the portion of the project they are willing to tackle. At a cost of about $600 million, they want to build a mobile servicing center, following up the success of Spar Industries, a Toronto firm, in developing the 50-foot robot arm for the shuttle. The new manipulator will be rigged with two articulating arms for greater flexibility than the simpler unit built for use in the shuttle cargo bay. It will also be mobile—crawling along the girders on the outside of the space station to get to its work site—and it will be rigged with two identical arms with swiveling joints similar to the human wrist and elbow. Eventually, the Canadian engineers plan to include delicate "touch sensors" so the astronauts on or near the space station will be able to "feel" the stresses and pressures when the arm is picking up a heavy load or straining to tighten a bolt.

The main robot will have arms 50 or 60 feet long. It will be accompanied by a "little sister" robot 20 feet in length that can operate independently of its bigger brother. The smaller robot can be "picked up by the large arm and used to work on payloads to perform more dexterous tasks than the large arm can," says William H. Gregory at Spar Industries. Like a fiddler crab, the little sister will have a non-symmetrical body. "As configured now it has one coarse arm with 7 degrees of freedom and one dexterous arm probably with 8 degrees of freedom for fine detail work."

Spar's engineers are planning to design the larger arm to lift the entire contents of the shuttle cargo bay—as much as 65,000 pounds. They will employ "flexstructures controls" so that the motions of the arm will be sensed through accelerometers and fed back into the control system. Thus, the astronauts in charge will be able to "feel" its responses and sense any problems it may encounter. Many of today's earthbound teleoperators (remotely controlled robots) have similar capabilities, but they are not built on such a massive scale.

What jobs will be assigned to the space-station robots? Their most vital contribution will be in the construction of the space station itself. Consequently, they will be among the first pieces of equipment to arrive on the scene. Although the robots will be large and ungainly-looking, they will be able to undo small bolts and screws and remove boxes, take them apart, and replace faulty circuit boards and other components.

"An important aspect is designing spacecraft interfaces that can be worked on by servicing arms to make the task as simple as possible," says James A. Middleton, space station program manager at Spar's Remote Manipulator Systems Division. Design simplicity is the key. "We would like to have the units mounted rather simply, with snap fasteners or something like that, where you can unclick them relatively easily."

Most external repairs and modifications to the manned space station will be handled by large robots crawling along its girderlike beams, but space-suited astronauts will occasionally have to go outside to make delicate repairs or handle complicated operations beyond the capabilities of the space station's remotely controlled robots. Fortunately, ample experience indicates that human beings can function effectively in space even when they are wearing bulky space suits.

The primary purpose of Canada's "intelligent" robot arm is to relieve the space-station crews of tedious and tiring tasks. As William H. Gregory of Spar Industries observes: "Machines can do the detail work, like unscrewing bolts, and the astronauts will be able to function as managers or supervisors of these operations."

Many of Canada's best experts are convinced that on-orbit servicing with free-flying robots will become the next important task for spaceborne teleoperators. Salvage operations will be economically viable with short payback periods. But perhaps more important, the capability for on-orbit repair will permit simplification in the design of satellites themselves.

A PRIVATELY FINANCED SPACE STATION?

Not surprisingly, most proposed space-station configurations have come from the governments of the world's major spacefaring nations. However, as the *New York Times* noted in January 1988, at least one attention-getting concept is being masterminded by private enterprise. "Five years ago, a young Texas company . . . wanted to open the heavens to American industry," reported *Times* staffer William Broad, "by creating a cheap, private, no-frills space station where the marvels of weightlessness could be used to purify metals, grow rare crystals, fashion new semiconductors, make scarce drugs, form exotic compounds, and invent altogether new types of materials."

That young Texas company, Space Industries, Inc. (Houston, Texas), is headed by ex-NASA expert Max Flaget, whose brainchild, according to the *New York Times*, would "be the first private entry in the international race to commercialize space . . . a prototype for orbiting industrial parks of the 21st century."

Measuring 250 feet in length with a power rating of 11,000 watts, the proposed industrial space facility will be an automated factory unmanned most of the time. But every six months or so, shuttle astronauts will come aboard to perform routine maintenance, replace obsolete instruments, and bring fresh supplies to its automated production machines.

Just before Christmas 1987, Congress directed NASA to spend $24 million exploring the possibility of leasing part of the proposed station. Congressional experts who backed the leasing arrangement felt that it would guarantee a major customer for the privately owned station and a reasonably prompt ride into space aboard the shuttle. They also felt that such a commitment would encourage commercial customers to sign similar leases. The small space station could be launched with one or two shuttle flights as early as 1991 at a cost of about $700 million. This compares with 18 to 20 shuttle trips to assemble the larger NASA station with a completion date of 1997 and a total price tag lying somewhere between $16 and $26 billion.

Proponents of the industrial space facility do not see it as a competitor for the much more ambitious NASA station, but rather as a precursor. "It's not as exotic or versatile," says former astronaut Joseph P. Allen, a Space Industries executive. "We're basically a mobile home with no plumbing. But we do have electricity and people can go in from time to time to do all kinds of experiments." Leaving the astronauts on the ground most of the time can be an advantage because astronauts move and breathe and, when they do, they jiggle the other equipment on board their station.

NASA officials, fearful that support for the smaller station might divert funds and attention from their version, have resorted to creative foot-dragging. But this approach has not been working, because Space Industries has both money and political clout. The Commerce Department has vigorously promoted the concept in the White House and it has attracted some powerful partners, including Westinghouse Electric and the Boeing Commercial Space Development Company. So far, these and other contributors have invested $30 million in the project. NASA officials may be providing only grudging support, but funds are not drying up and the congressional directive will almost certainly be enforced. According to space-industrialization expert Gregg Fawkes, completion of the small station is crucial because it will "put in place an important capability for the country," and it will be available much sooner than any other American station. "Moreover, it's private," he notes, "and that's a very dramatic turn of events."

THE RUSSIAN MIR

A python squeezes the life out of its victim—pig or money—not with brute force, but with steady, relentless pressure. Every time the monkey exhales, as it must to survive, the python casually takes up the slack. Soon the monkey has no room to breathe.

This almost painful analogy describes the Soviet Union's gradual but determined conquest of space. Seldom do the Soviets do anything very spectacular in terms of hardware or mission approach. Seldom do they take flashy risks, but their steady, unremitting pressure keeps them in the race against America's more soaring technology punctuated with dramatic fits and starts. When President Reagan launched the Space Station Program, he patterned his announcement after President Kennedy's call to action on Project Apollo. The ambitious goals he envisioned sounded fresh and new, even awe-inspiring. However, less than a year later, on February 18, 1986, the Soviet pythons from Tyratam in Central Asia casually launched their *eighth* space station.*

True, it was not of modern design. True, it rode into orbit on a modified version of a thirty-year-old booster. But it was soon traveling successfully around the earth, and it did herald a new era in the systematic exploitation of space.

"That the Soviets have made tremendous gains in their space program is undeniable," writes John Anderson of *Commercial Space.* "Development programs over the last decade include a space shuttle vehicle, a medium-lift launcher, a heavy-lift launcher, a reusable spaceplane that is one-third the size of the U.S. shuttle, and the large Mir space station to complement the existing Salyut 7."** Whereas the United States launches fewer than twenty satellites in a good year, the Soviets have

One of them blew up. The others have been occupied by cosmonauts for varying amounts of time.

Mir means "peace" in Russian.

SPACE STATION RESOURCE NODE DETAIL
(SHIRT-SLEEVE ENVIRONMENT)

When the shuttle docks with the space station, the astronauts will board it through a fancy air lock called the "resource node." The use of the large, tubular air lock will allow them to transfer supplies, equipment, and other materials in a comfortable "shirt-sleeve" environment that protects them from the vacuum of space. The astronaut near the top of the resource node is using the Canadian robot arm to move bulky items from the shuttle cargo bay to the space station. The small satellite in the background is flying in formation with the station. To its left is the orbital maneuvering vehicle, which transports tools and supplies to and from the space station, picks up disabled satellites, and performs orbital refueling operations.

been mounting a much more ambitious program. In 1986, for instance, they orbited about one hundred satellites while simultaneously maintaining and supplying two operational space stations. In late March 1986 they launched an unmanned cargo vessel bound for an automatic rendezvous with the Mir space station. It carried food, fuel, letters, water, and other supplies to Mir's astronauts.

THE RUSSIANS' CHILLY DACHA in SPACE

For the first few astronauts who came aboard, the American Skylab, with its shattered sunscreen, was a steambath too sultry for comfortable work. Excess heat was not the problem for Russia's stricken Salyut 7, which, while unmanned, suddenly lost power and began slowly augering in through the atmosphere.

Vladimir Dzhanibdkov, steel-nerved Russian cosmonaut, had ridden atop powerful rockets on four previous journeys into space. Usually Soviet space heroes settle into retirement after completing three orbital flights, but Vladimir's special skills were needed for a fifth time, and he was not difficult to persuade.

When he and his fellow space traveler Viktor Savinykh rendezvoused with Salyut 7, they faced a bone-chilling encounter. "When the air hit my face, I realized how bitterly cold the station was," Dzhanibdkov later told a reporter. "Moisture from my exhalations froze in a tiny cloud around my face. Ice was everywhere—on the instruments, control panels, windows. Mold from past occupations was frozen on the wall. We bundled up in fur-lined suits and hats until we looked like babies in Moscow winter." Beams from their flashlights pierced the gaping interior of Salyut 7, and the two shivering cosmonauts scrambled in after. Was the writhing leviathan doomed? Or could they somehow warm it up and make it habitable again?

"Water in both storage tanks was frozen solid. This worried us. We could work for days without food, but not without water." Actually, they both knew they had a backup plan. If they had to, they could drink the coolant water in their space suits. However, coolant water is about as drinkable as the water contained in the radiator of a Manhattan taxicab, and they preferred to think about something else.

To gauge the temperature, Dzhanibdkov and Savinykh spat on the walls and counted off the seconds until it froze. Back in mother Russia, mission control estimated 14 degrees Fahrenheit from their 10-second count. Next they tried to recharge the big batteries on board to restore heat, light, and ventilation. Unfortunately, when the station was in darkness, they were much too cold to work, so every forty-five minutes or so, when they traveled to the dark side of the earth, they had to retreat to their own spaceship to thaw frozen hands and feet.

Finally, the ice did begin to melt, but then they were trapped in a major flood. Water, once in such short supply, now gushed over everything. Well, at least they would not have to drink that repulsive coolant water from their sweaty space suits! Suddenly the relative humidity inside Salyut 7 soared to 90 percent and the hapless Russian cosmonauts felt their skin go clammy. "We fought it for a month," recalled Dzhanibdkov back on earth. "Finally, the station entered longer periods of sunlight and the interior began to dry." It had been a long, uncomfortable struggle, this fifth journey into space, but Vladimir was finally beginning to adjust. He was glad, at last, to be warm and dry. But still, when he drifted into sleep each night, he ached for the even warmer feelings of home.

THE SOVIET UNION'S PILOTED ORBITAL COMPLEX

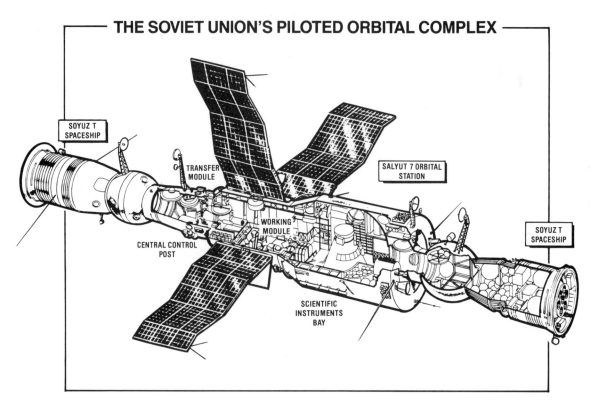

SOYUZ T SPACESHIP

TRANSFER MODULE

SALYUT 7 ORBITAL STATION

WORKING MODULE

SOYUZ T SPACESHIP

CENTRAL CONTROL POST

SCIENTIFIC INSTRUMENTS BAY

The Soviet Union's piloted orbital complex, a complicated and capable manned space station, has been on orbit in various forms over the past few years. Its crew normally consists of three Russian cosmonauts, but at times as many as six have lived and worked on board. The bulging Soyuz T spaceships on the two ends of the complex bring up fresh crews and supplies from earth.

"We've been Sputniked again," exclaimed Sandra Adamson, a director of the L5 Society, an organization packed with fresh-faced American college students itching for an all-out assault devoted to the colonization of space. NASA head James Fletcher is not quite so impressed with Soviet accomplishments. "Our space station is a *real* space station," he replied, when asked to compare the Mir with the American space station. However, as John Anderson of *Commercial Space* responded, "NASA's plans for a station still lie on the drafting tables while the Soviets' efforts are in orbit."

The Soviets have again taken what some Kremlinologists consider to be an inelegant "brute-force" approach and made it work to their advantage. The Mir, which is essentially a modified Salyut, is manned now, and it bristles with a total of six docking ports. If the Soviets keep launching large components at the rate they have been in the past few years, they will have an impressive 200,000-pound space station in orbit within a few years.

The Mir features comfortable quarters with numerous windows and private cubicles for those aboard. One Soviet space scientist has even characterized it as a

THE SOVIET MIR SPACE STATION

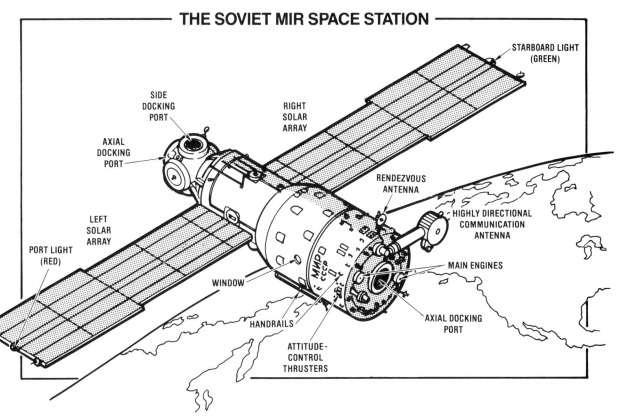

The Soviet Union's Mir is not nearly as sophisticated as NASA's manned space station, but there is an important difference: the Mir is actually in orbit with cosmonauts on board, whereas the more elegant American station is merely a sketch on the drawing board. Although it is small and cramped now, the Mir has six docking ports for later attachment of additional modules. At their present launch rate, the Soviets could have a 200,000-pound super-Mir in orbit within a few years.

"flying Disneyland." Soon it will be joined by an X-ray telescope, and shortly there-after, other modules devoted to meteorology, materials processing, and pharma-ceuticals production will be attached to those already in space.

The Soviets have high hopes for their orbital processing facilities. Perhaps in the long run the products made there will even favorably impact their balance of trade. Their Mir with its telescoping solar arrays seems strangely evil to American eyes, but when Flight Commander Kizim viewed its unique silhouette in space for the first time, he described it in lovely poetic terms: "As I came in close," he said on a TV broadcast, "it looked like a white-winged seagull, soaring above the world."

The image could have come from a once and future fantasy, yet is aired on the evening news. A U.S. astronaut looking like a modern knight-errant in shining space suit, sallies forth into the darkness, powered by a Buck Rogers backpack called the MMU (manned maneuvering unit). Armed with a space-age lance nicknamed the stinger, he spears a stray satellite and rockets back to the mother ship. There, silhouetted against the shimmering earth some 225 miles below, he spins along at 17,500 miles per hour, shouldering his prize like a sci-fi Atlas.

"Roaming the High Frontier"
Time, November 26, 1984

10

SATELLITE SALVAGE, RETRIEVAL, AND REPAIR

In late fall 1984, two American astronauts, Joseph Allen and his fellow skywalker Dale A. Gardner, using simple space-age paraphernalia, chased down two ailing satellites worth tens of millions of dollars each. Wrestling them into the shuttle cargo bay was a sweaty ordeal requiring seven hours of extravehicular activity, but when their exhausting rescue work was done the two delighted spacemen were not inclined to reach for a Michelob. Instead, standing on the end of the shuttle's 50-foot robot arm, they held a hand-lettered sign over one of the captured birds. In bright red letters on a white background, it read: FOR SALE.

Joseph Allen, smallest of the American space cadets, supplied most of the muscle power for the spaceborne rescue. Tipping the scales at only 135 pounds (about the same as his bulky space suit), Allen flashed a grin of appreciation when a colleague at Mission Control playfully announced over the air: "Joe Allen now qualifies as the first human in history to hold a 1,200-pound satellite overhead for one trip around the world."

A few days later the pages of *Time, Newsweek,* and the *Christian Science Monitor* burned with enthusiasm. As *Time* put it: "The mission was among the most spectacular in the 26-year history of the American space program." The Canadian magazine *Maclean's* also ran a major feature on the double-barreled satellite rescue, which made heavy use of the shuttle's 50-foot robot arm manufactured at Spar Industries in Toronto. "Man has been putting objects into orbit ever since the Soviets launched Sputnik I in 1957, but last week astronauts aboard the space shuttle *Discovery* reversed the procedure for the first time," wrote Hal Quinn of *Maclean's.* "The space salvage mission, during which two astronauts captured

176

communication satellites Palapa B-2 and Westar 6 and loaded them into *Discovery*'s cargo bay for the return trip to earth, secured $70 million worth of what had become space junk."

NASA's spaceflight engineers see a healthy financial future for the on-orbit retrieval and refurbishment of sick satellites. They charged only $5.5 million for capturing and returning Palapa B-2 and Westar 6—quite a bargain for the two insurance firms, Merrett Syndicates Ltd. of London and International Technology Underwriters of Washington, D.C., which had already paid Western Union and Indonesia a total of $180 million when the two satellites had failed to reach their desired orbits nine months earlier. When the mission was over, the insurance companies became proud owners of the two satellites, for sale to the highest bidder.

ECONOMIC RETURNS from ON-ORBIT SALVAGE and REPAIR

Palapa B-2 and Westar 6 were not designed for on-orbit servicing, retrieval, or repair. Consequently, Allen and Gardner had a hard time snatching them from the sky. They used a special jury-rigged mechanism called "the stinger" to latch onto the wobbling satellites. The stinger is a long, slender pole extending in front of the astronaut, who is pushed along by his backpack rocket. One end of the stinger carries a spring-loaded device similar to a molly expanding fastener that unfolds once it is inserted behind a surface. When the satellite is firmly attached, the entire end of the stinger is free to rotate, thus isolating the astronaut from the satellite's rotation. Otherwise, both astronaut and stray satellite would have to rotate at the same rate.

Tomorrow's satellites will be much easier to retrieve and repair, because they are being designed specifically with these possibilities in mind. Solar Max and the Hubble Telescope, for instance, are constructed from detachable modules and are rigged with special "grapple fixtures" so the astronauts can easily glom on to them in space. The Topex satellite, which will orbit beyond the reach of the shuttle, is being designed so ground controllers can signal it to fly back down to a convenient altitude for shuttle retrieval.

Within a decade, astronauts and orbiting robots will be retrieving large numbers of expensive satellites on a routine basis. These are some of the operations to be carried out in conjunction with future salvage missions:

- *Reboost maneuvers:* Large, low-altitude satellites gradually spiral in toward the earth because of drag with the earth's atmosphere. The space shuttle or a smaller upper stage will latch on to some of them and reboost them back up to higher altitudes.
- *On-orbit repair:* Tomorrow's satellites will be constructed with detachable modules so the astronauts can remove any inoperative component and replace it with a new, improved version.

- *Satellite resupply:* Many satellites use expendables such as hydrozene pro-pellants or cryogenic coolants. Today, when these fluids are depleted, the satellite dies; but in the future, replenishment will be possible on manned or unmanned resupply missions. In addition, some satellites devoted to zero-g manufacturing will require periodic visits for the swapout of raw materials for finished products. An orbital factory that makes flawless crystals for the electronics industry, for example, will need fresh supplies of silicon or gallium arsenide. At the same time, the astronauts or their robots will pick up the finished crystals for return to earth.
- *Salvage and retrieval:* If a disabled satellite cannot be repaired in space, the astronauts will pack it in the shuttle cargo bay and carry it back to earth, where it can be refurbished and repaired by expert technicians.

In future years, these servicing, salvage, and retrieval missions will become a big business—a business that will probably be open for competitive bidding.

To some extent, we can gauge the magnitude of this new business by noting that in 1984 and 1985, insurance companies paid $632 million in claims for satellites that failed to reach their intended destinations in space. Most of them, including Palapa B-2 and Westar 6, ended up only a few hundred miles above the strat-osphere, intact and nearly operational except for minor problems with compo-nents or upper-stage rockets. A few of them have already been salvaged at a cost of a few percent of their actual value.

At this moment, hundreds of other failed satellites are swarming around the earth. Many could be restored to useful service with simple reboost maneuvers, resupply of expendables, or minor repairs—either on-orbit or back on earth. An-other type of salvage mission that could be of great economic benefit is the re-trieval of radioactive or otherwise hazardous debris.

According to Nicholas L. Johnson, advisory scientist at Teledyne Brown En-gineering, "About fifty radioisotope power supplies, nuclear reactors, and fuel cores now in orbit pose both near- and far-term hazards." All but a few of them have been launched by the Soviet Union, which now boosts them into 600-mile orbits when they malfunction. This allows their radioactive materials to decay before they plunge through the atmosphere. Despite this precaution, however, failures of various types have caused as many as six of them to fall back to earth while still highly radioactive.

In addition, numerous spent stages are in orbit, some of which will eventually explode, producing hundreds of hazardous fragments. Nearly fifty explosions have already occurred in space, including a number of Agena upper stages built by McDonnell Douglas. Careful redesign of the Agena has largely alleviated this prob-lem. However, in November 1986 the third stage of a French Ariane suddenly exploded after coasting around the earth for about nine months. When it blew up,

Astronaut Dale A. Gardner, here wearing the manned maneuvering unit, cautiously approaches the Westar 6 over the Bahama Islands off Florida's Atlantic coast. Dwarfed by the giant Westar satellite, which weighs over half a ton on earth, Gardner was assisted by two other astronauts: 135-pound Joseph Allen, who supplied most of the muscle power for the salvage operations, and Dr. Anna L. Fisher, who operated the 50-foot remote manipulator arm from inside the cabin of the space shuttle Discovery.

the stage was in a 490-mile polar orbit, but the force of the explosion threw debris into orbits ranging from 270 miles to 840 miles high.

Following the mishap, which occurred just north of the equator between Africa and South America, radar antennas operated by the U.S. Air Force and the Navy detected at least 200 pieces of debris half an inch in diameter or larger. Of course, other pieces too small to show on radar screens were no doubt created by the explosion, which was most likely caused by the spontaneous detonation of propellants (hydrogen and oxygen) left over when the rocket had burned out nine months earlier.

Ariane's engineers are redesigning their upper stage now that they realize a problem exists, but if other satellite manufacturers get in similar difficulties in the future or if their payloads contain radioactive substances, they may want to hire companies that specialize in handling that type of hazard. Major oil companies do the same thing if one of their oil rigs catches on fire. The teams of "firefighters" they hire to extinguish the blaze are well paid for their skill, courage, and expertise.

SAVING the NAVY'S LEASAT

The successful retrieval of Palapa and Westar was in keeping with a long and exciting tradition of spaceborne retrievals, rescues, and on-the-spot repairs. In September 1985, for instance, astronauts James D. von Hoften and William F. Fisher "walked" in space two consecutive days in order to rescue the Navy's Leasat. In April of that same year, shuttle astronauts had attempted to repair the Leasat with a jury-rigged "flyswatter" hastily kludged together in space, but that attempt ended in failure. Fortunately, Fisher and von Hoften would have considerably better luck.

As the *Discovery* flew into darkness over Hawaii, von Hoften, who was tilted at an awkward angle on the end of the shuttle's robot arm, managed to snap a "capture bar" onto the Leasat. At one point in the rescue, Fisher was standing in restraints in the shuttle cargo bay flexing his "space muscles" as he effortlessly held the 14,500-pound satellite over his head! Later, when the satellite was nestled snugly in the cargo bay, the astronauts removed several screws to open two small panels. They were then able to link special connectors into the panel's exposed rockets to allow ground activation of the satellite. At this point von Hoften again rode on the end of the robot arm to hold the giant satellite over his head and release it into space.

DESIGNING TOMORROW'S UPPER STAGES for REBOOST and RETRIEVAL

Today's upper stages carry payloads into their final orbits, but that is about all they are able to do. However, as the space program evolves, we will need upper stages capable of performing more complicated in-space operations on their own or by remote control under the direction of operators on the ground or elsewhere in space. Big money will be available to companies that can perfect more capable

SOME SPECTACULAR SPACE-AGE REPAIRS

"Houston, we have a problem."

"Say again, Apollo 13."

"We have a problem."

It was a problem all right! Seconds before, an explosion had ripped through the Apollo service module, knocking out two of its three fuel cells and dumping the astronauts' precious oxygen supplies into black space.

At first they managed to remain fairly calm, but as their crippled spacecraft hurtled toward the moon, a new crisis unfolded: the lithium hydroxide canisters in the LEM and the service module turned out to be noninterchangeable, and as a result, the air the astronauts were breathing was rapidly becoming polluted. Fortunately, they were able to slap together a workable connection for the canisters in the service module, thus making them usable in the "lifeboat" LEM.

Over the next few years other astronauts successfully achieved similar on-orbit repairs. For instance, when the micrometeoroid shield was ripped off the Skylab during its journey into orbit, the astronauts erected a big cooling parasol to shade the Skylab from the harsh rays of the sun. In the next mission, astronauts Jack R. Lousma and Owen K. Garriott improved the sunshade by erecting two 55-foot metal poles from a large A-frame tent over their new home in space. Other Skylab astronauts repaired an ailing battery, retrieved exposed film from the Apollo telescope mount, and removed and replaced several gyroscopes used in stabilizing their wobbling craft. All of these complicated tasks were performed in full space suits outside the protective envelope of the Skylab module.

The retrieval and redeployment of the Solar Max satellite—which was filmed by the shuttle astronauts—provides another illustration of the skill and dexterity of man in space. But robots have performed in a similarly impressive way. For instance, when the TV camera on the robot arm showed a chunk of ice growing outside the waste-water vent on the shuttle orbiter, the Canadian arm helped the astronauts achieve the solution. Rather than risk possible damage to the shuttle's heat shield, should the ice come loose on reentry, the astronauts were instructed to use the robot arm like a giant hammer to knock the ice loose.

In another mission the robot arm was ready to release the ERBS (earth radiation budget satellite) into space. When its solar arrays got stuck, the astronauts used the robot arm to shake the satellite vigorously, then hold it up to the sun so its array could unfold. But before it released the satellite, the robot was again used to nudge a balky earth-mapping radar antenna into place.

upper stages, which will be, in effect, orbiting robots. A few versions of these versatile space-age robots are already beyond the planning stages.

Grumman Aerospace, for instance, has proposed a boxy remote manipulator called the proximity operations vehicle (POV) to be operated by the shuttle astronauts, who would watch and respond to television pictures transmitted to them by cameras aboard their remotely controlled vehicle. Four long, spindly arms attached to the Grumman spacecraft are each tipped with four gaseous nitrogen thrusters to control its flight path and its orientation. When the proximity operations vehicle reaches a disabled satellite, it takes it in tow with its grappling device for a quick trip back to the orbiter. A control panel on the shuttle provides the astronauts with pictures from either of two television cameras carried aboard the craft—one pointing in the direction of its travel, the other pointing aft.

Grumman's device minimizes harmful contamination and saves appreciable amounts of fuel. The gaseous nitrogen propellants it uses are not very efficient, but the vehicle itself is so sleek and light that moving it in space is much easier than lugging around the massive shuttle orbiter—even though the shuttle is powered by much better propellants. Rudolph Adornato, Grumman's manager of satellite services, makes this telling comparison: "The propellant used by the proximity operations vehicle for a typical rendezvous mission would be less than 100 pounds. For the shuttle its more like 500 to 1,200 pounds." In Rudolph Adornato's opinion, his company's creation will in the future become a far more capable spacefaring robot. "Later versions equipped with sets of grappling arms could even repair satellites without bringing them back to the shuttle."

The proximity operations vehicle would be designed to fly in low-altitude orbits. However, tomorrow's most profitable robot repair vehicles will operate at the geosynchronous altitude. At this moment more than a hundred communication satellites are rimmed around the geosynchronous arc. On the average it costs about $300 million to replace one of them when it malfunctions, even though in most cases the failed component is worth only a few thousand dollars.

According to a recent article in *Aviation Week,* a robot repair vehicle permanently based in a geosynchronous orbit could save communications companies at least $1 billion a year. The satellites at the geosynchronous altitude are all in the same plane, so the propulsive energy required to travel from one of them to another is quite modest. Satellites bound for geosync could carry new tools and fresh supplies for the robot—which would never leave the geosynchronous arc.

Under the direction of NASA, researchers at MIT have designed a prototype device for on-orbit repairs. It is called the telepresence servicer unit. A remotely controlled orbital robot, it will be able to repair and service many different kinds of satellites. According to the MIT team, it will be about as capable and dexterous as an on-site astronaut assigned to the same task. Two racks run along its midsection. One carries spare parts; the other carries several different kinds of "end

PROPOSED FACILE HAND FOR SPACE STATION ROBOTS

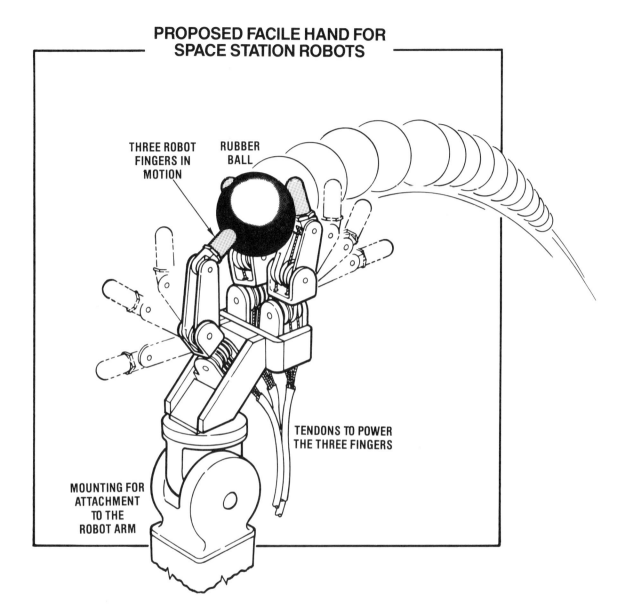

THREE ROBOT FINGERS IN MOTION

RUBBER BALL

TENDONS TO POWER THE THREE FINGERS

MOUNTING FOR ATTACHMENT TO THE ROBOT ARM

This facile three-fingered robot hand is being developed jointly by Stanford University and the Jet Propulsion Laboratory for possible use in connection with Canada's 50-foot remote manipulator arm carried in the shuttle cargo bay. Its two flexible fingers and its single opposing "thumb" are powered by "tendons" similar to the ones running along the back of the human hand. Tendon control gives the hand greater flexibility and eliminates the need for many of the special-purpose fittings the robot arm would otherwise need for tomorrow's complicated missions.

effectors"—hands—for the robot. MIT's spacefaring robot has four arms. Two of them will be directed to grapple with the ailing satellite; the other two will perform any necessary repairs.

The use of robots in space may seem futuristic and strange, but actually the Russians sent a robot to the moon nearly twenty years ago. It was a big wire-wheeled cart that ambled around the lunar surface for several months under real-time teleoperator control of the scientists in the Soviet Union. Canada's 50-foot remote manipulator system is another example of a remotely controlled robot in space. Its end effector is simple now, but the Jet Propulsion Laboratory is working on an improved version—a three-fingered hand whose joints are manipulated by tendons similar to the ones running down the back of the human hand.

Eventually the proximity operations vehicle may fly in space. But in the meantime, TRW is working under NASA contract to build another, less capable, upper stage called the orbital maneuvering vehicle (OMV), with a 1991 delivery date. The orbital maneuvering vehicle will be an unmanned "space tug" capable of delivering and retrieving payloads up to an altitude of 2,000 miles. In its initial configuration, the OMV will pick up disabled satellites and return them to the shuttle for on-orbit repair or return to earth. It will also be able to reboost satellites into higher orbits when atmospheric drag causes their orbits to decay.

Later versions will be equipped with manipulator arms to provide on-the-spot servicing and maintenance of satellites, including replacement of subsystems and propellant resupply. Operators on the ground will direct the craft by remote control after it has been released from the shuttle or the manned space station.

Most of today's satellites are not designed for on-orbit salvage, retrieval, or repair. But many will be in the future, and when they are, their engineers will probably gravitate toward standardized components and modular design. In a few cases, the modular-design concept has already been used, and one of the satellites that used it has already been repaired in orbit. It was the Solar Max, a "multimission modular spacecraft," as masterminded by NASA's Goddard Spacecraft Center in Greenbelt, Maryland.

With ample help from a number of aerospace contractors, most notably Fairchild, the Goddard designers have modularized their satellites, thus saving millions of dollars even if the satellite is never retrieved or repaired. They have accomplished this by partitioning the spacecraft by function and packaging the devices needed to handle each function in a separate detachable "box" with simple interfaces and only two or three attachment points.

This simple but powerful design philosophy has already been used in connection with several low-altitude satellites, including the Landsat, Topex, Gamma Ray Observatory, and Solar Max—which was successfully repaired on orbit by shuttle astronauts George Nelson and James von Hoften. Once Nelson had arm-wrestled

RUSSIAN ROBOT EXPLORING
THE SURFACE OF THE MOON

On November 17, 1970, Soviet space scientists successfully hurled an unmanned spacecraft onto a rendezvous trajectory with the moon. It carried the Lunohod, a remotely controlled wire-wheeled robot cart designed to amble along the lunar landscape. For several weeks thereafter, Russian technicians back on earth "drove" their lunar go-cart among the boulders on the moon by remote control. Although the experiment was a success, controlling the movements of the lunar buggy was considerably more difficult than Russia's mission planners had anticipated. The operators had to plan ahead with extreme care, because the television images coming from the Lunohod required 1.5 seconds to reach the earth and a similar amount of time was needed for the operator's control signals to get back to the moon. Imagine how hard it would be to drive your car if you had to make each steering adjustment three seconds in advance.

the cranky 5,000-pound satellite into submission, the two astronauts moved it into the shuttle cargo bay, where they skillfully replaced a faulty attitude-control module and its main electronic box. Thirteen days later the refurbished Solar Max, now safely back in orbit, observed the largest solar flare seen on the sun since 1978. Multimission modular spacecraft design was now a proven approach, and, as one commentator put it, "The age of the throwaway satellite was over."

A modular satellite design typically involves a weight penalty of about 15 percent, but it has a number of compensating advantages, including cheaper test programs, more practical on-orbit maintenance, and relatively easy upgrading even after launch. If extensive on-orbit repairs are to be accomplished in future years, component standardization and modular design with simple quick-release modules will probably turn out to be the key.

DAVE THOMPSON'S $30 MILLION TRANSFER ORBIT STAGE

"Can three Harvard MBAs and a Texas wildcatter take on the aerospace establishment? Tune in for the Adventures of Orbital Sciences." This teasing headline was written by Julius Ellis in *Air and Space,* published by the Smithsonian Institution in Washington, D.C. The saga it describes started when the young founders of Orbital Sciences Corporation, Bruce Ferguson, David Thompson, and Scott Webster, with widely admired confidence and optimism, formed their fledgling company in 1982. Their business was building a high-flying rocket called the transfer orbit stage.

Most upper-stage rockets are financed and sold by old-line aerospace companies, the same companies that build big boosters. But the transfer orbit stage, as masterminded by the founders of the Orbital Sciences Corporation, clearly illustrates how ordinary private citizens—if they have enough courage and intelligence—can gain entry into today's businesses in space.

The first meeting of Ferguson, Thompson, and Webster occurred in a classroom at Harvard University in 1979 when they participated in a NASA-sponsored project that evaluated the many opportunities for the commercialization of space. Some of their classmates scoffed at the concepts being presented, but these three close friends quickly focused on a near-term opportunity—an upper stage to be launched out of the space shuttle.

The talents of the three young students meshed together nicely for a joint venture in space. Thompson had graduated first in his class at MIT in aeronautics and astronautics, Webster was a mechanical engineer, and Ferguson pursued a joint degree in law and business.

David Thompson had been a self-proclaimed space cadet ever since his boyhood days when he built a crude 7-foot rocket that hurled squealing monkeys on half-mile parabolas over the rich farmlands outside Spartanburg, South Carolina. He always enjoyed pretending he was Christopher Krafft at Mission Control, but he never thought about trying to form a space company until he enrolled in that class at Harvard. Nor had he thought about "holding a board meeting in space," a dream he eventually shared with the two other self-styled space cadets.

"Upper stages seemed ideally suited to private investment because of their fairly simple technology, modest development cost, and large customer base," Bruce Ferguson observed in a recent interview. "Yet only McDonnell Douglas had taken the initiative to fund its own shuttle upper stage." Lightweight payloads were adequately covered by the payload assist module (McDonnell Douglas), and heavier ones were covered by Boeing's inertial upper stage. Consequently, the dynamic trio concluded that a midsized booster might find a comfortable niche in the market. Their studies showed that it could have a number of commercial customers and was suited to government missions too.

When they graduated in 1981, they trailed off in separate directions. They might have stayed apart if they had not won a $5,000 award from the Space Foundation, a nonprofit organization of Houston business executives. The award barely covered their trip to Houston to attend the ceremony, but the honor it bestowed inspired the young entrepreneurs to moonlight for a while on their upper-stage rocket.

Later, when they delivered their first appeal for funds to Sam Dunnam, president of the Space Foundation, he directed them to Fred Alcorn, a Houston wildcatter who was willing and able to engage in high-risk ventures. "I may have been naive," Alcorn remembers. "But the young men's ideas made so much sense, I knew right away I wanted a piece of the action."

On the basis of a proposal outlined on a deli napkin, Alcorn gave them $30,000—and a promise of more money if and when NASA gave its blessing to the project. Later, Thompson and Webster heard a presentation by a NASA engineer outlining the need for a midsized upper stage similar to the one they already had in mind. The representatives at NASA patiently listened to their presentation, but were rather noncommittal. Nevertheless, they quit their jobs and secured another $250,000 from the deep pockets of Fred Alcorn, plus a $2 million line of credit from his bank.

Even so, funds were gradually growing thin until a positive article in the *New York Times* led Nathaniel Rothschild, a member of Europe's noted banking family, to form an investor group to pump in another $1.8 million of painfully needed capital. This was followed by a limited partnership good for another $50 million— the largest amount of money ever raised in this manner in the aerospace industry.

The first transfer orbit stage has already rolled off the production lines. Eventually it will trace out a graceful trajectory bound for Mars. Unfortunately, the *Challenger* disaster wiped out much of the rest of the little company's potential

THE ORBITAL MANEUVERING VEHICLE: FUTURISTIC ROBOT FOR ON-ORBIT SALVAGE AND RETRIEVAL OF DISABLED SATELLITES

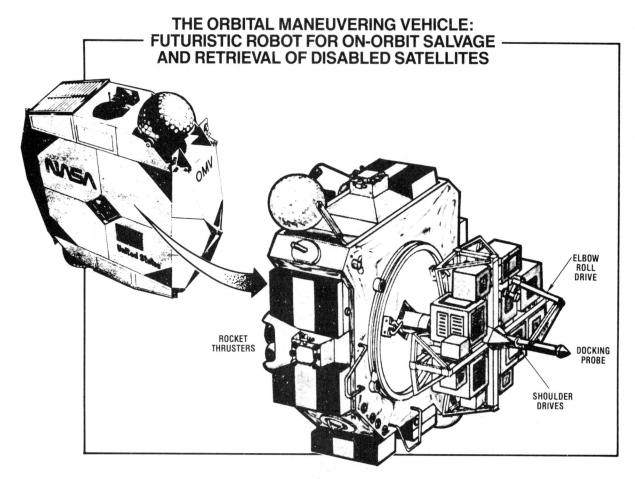

The orbital maneuvering vehicle being built at TRW will be a spacefaring robot designed to fly higher than the shuttle and to capture and retrieve ailing satellites. Once captured, they may be returned to the space station for refurbishment and repair, or they may be placed in the shuttle cargo bay for return to earth. When the repair work is done, the healthy birds can be returned to their original locations in space by the OMV.

business. At that fateful meeting in Washington, NASA had pinpointed a need for ten additional stages valued at $30 million each, including the one their representatives eventually agreed to buy. Still, if Ferguson, Thompson, and Webster are discouraged, they never seem to let it show. They are confidently looking toward other NASA missions now emerging from the drawing boards. In the meantime, they are talking to the Department of Defense, which may have as many as ten missions suitable for use of the transfer orbit stage. With a company of only thirty employees the three MBAs have made big waves in aerospace, beating the giants of the industry on their own turf. Thompson, Ferguson, and Webster still gaze upward with their eyes focused on the stars. "We can pull off that board meeting in space by the year 2000," Thompson concludes. "I don't know exactly when, but we'll manage somehow."

THE HAZARDS of ORBITING SPACE DEBRIS

On July 2, 1982, during the final day of their mission, astronauts Ken Mattingly and Henry Hartsfield aboard the space shuttle *Columbia* flew uncomfortably close to a spent Russian Intercosmos rocket high above the northwestern coast of Australia. By coincidence that same region of space had experienced an earlier encounter with space debris when America's Skylab crashed in the outback in 1979. Astronauts Mattingly and Hartsfield were warned in advance, but they were unable to catch a glimpse of the Intercosmos rocket as it whizzed by their spacecraft at 7,000 miles an hour.

Six months later, Russia's Cosmos 1402 abruptly slammed into the earth. Like its sister ship Cosmos 954, it was a spy satellite powered by a nuclear reactor containing radioactive uranium. But unlike its sister ship, it crashed in the sea—not on the territory of an innocent nation. In 1978 when Cosmos 954 fell in northern Canada, the Canadian government expended $6 million cleaning up the mess. Later, with some reluctance, the Soviet Union reimbursed Canada for half that amount.

The U.S. military tracks about 6,000 man-made objects in space as big as a watermelon or bigger. A few hundred of them are functioning satellites. The rest are a varied lot: spent rockets, protective shrouds, clamps, fasteners, fragments from space vehicle explosions, even an astronaut's silver glove. In addition to the 6,000 objects of trackable size, tens of thousands of smaller ones are believed to be swarming around our planet in space.

These orbiting objects are hazardous, but not to the people living on the earth. On the average, human beings occupy the earth with only seventeen tiny bodies per square mile. The Skylab was among the largest man-made objects ever to plunge through the atmosphere, but scientific calculations indicated that the probability of any specific individual being hit was only about one in 200 billion. Actually, no calculations at all are required to show that the hazard of being bashed by orbital debris is extremely small. More than 1,500 large hypervelocity meteorites are known to have plunged to earth—roughly eight per year for the past 200 years. Many of them shattered on reentry, but not one single official death certificate reads "death by meteorite." And yet, if we go back far enough, there is one reliable reference to human injury and death caused by falling meteorites. It is related in the Bible's book of Joshua, in a passage describing how terrified soldiers fleeing from battle were killed by "stones from heaven."

SPACE DEBRIS: THE GROWING HAZARD in SPACE

If you own a good pair of binoculars, you can get a firsthand look at the destructive potential of hypervelocity projectiles. Many of the craters on the moon are rimmed with white spokes formed centuries ago when lunar subsoil was hurled outward by large meteorites slamming into the surface of the moon. Their average impact velocity has been estimated at 44,000 miles per hour.

Your binoculars will also help you observe evidence of the population explosion of man-made objects in space. Look toward the southwest as the sun begins to sink below the horizon. Four or five times an hour you will spot an orbiting object of earthly origin glistening in the light of the setting sun. Now wait a few hours and note the number of stars visible to the naked eye. If the sky is dark and clear, and there are no city lights to create glare, you will be able to see about 2,000 stars—roughly the same number as the man-made objects orbiting in one hemisphere. At this moment the technicians at NORAD are tracking more than 6,000 man-made objects in the vicinity of the earth. These objects include hundreds of functioning satellites plus a larger number of spent rockets, dead space vehicles, shrouds, clamps, fasteners, and even Ed White's silver glove, which came off during his walk in space. Each year about 800 new objects are added, and roughly half that number plunge back to earth. Fortunately, most of them burn up before striking the ground. Objects as small as basketballs can be tracked by NORAD radars, but much smaller objects can present a hazard to travelers in space. Because of their savage velocities, even fragments smaller than garden peas can damage an artificial satellite. Most experts believe the total number of objects of destructive size is at least 15,000, perhaps substantially more.

Sixty percent of the trackable objects in NORAD's inventory have resulted from explosions in space, at least fifty of which are known to have occurred. Russian "killer satellites," large, deadly sawed-off shotguns, created one-third of the explosions when they were tested in space. Most of the others were caused by unplanned explosions of propellant tanks on American upper stages. A few of these rockets were thought to be dead in space for three years or more before they exploded. According to *Spaceflight* magazine, astronauts from the Soviet Union may have further aggravated the problem of space debris by releasing garbage from the manned space stations. Our radars are not sensitive enough to make a positive identification, but Russian watermelon rinds may be mingled with the other objects our radar operators sometimes see streaking across their screens.

Here on earth, we are relatively safe, but in space, man-made objects are extremely hazardous. A collision with even the tiniest fragment can be instantly catastrophic because orbiting satellites travel at such enormous speeds. According to NASA engineer Donald Kessler, at Houston's Johnson Space Center, "the impact velocity between two objects in orbit in the vicinity of earth would average 22,000 miles per hour." A collision between two 1-pound projectiles closing on one another at that speed could create the same explosive energy as the detonation of 6 pounds of TNT!

A few years ago the engineering staff at the General Motors Defense Research Laboratory conducted experiments to gauge the probable hazards of space debris. In one test they fired a quarter-ounce plastic cylinder from a special gun at 17,000 miles per hour into a slab of aluminum. The impact created a 3-inch crater and blasted out hundreds of hypervelocity fragments weighing a total of 1.1 pounds—seventy-eight times the weight of the original projectile! Don Kessler and his colleagues are afraid that similar collisions in space could create swarms of lethal projectiles around the earth, thus making future space operations hopelessly risky.

Collisions are most likely to occur near the equator, because every object that travels around the earth must make two equatorial crossings per circuit. The most hazardous altitude is 530 miles. If you are in orbit at that altitude, you are more likely to be pelted by man-made space debris than at any other location in space.

If you do manage to become an orbiting tourist, what are the chances your vacation will be marred by an untimely collision? Donald Kessler estimates that for each week it spends in orbit, the space shuttle has about one chance in 500,000 of slamming into a destructive particle. This is not an insignificant risk, but even if every collision turned out to be fatal, you would still be about as safe in orbit as you are here on earth.

If you spend a week in a foreign country, your chances of being attacked and killed by terrorists are roughly the same magnitude, and if you stay home for a week, your chances of being killed in a traffic accident are about twice as great. Wherever you are, in space or on the ground, your chances of dying in any given week are about one in 3,500—roughly 150 times greater than the hazard of deadly space debris.*

Of course, large space vehicles have a proportionately greater risk of colliding with fragments in space. The solar power satellite (SPS), a spider-beam array the size of Manhattan Island (21 square miles), is the largest satellite yet proposed. If it is ever built, it will capture 5 billion watts of electricity from the sun for use by the

---

*At hazardous locations in space, the chances of being hit by a deadly meteoroid are about one-tenth as high as being hit by a man-made debris fragment of comparable size.

LABORATORY SIMULATION OF HYPERVELOCITY IMPACTS

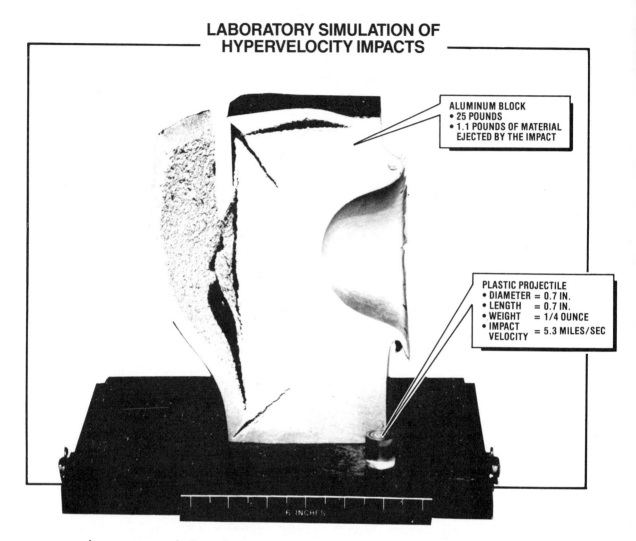

ALUMINUM BLOCK
- **25 POUNDS**
- **1.1 POUNDS OF MATERIAL EJECTED BY THE IMPACT**

PLASTIC PROJECTILE
- **DIAMETER = 0.7 IN.**
- **LENGTH = 0.7 IN.**
- **WEIGHT = 1/4 OUNCE**
- **IMPACT VELOCITY = 5.3 MILES/SEC**

6 INCHES

In an attempt to duplicate the impact conditions of colliding space debris, researchers at General Motors fired a quarter-ounce plastic projectile into this flat slab of aluminum at a muzzle velocity of 17,000 miles per hour. When the plastic cylinder hit the aluminum surface, it blasted out a thumb-shaped crater and created hundreds of aluminum fragments outweighing the projectile seventy-eight to one. These impact conditions are roughly comparable to what would happen if Ed White's stray glove slammed into one of our weather satellites at an angle of 60 degrees—an impact geometry that is not at all unlikely.

people living on earth. Unfortunately, calculations carried out by the engineering staff at NASA's Marshall Space Flight Center in Huntsville, Alabama, indicate that a typical solar power satellite would smash into twenty-seven pieces of space debris during its thirty-year orbital life—fifteen during construction in a low-altitude orbit, eight while it was being moved to its final destination 22,300 miles above the earth, and four more after it arrived there and was generating useful amounts of electrical power. This hazard would complicate the design of the solar power satellite because it would have to be designed to avoid impending impacts or to survive collisions in space.

Smaller satellites do not experience the same level of risk, but, because there are so many of them, taken collectively they, too, are exposed to substantial hazards from orbiting space debris. Indeed, evidence indicates that small man-made fragments may have already smashed into four satellites in space. For instance, a section of the solar panel on GOES B, an American weather satellite, was suddenly damaged, apparently from an unexpected impact. In another incident in July 1975, the PAGEOS balloon, after nine peaceful years aloft, suddenly broke up in a region known to contain large amounts of space debris. A third incident occurred in connection with the Soviet's ill-fated Cosmos 954, which crashed in Canada in 1978. Its widely publicized adventure started on January 24 of that same year when it suffered a sudden depressurization, which some experts believe may have been caused by a collision with orbiting debris. Perhaps the best-known collision in space occurred in 1983 when space debris pitted a window of the *Challenger,* leaving a crater one-tenth of an inch across. Later analysis showed that it was caused by a paint flake no larger than a grain of sand moving toward the shuttle at about 10,000 miles per hour.

Collisions in space can be a bothersome design problem today, but they could become considerably more hazardous in future years. Part of the difficulty arises from the fact that on each mission, the Russian Proton or the American shuttle carries several tons of material into space. But in the long run, the cascading effect of orbital collisions may turn out to be a much larger contributor to tomorrow's space debris. Like an explosion, a collision between two orbiting objects can create hundreds of additional fragments, which, in turn, can further multiply from new collisions. Ultimately, our planet could be wearing a deadly girdle of gravel-size scraps of metal similar to the girdle of asteroids now encircling the sun. Within forty years or so, millions of small particles could be barreling around the earth in such dense swarms that a large manned space station could expect daily collisions.

Val A. Chobotov, manager of the Space Hazards Office at the Aerospace Corporation in Los Angeles, has made several careful studies of the space-debris hazard. His reports indicate that if the debris in space continues to accumulate at the current rate we will experience an "eightfold increase in the collision hazard in twenty years." Chobotov outlines a rational policy of control in which he pleads for "a consistent and universally observed space object management policy which could ensure that future missions would be protected from unacceptable collision hazards in orbit."

DEBRIS RETRIEVAL CONCEPTS

Several researchers have suggested methods for removing some of this hazardous debris, including "scavenger" rockets that would fly through space scooping up stray bits of garbage. Marshall Kaplan, president of Space Tech, Inc., is working on a preliminary design for a space "scavenger" 20 to 30 feet across. Once a fragment is captured by his device, it can be carried safely back to earth, deorbited in an uninhabited area, or moved to a safer location in space.

The main problem with debris retrieval is that any scavenger rocket must switch from one orbit to another to catch each new object. Changing orbits consumes large amounts of propellants. This suggests that it may be more practical to attach the retrieval rocket directly to the payload *before* it is launched. Russian and European engineers have already used this approach. NASA studied the possibility of using it in connection with the Saturn S-II that went into orbit with the Skylab, and they will be using it with the Topex, a French-American oceanographic satellite that is being designed with a propulsion system capable of moving it to a lower altitude within grappling range of the shuttle.

Thus we see that when a satellite begins to die, it is possible to deorbit it or move it to a safer location in space—if prior provisions have been made. However, the necessary rockets are heavy and costly, and they must operate flawlessly several years after the mission begins. Fortunately the space shuttle can cut down on the rate of growth of space debris. When it returns to earth, it will bring back many of the components that expendable rockets normally leave in space. Still, the most promising way to reduce the accumulation of orbital "garbage" is to eliminate spacecraft explosions. In addition, international treaties could outlaw killer satellites, and more careful design could minimize propellant-tank explosions.

A few geosynchronous satellites have performed evasive maneuvers to avoid being hit by their lumbering neighbors along the geosynchronous arc—but designing a satellite to duck when it is on a collision course with any random hypervelocity fragment the size of a cornflake will be extremely challenging, to say the least. Making our satellites impact-resistant is possible, but heavy armor plating would be required—although double-walled construction can substantially reduce the weight. The first wall shatters the projectile into smaller fragments; the second absorbs their dispersed energy. This approach can reduce the weight of the armor plating by as much as 80 percent.

USING SPACE DEBRIS as an ON-ORBIT RAW MATERIAL

In his book *The Secret Home,* David Bodanis describes a population of tiny dust mites that live in our beds and carpets and "feed on the tiny rafts of human skin that fall off your body at a stupendous rate whenever you walk—tens of thousands of skin flakes per minute." If you are a typical American, you are sharing your bed (and your skin!) with about two million of these tiny mites, which are so small and unobtrusive that they were not discovered until 1965.

From our point of view, the flakes of skin we shed so prodigiously are not of much importance, but the little creatures living in our beds and carpets see them in a completely different light. As Bodanis puts it, "for the waiting mites they are manna."

Some of the spacefaring "nations" of tomorrow that will live above us in earth orbit may, in a similar way, lie in wait for the discarded particles we send in the opposite direction. The materials we rocket upward from the earth could become for them useful components and raw materials—disabled satellites, rocket casings, payload fairings, the astronauts' silver gloves; anything that drifts by their home in space that can be repaired, reused, or melted down for its metals. At today's prices, launching a payload into orbit costs something like $3,000 a pound. Tomorrow's launch costs will probably decline, but transporting equipment and supplies up to the final frontier will always be expensive. Consequently, almost any materials, even those requiring extensive refurbishment or reprocessing, will probably be snatched up with gleeful enthusiasm by tomorrow's spacefaring populations.

In fact, materials from earth could become so valuable that some rockets may be partially loaded with useful "ballast" for later use by the people living on the space frontier. Many of these materials will be delivered to the doorstep of tomorrow's citizens of space, but others will probably be left in any handy "drift orbit" or placed aboard other orbiting satellites in case they may eventually prove useful.

SAVING the SHUTTLE'S EXTERNAL TANKS

Many aerospace experts feel that discarding the shuttle's external tank—that giant bullet-shaped container for hydrogen and oxygen nestled below the orbiter —is a shameful waste of precious resources. On each flight the tank is released from the orbiter when most of its fuel is expended. It then falls in burning pieces over the Indian Ocean. With a little extra boost, the tank could be carried into orbit, where it might have a number of useful purposes. Pushing it into orbit would not even be costly. When it is released today, it has already reached 98 to 99 percent of orbital velocity.

Ben Bova, president of the National Space Society, argues forcefully for preserving the external tanks for use of future generations: "For a minuscule decrease in the shuttle's payload capacity, these 30-ton [empty] tanks could be inserted into orbit, where they would form the shells for working facilities: a 'prefab' space station. Each tank offers nearly 71,000 cubic feet of volume, seven times the space available in the shuttle's payload bay."

Members of the National Commission of Space share Bova's attitudes toward preserving the external tanks. In their 1986 report to the White House, they conceded that "there are hazards and costs that weigh against saving the tank," but nevertheless, they requested serious NASA studies to see if the valuable materials they contain can be saved for future generations. "We feel that so great a resource cannot be ignored and propose that a new look be taken," reads the report, which goes on to point out that over the next decade, 20 million pounds of potentially valuable tankage will be discarded. "At standard shuttle rates it would cost about *$35 billion* to lift that amount of mass as cargo into orbit."

Instead of sending the big metal tanks to oblivion on each shuttle flight, commission members felt that preserving them for later use may be far more advisable. The tanks could, for example, be used as raw stock for making heavy girders or for radiation shielding, and their residual propellants could be siphoned off for use aboard the space station. "We cannot set limits now on what use could be made of shuttle tanks in orbit: ingenuity and the profit motive might produce useful ideas," they concluded.

Someday dozens of these large cylindrical tanks may be drifting around the earth like spent cartridges, floating raw materials held in long-term storage. The materials they contain could be quite useful to the spacefaring nations of Century 21. Perhaps they will turn out to be as useful as the little flakes of skin we inadvertently provide for the grateful mites living so snugly in our carpets and beds.

Because of the attractive prospects of using the external tanks, a new company dedicated to making them into "orbital research laboratories" has already been formed in Boulder, Colorado. It is called ETCO—External Tank Corporation—and it is headed by Thomas Rogers, a private consultant from McLean, Virginia. The aim of his so-called Space Phoenix Program is to gain title to the external tanks (for free) after NASA agrees to boost them into orbit. Negotiations with NASA representatives are already underway to secure the rights.

ETCO is seeking equity funding: $500,000 in private investments to finance the next phase of the venture. Rogers and his colleagues believe this is a good investment for corporations that intend to be active in civilian space pursuits. "They can invest in ETCO's future at very modest cost," he points out, "the external tanks could yield tens of billions of dollars in benefits over the next two decades."

The new company has been circulating a prospectus among potential investors that projects annual profits of more than $30 million in the 1990s based on lease fees from two connected empty tanks. Among the potential tenants ETCO representatives have approached are the managers of large hotel chains, who could conceivably use the space facilities in the future. Research scientists, however, are far more likely to take up residence in the orbiting tanks. Their natural rigidity makes them ideal for conversion to orbital research facilities.

USING THE SHUTTLE'S EXTERNAL TANKS AS A
SPACEBORNE LABORATORY

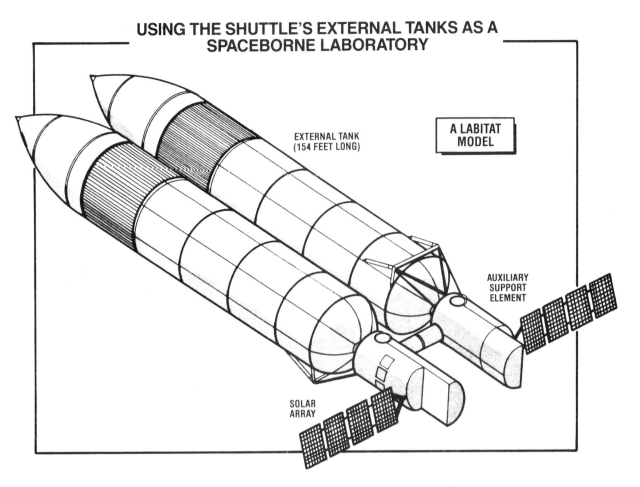

EXTERNAL TANK
(154 FEET LONG)

A LABITAT
MODEL

AUXILIARY
SUPPORT
ELEMENT

SOLAR
ARRAY

The External Tank Corporation (Boulder, Colorado) is negotiating with NASA to take title to the shuttle's external tanks for use as orbiting laboratories. According to ETCO's calculations, a single pair of external tanks with a pressurized volume of 142,000 cubic feet could bring in profits of about $30 million per year by the mid 1990s. The corporation plans to provide servicing and repair for the outside structure of the two-tank complex, but the users who lease space inside will be responsible for maintaining the experimental equipment within their cavernous volume.

The External Tank Corporation estimates that for $100 million, it could turn a pair of tanks into a spaceborne laboratory. The cost of maintaining and operating the basic "Labitat," as ETCO's officials are calling it, is estimated at $15 million per year. This would include a crew of two, as well as operating costs and repairs; if any are needed. Additional costs for consumables, internal facilities, and special equipment would be borne by the users.

In their current round of financing, ETCO is offering 5,500 shares, just under 10 percent ownership in the company, through a foundation owned by the University Corporation—a consortium of fifty-five universities and other private companies. "The company's financial plan is based on annual operating expenses of about $188 per cubic foot per year, and revenues of $565 for commercial use," says *Aviation Week.* "Based on these estimates, the company projects gross profits of $26–$32 million per year in 1992–96."

Speaking at a standing-room-only press conference in Washington, D. C., President of Society Expeditions, T. C. Swartz, announced the world's first space-tourism program: "Project Space Voyage." Developed behind the scenes during the past two years by a team of aerospace engineers, the project entails an earth-circling, three-day journey by 24 to 32 passengers in the mid-1990s. As many as three to five flights each year is considered feasible, with an eventual target of 300 passengers annually.*

"Commuting into the Cosmos"
Space World, August 1985

11

CENTURY 21

Many thought it would take generations, perhaps centuries, before ordinary people would enjoy fun-filled vacations in space. Actually, plans are already in the works to give space-age tourists—"rubbernecking vagabonds of the vacuum," as *Space World* calls them—a chance to pierce the stratosphere.

Now that your favorite tote bag is packed and the next-door neighbor has agreed to feed your cocker spaniel, how much will a round-trip ticket likely set you back? Dr. William Brown, director of technological studies at the Hudson Institute, believes that "at least one hundred passengers per year will be willing to spend one to two million dollars to depart the earth and head for orbit." Dr. Brown goes on to observe that these hefty infusions of cash from the first few well-heeled travelers will serve as a "spark plug for greater activity," driving ticket costs down to a much more affordable level.

When it became apparent that ordinary private citizens would soon be flitting through the cosmos, officials at Space Expeditions, a Seattle-based offshoot from Society Expeditions, an innovative travel company, felt compelled to enter the race. For years president T. C. Swartz of Society Expeditions had been organizing cultural pilgrimages to such remote locations as the Galapagos Islands, Antarctica, the Amazon, and even the North Pole.

Initially, their marketeers concluded that William Brown's $1 million price tag was about right for the three-day space mission they had in mind. But that was before they initialed a transportation agreement with Pacific American Launch

*In the meantime the name of the space tourism company has been changed to Space Expeditions, and it is no longer affiliated with Society Expeditions.

Systems of Redwood City, California, and before they shortened the trip to twelve hours in space. Now that these details have been ironed out, their new price quote is a more modest $50,000 per passenger.*

A 10 percent deposit ($5,000 down!) reserves a window seat on an early flight. It also freezes the total tab at $50,000, no matter what happens. First blastoff (Space Expeditions calls it a "departure") is scheduled for October 12, 1992. In the meantime, if you "get the willies, go broke, or decide on a Paris vacation instead, your deposit is fully refundable all the way up to one year prior to the actual voyage—with no penalties."

The powered portion of your flight will last only six minutes. During that time you will feel a 3-g acceleration, not entirely pleasant, but scarcely worse than the carnival rides we happily stood in line to board in childhood years.

What feelings will you experience during your extraterrestrial journey? McDonnell Douglas engineer Charles Walker, who twice cruised in space aboard the shuttle, had this to say the second time he stepped out onto the runway at Edwards Air Force Base: "I just can't imagine what else can be more awesome to the thinking, conscious person than riding one of those things into earth orbit. It's the biggest, fastest elevator ride you can ever imagine!"

What was his greatest preoccupation as the shuttle circled the earth? "A basic need of space tourism is viewing the scenery," Walker concluded shortly after he slipped the surly bonds of earth. "One of the first things you start doing is taking pictures of your crewmates and of the earth. You've got to have pictures for your photo album."

Watching the constantly changing view has always been a favorite pastime of both American and Russian astronauts in space, where the scenery passes by at 5 miles per second. This means that an entirely new scene comes into view every forty-five seconds through the 2-foot window. Small wonder shuttle astronauts seldom ever get bored.

Here on earth we are surrounded by objects of reasonable size: trees, bushes, buildings. "But from the shuttle, the scale is totally different. Yet, if you use binoculars, you can begin to pick out buildings, roads, and even cars. Take your eye away from the eyepiece, and there's the world again . . . almost all the world curving away in front of you."

Professional experts, including former astronauts, will go along on each Space Expeditions flight to point out the most interesting features in the sky above and the mud below. Active volcanoes will be clearly visible. So will cyclones and hurricanes, Arctic icebergs, mining operations, center-pivot irrigation, the Caribbean Islands sprinkled off the Florida coast, the Panama Canal, the Great Wall of

---

* The tourists who sign up will also get about a week of training, entertainment, lectures, and debriefing before and after their junket into space.

China, the Egyptian pyramids. Nightfall, which comes along again every ninety minutes, opens up further possibilities: comets, stellar constellations, air-glow phenomena, the Northern Lights, and interesting planetary features such as the "canals" on Mars, the rings of Saturn, the Sea of Tranquillity, the moons of Jupiter, and the creamy clusters of stars in the Milky Way.

You will also, of course, frolic in zero g, as all the other astronauts have done, performing simple but interesting scientific experiments, tossing balls and silverware, and catching tasty morsels of food and pink globules of champagne in midair porpoise-fashion.

But how can we, or anyone else, afford the $50,000 ticket price? For one thing, we will have much higher incomes than you might ever imagine. Members of the President's National Commission on Space predicted surprisingly high degrees of future prosperity: "It [is] reasonable to project a 21st Century America with a . . . Gross Domestic Product of $12,900 billion, and a GDP per capita close to $40,000, in today's dollars." Thus, in the world of tomorrow, the average couple will be paid at least $150,000 per year, most of it disposable income. With barely one year's take-home pay, they could honeymoon at the fringes of space—or venture there for an unforgettable summer vacation.*

COLONIES in SPACE

Tourists in the twenty-first century will be flocking into space for short visits, but in addition, if today's aerospace visionaries are right, surprisingly large numbers of other people will be living and working there on a more or less permanent basis.

In his book *Colonies in Space,* Dr. Tom Heppenheimer discusses one design for a colony capable of housing 10,000 people in shirt-sleeve comfort. It consists of an inner-tube-shaped space station 2 miles in diameter turning at one revolution per minute to provide natural gravity for its inhabitants. It is called the Stanford Torus.

The sun's rays are selectively reflected into the torus with a large flat circular mirror. Hollow spokes radiate from the bulging rim inward to a central hub, where the maximum g-level is about one-sixteenth of what we experience here on earth. The spokes contain power cables, heat pipes, and "elevators" for transporting the colony's inhabitants. All told, the spokes enclose about the same volume as the Empire State Building. They, the torus ring, and the central hub span 300 acres, roughly the same as a compact college campus.

"Here is a city of 10,000, a small, bright island in the emptiness of space," writes Heppenheimer. It certainly sounds appealing, but what will life be like aboard the

*In January 1988, some dedicated tourists paid as much as $360,000 each to book passage on the round-the-world voyage of the luxury liner *Queen Elizabeth II.*

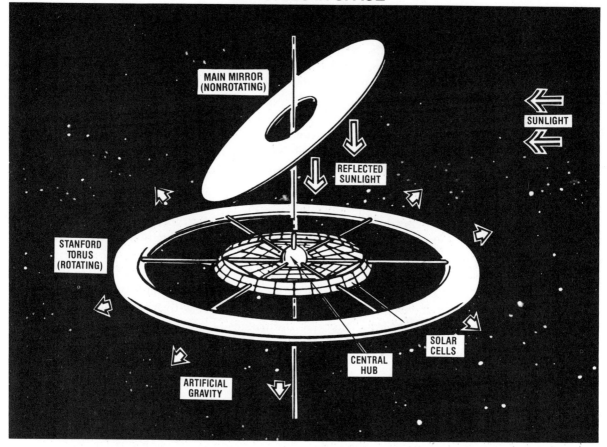

This giant space colony is designed to support a self-sustaining society of humans working and living in space. Constructed primarily of lunar materials, its tire-shaped outer rim would house 10,000 people in relative comfort with g-levels resembling those here on earth. The central hub is set aside for growing crops, recreation in reduced g, and nature visits by the colony's inhabitants.

space colony? According to the vision of Dr. Gerard O'Neill of Princeton University, the colonists will have pleasant apartments set among ample gardens and lakes. They will enjoy "home-grown" fruits and vegetables, meat and poultry, and eggs with plenty of milk and cottage cheese.

Farming areas will be somewhat limited, but by carefully controlling the temperature, humidity, and growing season—and even the concentration of carbon dioxide in the air—the entire 10,000-member colony can be supported on 60 acres of arable land.

This gives a comfortable pad, because the Stanford Torus is designed with 200 acres available for farming and grazing. Most of the colonists' animal protein will come from rabbits and chickens, but fish will also be bred and raised on board. The rabbits will eat mostly alfalfa; the milk will come mostly from goats. Cheese, butter, and cream will be available in abundance. The space farms will even provide special guests with peach yogurt and strawberry ice cream.

In the weightlessness of space it may be possible to raise fish without water! "On earth when a fish is taken from water, gravity makes its gills collapse so that it cannot get oxygen," explains Tom Heppenheimer. "In weightless space, these same fish might easily 'swim' through an atmosphere of 100 percent humidity, keeping comfortably moist. . . . There will be enough to supply everyone on board with ten one-ounce fillets per week." *

The colonists will live in houses and apartments constructed primarily from lunar materials. Some trees will be grown, but even so, wood will be a rarity. So will the plastics seen in such abundance in most science fiction films. Plastics are made from hydrocarbons, unavailable in the materials found in the moon's crust.

Fortunately, colorful concrete and stucco can be constructed from lunar rocks. So can "beta cloth," a synthetic made from spun glass that resembles denim fabric. Beta cloth is too scratchy to serve as lingerie, but it will do nicely for upholstery and drapes. It can also be tufted on a thick mat for carpeting.

For all its expert design, the 10,000-man space colony will be a bit cramped. With only 500 square feet of usable space per person, it will have about the same population density as a small French or Italian village. These densely populated settlements minimize feelings of crowding in many of the same ways the colony will, by adopting clustered, multilevel construction, by placing central courtyards at strategic spots with ample trees and grass, and by eliminating all automobiles. The colonists will not miss their personal cars, because no point in their settlement will be more than 2 miles from any other and because bicycles and public transportation will be widely available.

Despite its small size, the colony sounds entirely tolerable, but what's cooking on a Saturday night? Quite a lot, according to Dr. Heppenheimer. In his opinion, the colonists will be "no cadre of grimly self-sacrificing robots." They will be ordinary human beings like you and me, and they will seek out the same kinds of diversions—with a few interesting twists. In particular, they will enjoy sex in zero g with its fluid motions and its endless possibilities for acrobatic positions. "Weightlessness will bring new forms of erotica," says Arthur C. Clark. "And about time, too!"

Small alcohol-powered space shuttles will allow the colonists romantic outings among the stars. Most will stay within sight of their orbiting home, but the more

*This suggests an interesting high school experiment for a Getaway Special aboard the space shuttle. An assortment of small fish could be carried into space in a tank of water, then released into an atmosphere at 100 percent relative humidity. The entire process could be filmed for later study by the students. Even a negative result would be interesting, and would teach them something useful: social graces at a fish funeral.

adventuresome may go deeper into space. A few may run out of gas or become panicky and dial 911 for rescue by the space patrol.

Except for special occasions, liquor from earth will be prohibitively expensive, something like $100 per fifth. But moonshine will be readily available from anything on board that will ferment—apples, peaches, potatoes, wheat.

Other popular recreations will likely include swimming, diving, parties, movies, and dining in fine restaurants on meat, fish, fresh fruits, and vegetables. There will also be weddings in space, theater groups, basketball games, and indoor tennis. And, of course, the colony will have its own radio and television stations to relay the latest variety shows and soap operas from earth. A few popular programs will also originate from broadcast studios aboard the space colony.

How will tomorrow's colonists earn their keep? Space factories are one often-proposed possibility. Another promising prospect is for them to capture and resell some of the abundant solar energy that surrounds them in space.

SOLAR POWER SATELLITES

Harvesting the sun's energy up there can be much more efficient than it is here on earth. This is true, in part, because carefully chosen orbits are illuminated by the sun at full intensity 99 percent of the time. By contrast, a collector on the ground loses some of the sun's energy because of darkness, atmospheric filtering, and shadowing created by clouds. The net result is that a solar collector at the geosynchronous altitude is exposed to about six times as much solar energy as it would be in the sunniest part of the Arizona desert.

One promising way to harness this energy is the solar power satellite (SPS), brainchild of Peter E. Glaser, vice-president of Arthur D. Little, Inc., of Cambridge, Massachusetts. A solar power satellite is a giant orbiting powerplant that converts the sun's energy into electricity using solar cells (or thermal conversion devices). This energy is then beamed to collectors on the ground by microwave relay links.

A solar power satellite is enormous by conventional standards. Each one spans 21 square miles, or about the area of Manhattan Island. However, it doesn't have to resist gravity or other terrestrial forces such as wind, snow, and rain, so it can be extremely light for its size. If a solar power satellite (including its supporting framework) were compressed into a flat sheet of the same size it would be thinner and lighter than the aluminum foil you buy in your local supermarket.

The electrical power obtained from the first few "powersats" will make only a small contribution to our country's energy needs. However, as more and more are built, they could have a significant impact on the world economy. Industry experts estimate that electricity from space could provide 20 percent of our country's energy needs within thirty years after the first unit becomes operational.

SWIMMING and DIVING in ZERO G

The surface of the water in the space colony's swimming pool will not be flat. Instead, it will curve into a cylinder, a cylinder that surrounds the central hub, where gravity will be only about one-fiftieth of a g. Standing on the deck, you will make a curious observation: as you raise your eyes, you will see the surface of the pool curving upward and arching over your head. Directly above you swimmers will be shouting and splashing in the water.

On earth when a swimmer jumps into a pool, he plunges through the air, there is a big splash, and then the water quickly becomes flat again. But when a swimmer jumps into a pool at 2 percent gravity, he will rise in breathtaking slow motion dozens of feet above the board before arching back down again. When he finally does impact, he will make a noticeable hole in the water, a hole that will take a second or so to fill.

Water fights will be great fun in the colony's swimming pool. "A double handful of water will more or less hold together under its surface tension, forming a glistening blob which squirms and wiggles in its flight," observes Dr. Tom Heppenheimer in his book *Colonies in Space*. Moreover, as it moves along through the air, it will not be pulled down by gravity; consequently, water fights will be carried out at surprisingly great distances.

In the reduced gravity a dedicated diver can learn to spring back and forth from one diving board to another in Rodney Dangerfield style. Another daring diver may aim for the water, but he will set himself spinning so fast he will not know where he is going to land. But several seconds later, he will splash down safely in the water. Some divers will attempt a vertical dive! "This consists of bounding up from the board with sufficient speed to travel through the 'center' of the pool and on to the water that lies overhead."

More placid swimmers will congregate in the zero-g portion of the pool—an empty space running through the center of its cylindrical shape. Once there, they may decide to build their own private swimming hole by bringing up water in their cupped hands and dumping it into the empty spot in zero g. Perhaps someone will even be creative enough to try to put himself in the middle of such a globule with his arms, legs, and head sticking out.

Walking on water will be another popular sport at the colony's swimming pool. If you slap the water sharply with the soles of your feet, you should be able to stay on top—to the delight and amazement of visitors from earth. But be careful. If you don't step carefully, you might trip over a wave and embarrass yourself!

One version of the solar power satellite designed at Rockwell International weighs 80 million pounds and generates 5 billion watts of usable electrical power—about twice the total generating capacity of the Grand Coulee Dam. Engineering calculations indicate that a collector of equal capacity located on the ground would have to be hundreds of times heavier than its space counterpart.

Gallium aluminum arsenide solar cells are used in the Rockwell concept with a concentration ratio of two to one. This means that half the collector area consists of polished metal reflectors that focus extra sunlight on the other half, which is covered with solar cells. Solar cells made of gallium arsenide are superior to conventional silicon cells because they are more efficient and because they can be made to heal themselves when they are damaged by radiation in space.

The solar arrays track the sun. The energy they collect is beamed to the ground from a 3,000-foot swiveling antenna attached to the center of the satellite. Fears have been expressed concerning safety to the biosphere, but the beam would actually contain less energy than ordinary sunlight. Nevertheless, extensive tests will be necessary to demonstrate safety to wildlife before construction could begin.

The energy from each satellite will reach the ground continuously day and night. It will be in a form that could be converted into electricity at about 85 percent efficiency. This compares with the 15 percent efficiency level typically achieved in producing electricity directly from sunlight using solar cells.

Peter E. Glaser, who first proposed solar power satellites, characterized them as resembling "giant butterflies miles long." In his version, sixty of his space-age butterflies would be rimmed around the geosynchronous arc. Ultimately, they could supply a substantial fraction of America's energy without dependence on foreign powers. However, this energy independence would not come cheap. According to Glaser, "Costs are now estimated at perhaps $1 trillion or more—about forty times what was spent on the Apollo program."

Put in different terms, the cost per installed kilowatt would be at least $3,100 compared with about $2,000 per kilowatt for a new coal-fired powerplant. Some powersat studies set costs as high as $16,000 per kilowatt of installed capacity. Of course, sunlight, unlike coal, is free. But even so, in the first cut, Glaser's butterflies did not turn out to be very attractive compared with more conventional ways of obtaining energy.

Why were costs so high? For one thing, solar cells are notoriously expensive. For another, sunlight is not a concentrated source of power—even if it is six times as plentiful in space.

But one of the biggest factors is the high cost of launching the necessary machinery into space. The shuttle is not nearly big enough to support this enormous

This version of the solar power satellite, designed by scientists at Rockwell International, generates 5 billion watts of electricity using gallium arsenide solar cells for energy collection and klystrons to beam the energy to a large antenna on the ground. It weighs 80 million pounds and covers an area of 21 square miles. Solar power satellites, as first proposed by Peter E. Glaser of Arthur D. Little, Inc., were seriously studied by NASA, but shelved temporarily because of the high cost of solar cells and spacebound transportation.

project. Larger, more economical rockets would help some, but Dr. Gerard O'Neill of Princeton University has suggested an alternate approach. If lifting the necessary materials from the earth is too expensive, why not instead get them from the moon?

USING MATERIALS from the MOON

In space, distance does not determine cost. Costs are determined by the energy that must be expended, and Dr. O'Neill correctly noted that only about one-twentieth as much energy is required to move materials from the moon as bringing them from much closer supplies on the earth. Under this reasoning, large components for the powersats should be built in space, rather than on earth. Moreover, as we shall see, Dr. O'Neill developed a clever plan for transporting the necessary raw materials from the moon without using costly rockets.

First, space engineers will build a geosynchronous "construction shack" capable of housing 2,000 workers. Their job is to make and assemble useful components for the solar power satellites, using ores sent to them from a smaller contingent of miners on the moon. Ore from the moon will be hurled into space by O'Neill's "mass driver" where it will be caught by a large funnel-shaped net. The mass driver is similar to the particle accelerators used in nuclear research, but it is built on a much larger scale. It uses a train of electromagnets sequentially activated to accelerate metal buckets filled with lunar materials to escape velocity.

The mass driver uses electricity rather than rocket propellants to move masses off the surface of the moon. The only mass that must be accelerated is the buckets and the moon rocks themselves. Incidentally, the mass drivers can also be used in space to transport bulky cargoes. When it hurls rocks or anything else to high velocities, the mass driver itself is pushed in the opposite direction. Thus in space it behaves like a big, clumsy rocket.

Another unique feature of O'Neill's concept for mining the moon is that the original facilities can duplicate themselves using mostly lunar materials. The resulting "bootstrapping" effect allows large numbers of facilities to be built in a surprisingly short time.

For years, concepts for large moon bases have been kicking around the aerospace industry, but most of them are very costly, and most require enormous amounts of capital before any of the money comes back to the investors. These ambitious projects may eventually come to fruition, but in the meantime more modest plans have also been proposed. Aerospace expert Michael Duke and his colleague Wendell Mendell, for example, have been urging NASA to build a much smaller lunar base staffed by about twenty moon miners who would process lunar soil into steel, glass, cement, and liquid oxygen for fuel and life-support systems in space and on the moon. The twenty moon miners would live and work in a small, self-sustaining ecological system, recycling wastes and raising much of their own food, including rabbits and tomatoes. Space ferries would deliver building materials and oxygen from the lunar base to stations swinging around both the moon and the earth.

Oxygen is so important in space because it makes up six parts of the seven-part hydrogen-oxygen rocket-fuel recipe. Some estimates indicate that over the next few decades, half the weight we will be transporting into space will be liquid oxygen. A lunar base is an ideal location for the production of composites, computer chips, and pharmaceuticals. Astronomers and nuclear physicists would also benefit from the radio isolation and the low levels of seismic activity.

Asteroid mining is farther in the future. Its major benefit over mining the moon is that some asteroids contain large quantities of precious metals and hydrocarbons —which opens up new and exciting possibilities for space-made materials such as plastics, dyes, drugs, and the like. Dozens of asteroids are known to pass near the earth, each big enough to supply orbiting industries with raw materials for hundreds of years. Many of them have been discovered in the past decade, so there are probably hundreds of others bobbing around in space.

LUNETTA and SOLETTA

If solar power satellites prove impractical or uneconomic, there are other ways to harness the sun's abundant energy in space, including Lunetta and Soletta ("little moon" and "little sun"). Both were invented by Dr. Krafft Ehricke, one of the German rocket scientists brought to the United States as a part of "Operation Paperclip" at the end of World War II.

A Lunetta is a large, flat film of plastic coated with sodium that reflects solar energy to the earth with an intensity of about thirty full moons. Its purpose is to provide illumination for specific localities on earth. Construction sites or harvest areas, for example, could be bathed in light so that useful work could be accomplished twenty-four hours a day. Extra illumination could be particularly important in the vicinity of the Arctic Circle, where darkness shrouds the landscape for months at a time. In another promising application, the Lunetta would provide night lighting for urban areas, thus eliminating the need for high-intensity lights on the city's streets and freeways.

The Soletta, giant big brother to the Lunetta, reflects solar energy to selected regions comparable in intensity to the sun itself (about 1,000 full moons). In theory, this extra reflected sunlight could be used to illuminate solar collectors to generate electrical power.

However, a more attractive possibility is to use the Soletta's energy to accentuate food production. Land-based crops such as wheat or sugar cane would give larger yields if they were illuminated by the Soletta, but there is an even more attractive possibility: illuminating certain remote regions of the oceans where upwelling currents pull concentrated nutrients to the surface from the ocean floor. A simple 14,000-square-mile reflector could produce 24 million tons of extra edible fish each year in such a region. This would provide sufficient animal protein to feed 65 million people for their entire lives.

SPACEBORNE TETHERS

Spaceborne tethers provide us with another means of exploiting the vast economic potential of space. A tether is a long, flexible cable connecting two orbiting masses. In the 1960s the Gemini astronauts used the first primitive tether in space when they cable-connected their craft to an Agena upper stage, then swung around it in an attempt to create artificial gravity. The experiment was successful, but it was not a very smooth ride. One of the astronauts radioed Mission Control that their tether was "bucking like a wild horse."

Soon a 60-mile tether will be draped down below the shuttle to sample the earth's upper atmosphere. In the first shuttle test, however, a 12-mile tether will be reeled out in the *upward* direction. Those of us who have spent our lives conditioned to distinguish between "up" and "down" may find this a little strange, but in the weightlessness of space it should work just fine.

Italian space experts are working on a reusable 1,200-pound satellite to be dangled from a tether attached to the shuttle. After each mission it will be reeled in again like a fishing lure, using a mechanism being developed at Martin Marietta. Between missions new instruments and sensors will be installed.

If a tether is made of an electrically conducting material, it can be used to convert orbital energy into electricity in a highly efficient way. The tether behaves like a dynamo, cutting through the earth's magnetic field as it coasts around the earth. It loses altitude in the process, which must later be restored. Tethers can also be used to sling payloads to more favorable locations in space. The shuttle, for example, could whip around the space station on the end of a long tether before it is suddenly released. As a result, the shuttle will enter its deorbit trajectory while the space station is hurled into a higher, decay-resistant orbit. Both results are beneficial, and both are achieved without using any propellants. According to a study conducted at NASA's Marshall Space Flight Center in Huntsville, Alabama, "deorbiting the shuttle by tether could save $140 million per year."

Tethers can also be used to conduct "wind tunnel" tests in the upper atmosphere at hypersonic speeds, speeds that are impossible to duplicate here on earth. Moreover, oil and mineral explorations can be improved with spaceborne tethers. A magnetometer dangled down from the shuttle will be able to map subtle variations in earth's magnetic and gravitational fields. When pieced together by computers, these variations can paint a mosaic picture of subsurface geological structures concealing petroleum, manganese, and geothermal steam.

THE ROTATING CABLE

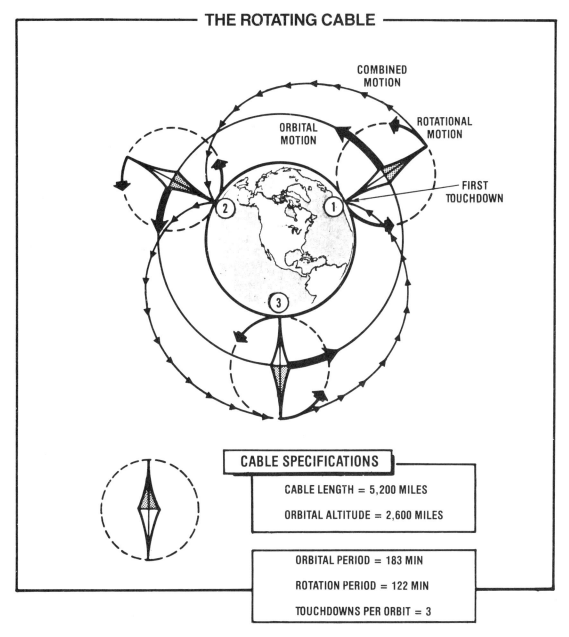

COMBINED MOTION

ROTATIONAL MOTION

ORBITAL MOTION

FIRST TOUCHDOWN

CABLE SPECIFICATIONS

CABLE LENGTH = 5,200 MILES

ORBITAL ALTITUDE = 2,600 MILES

ORBITAL PERIOD = 183 MIN

ROTATION PERIOD = 122 MIN

TOUCHDOWNS PER ORBIT = 3

A long, rotating cable in the proper orbit could act as a two-way "elevator" for hauling payloads from earth into space and bringing useful materials back in the reverse direction. In this sketch a 5,200-mile cable travels around the earth in an orbit 2,600 miles high. It rotates every 122 minutes so that one of its two ends touches the ground three times per orbit. When a touchdown occurs, crews aboard high-flying airplanes would have a minute or so to exchange payloads for the next trip into space.

THE ROTATING SKYHOOK

Someday long tethers may be used to pluck heavy weights off the surface of the earth, thus greatly reducing the cost of launching payloads into space. One scheme, proposed by scientists Hans P. Moravec and Robert L. Forward, uses a cable 5,200 miles long in a 2,600-mile orbit.

As it circles the earth every 183 minutes, the giant cable rotates 1.5 times, behaving like a single straight spoke on an invisible rotating wheel. Like a wheel, its lower end has zero velocity where it touches the ground.

Once every sixty-one minutes, one of the two ends of the cable dips down toward the earth, and when it does, payloads can be attached to it for transportation into space. To earthlings, the rotating cable would seem to pierce the sky coming straight down, pause for a few seconds, then shoot straight back up again. The cable stretches 100 miles (2 percent of its length) under the pull of gravity to give high-flying airplanes about a minute to attach and detach payloads from its lower end. The other end would carry payloads in the opposite direction—from space down to the surface of the earth. These payloads would come from orbiting factories, the moon, or the asteroids.

The imaginative scheme of Moravec and Forward could eliminate the need for massive rockets for carrying payloads into space, but a huge flexible cable is required. They estimate that a cable weighing 7,500 tons will be needed to lift 100-ton cargoes into space. If graphite crystalline fibers are used, a twelve-to-one taper ratio will be needed to support the weight of the cable and its 100-ton payload. This means that the diameter of the cable at the center is twelve times larger than the diameter at the two tapered ends.

Loading rotating skyhooks with fresh payloads will be a frantic activity creating constant harassment for the airborne servicing crews. Fortunately, a more placid and peaceful design for a skyhook has been devised.

STATIONARY SKYHOOKS

Objects in space usually travel thousands of miles per hour, but 22,300 miles above the earth a satellite can be made to hang ghostlike and motionless in the sky. Its angular speed exactly matches the earth's rotational rate. At this moment, dozens of geosynchronous satellites are hovering above the earth's equator.

Suppose we could equip one of those geosynchronous satellites with cable-making machines. If the cable was strong enough to support its own weight, it could be draped all the way down to the surface of the earth. While this was happening, another cable-making machine aboard the satellite would drape a sec-

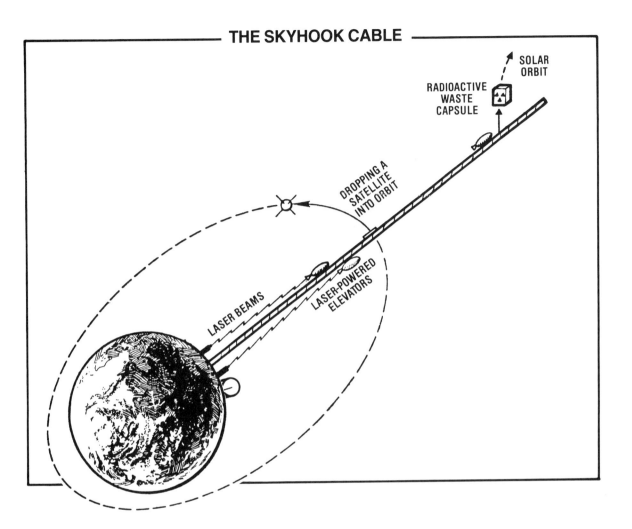

THE SKYHOOK CABLE

In this sketch, laser-powered elevators are crawling upward along the stationary skyhook cable to carry satellites into space. At any altitude above 18,000 miles, such a satellite can be "dropped" into an elliptical orbit. A variation of the same technique would allow us to hurl radioactive wastes into orbit around the sun. Any waste capsules hoisted to an altitude of 29,000 miles or higher will automatically achieve earth escape velocity, never to return.

ond cable in the opposite direction, radially upward away from the earth. During construction, we would have to control the building rates of the two opposing cables to keep them in balance. Once they were both in place, the lower one could be firmly anchored to the ground. It now becomes a stationary skyhook; payloads can be hoisted upward along the cable and "dropped" into orbit.

Elevators powered by linear induction motors will crawl up the cable. Their energy can be shunted through the cable to the elevator or beamed to it from powerful lasers located on the ground. Today we spend about $4,000 per pound to orbit a satellite. But when the stationary skyhook is in place, it may cost less to send a satellite into orbit than it does to airmail your Aunt Nellie's Christmas present across the country.

The elevators will consume, at most, only a few dollars' worth of electricity for each pound they carry up the cable. This dramatic cost reduction will open up many new possibilities for space industrialization, including recreation and tourism. In one exciting scheme, we would use the cable to get rid of radioactive wastes. At any point along the skyhook above 29,000 miles, hazardous cargos can be released onto an escape trajectory, never to return to earth.

What holds the skyhook cable in place? To grasp the fundamental principle, consider a cable of uniform cross section stretching vertically upward 100,000 miles high. We now hire an enthusiastic space cadet to climb a staircase inside the cable. Every time he takes a step, his weight declines slightly because the earth's gravity gets weaker, and the spinning cable slings his body outward with greater force.* By the time he reaches the geosynchronous altitude, 22,300 miles above the earth, he becomes weightless and will float around inside the room. If he climbs to an even higher altitude, he will be standing on the ceiling—the centrifugal force slinging him outward exceeds his body weight.

The materials making up the cable are affected in essentially the same way. Specifically, if we move a steel plate from the base of the cable and reattach it at the geosynchronous altitude, it will be weightless. If we attach it above that altitude, it will pull the cable *upward* against the pull of gravity. Since both of the forces on the cable—gravity and centrifugal force—tend to stretch it, it doesn't have to be rigid to stay in place. Unfortunately, a uniform cable made of conventional materials would not be strong enough to support its own weight. However, if we can build it with composite materials and taper it, we may someday be able to build a practical stationary skyhook.

A composite is a material composed of two or more distinct substances, each of which maintains its structural identity. Most are man-made, but bamboo is a naturally occurring composite material. A bamboo pole is composed of fibers of cellulose held together by lentin, a plastic matrix. Man-made composites are more rugged and considerably stronger, especially those that contain tiny cylindrical whiskers of graphite and boron. The thinner the whiskers, the stronger the material tends to be.

* It may not seem that a stationary skyhook cable would be spinning, but it spins around the center of the earth to keep up with the earth's rotation.

THE MAKING of the SKYHOOK

Composite materials capitalizing on the remarkable strength of thin metal whiskers will be required to build the skyhook; but even with superstrong composites, special approaches will be needed to construct a skyhook that can support its own weight.

The first hint that composite materials might be extraordinarily strong was provided by a talented British materials expert. This is how *Scientific American* described some of his earliest experiments: "In the late 1920s A. A. Griffin showed that threadlike forms of a material are many times stronger than the bulk form in which materials are generally used. This is particularly true of brittle materials."

Griffin's superstrong slender rods were scientifically interesting, but they were not very practical. What good is a slender rod that can withstand enormous tension if the slightest crosswise force causes it to shatter into useless splinters? Eventually a solution was found when later researchers mimicked nature's design of bamboo. They embedded the tiny rods in a plastic matrix to produce composite materials with high shear resistance and good ductility. Today millions of pounds of composites are being produced. They are found in automobiles, tennis rackets, cafeteria trays, and golf clubs, in addition to airplanes and other high-technology vehicles.

Some of the properties of composites are contrasted with those of conventional materials in a technical exhibit in the main lobby of the Rockwell International facility at Seal Beach, California. A steel rod 1.4 inches in diameter is compared with a flat composite slab 1 inch wide and one-sixteenth of an inch thick. The two rods are equally strong, but the composite weighs less than a hundredth as much!

Although today's composites exhibit amazing strength, they are not strong enough to support a skyhook cable with uniform cross section. Fortunately, the stresses in the cable peak at the geosynchronous altitude, decreasing above and below. Consequently, the cable can be tapered to match stress with strength. The first American to propose this approach was Professor John D. Isaacs, at the Scripps Institute of Oceanography. "How did you think of tapering the cable?" Isaacs was asked by another scientist at a Lake Arrowhead resort. "To an oceanographer, it was obvious," he modestly replied. "We've been tapering suboceanic cables for the same reason for many years."

Professor John D. Isaacs and his colleagues at the Scripps Institute of Oceanography were the first Americans to propose tapered skyhooks.* They also calculated the best tapers and the weights of skyhooks constructed of various materials. Their beryllium cable weighed only 9 tons. Graphite and quartz skyhooks were 70 tons and 182 tons, respectively.

These cables were barely able to support their own weights in high winds, but Hans Moravec and Robert Forward have designed a much larger stationary skyhook made of crystalline graphite fibers with a lifting capacity of 100 tons. It weighs 600,000 tons and has a sharp taper stretching just beyond the geosynchronous altitude. "Graphite fiber technology is developing so rapidly that a rotating space cable will soon be feasible," Moravec concluded when he completed the design. "Shortly after that we may be able to make cables strong enough to weave a stationary skyhook."

Lowering launch cost to get into space more cheaply is important, but generating energy without creating excessive pollution could be far more crucial to the future of our high-tech society.

The muscle power of every man, woman, and child in the United States is multiplied 250 times by the machines we have developed to help us do our work. Each of us has, in effect, 250 mechanical servants devoted to making our lives easy and interesting. However, if we don't soon devise practical substitutes for our dwindling fossil fuels, our mechanical servants could become so much useless scrap. Fortunately, our future does not have to turn out that way. Handled correctly, the rotating earth itself can be made to yield limitless supplies of inexpensive energy —as pollution-free as a Sierra waterfall.

THE SKYHOOK COMPLEX

The earth is a giant flywheel; locked within its spinning mass is enough energy to supply all our needs for the next 800 million years. But how can we tap the earth's flywheel energy supplies? Project Skyhook provides the proper key. First we will use the laser-powered elevators to increase the cable's diameter to give it greater strength. Then we will add six parallel pipeline sections to its outer edges. The final result will resemble a giant drinking straw that splits the sky to a height

---

*They were the first Americans, but Yuri Artsutanov, a brilliant Russian graduate student at the Leningrad Technological Institute, had carried out similar calculations six years earlier. Moreover, two young aerospace engineers, Tom Logsdon and Robert Africano, lectured to Los Angeles high school students on untapered (uniform) skyhooks at the California Museum of Science and Industry a full year before Isaacs and his coauthors published their first article dealing with stationary skyhooks.

THE CONSTRUCTION OF THE SKYHOOK PIPELINE

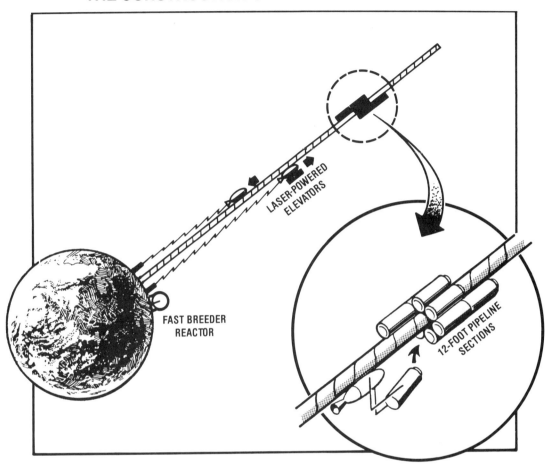

Most of today's pipelines lie parallel to the ground, but the skyhook pipeline will protrude vertically upward into the sky. First the laser-powered elevators will carry extra structural materials up the skyhook to enlarge its cross section. Then they will take 12-foot pipeline sections aloft and fit them together in a hexagonal pattern along the cable's outer perimeter. The final structure, which resembles a giant drinking straw splitting the sky to a height of 120,000 miles, will provide mankind with inexhaustible supplies of clean and inexpensive electrical power.

of 120,000 miles. When it is finished, pumps and turbines will be installed at intervals inside each tube.

The pumps will suck water from the oceans and lift it upward to a height of 22,300 miles. Above this altitude the centrifugal force slinging it outward exceeds the earth's gravitational pull, so that the water will "fall" *upward* inside the pipeline. As it falls, it will spin a train of turbines to generate electricity.

By the time the water reaches the 90,000-mile altitude, the electricity it has generated just matches the energy required to pump it upward the first 22,300 miles. From this point on, more and more extra electricity will be produced. By the time a pound of water reaches the 120,000-mile level, the net energy it has contributed will equal the energy released when we burn a pound of gasoline. Thus, the skyhook pipeline, in effect, allows us to convert seawater into gasoline! The extra energy is beamed back to the ground, where it drives the wheels of our civilization.

But won't we soon empty the oceans? Not likely. The top inch of ocean water will fill all our energy needs for more than 2,000 years. Purists may object, but it is hard to see how a 1-inch reduction in sea level over a 2,000-year interval could make much difference to our fellow earthlings. Nevertheless, detailed environmental-impact statements will be required before construction begins.

As the pipeline siphons off millions of tons of water from the oceans, the earth's spin rate will change slightly. But we could keep the pipeline running at its full productive capacity for millions of years without noticeably altering the length of the day. Raw materials brought down to earth from other bodies in space could also compensate for these changes.

At the geosynchronous altitude, extra weights can be attached to the skyhook without creating extra stress. Consequently, that level will evolve into an important center of commerce and trade. Eventually, the activities there will include product manufacture, power generation, tourism, medical treatment, and greenhouse gardening, to name only a few.

Most products manufactured in the skyhook factories will be enjoyed by the people on the earth. Others, however, will remain in space. For example, large parabolic antennas for use in communication satellites will be constructed at the skyhook factories, where there will be no gravity to twist or distort them. Similarly, some of the electronic circuits used in our space vehicles will be assembled "at the site." High-strength components for the skyhook pipeline could also be fashioned in orbiting factories. Particularly attractive candidates will include turbine blades and precision ball bearings for its pumps and generators.

As space-age visionaries have often pointed out, the treatment of heart-attack victims in space could yield stunning medical benefits. In a weightless condition, the stress on a victim's heart could be minimized, thus enabling his body to repair the damage. Patients hoisted up the skyhook would never be subjected to more than 1 g, the same g-level we all experience every day. A cable-based treatment center would have another important advantage over its orbiting counterpart. Once a patient has passed the crisis stage, we can gradually reacclimate him to the earth's gravity by slowly lowering him down the cable. If necessary, this process could span weeks or months with periodic stops at outpatient clinics along the way.

Patients suffering from partial paralysis will enjoy their treatment in the skyhook hospitals. By carefully controlling the gravity levels, doctors can gradually strengthen inactive arms and legs. Thus patients will be able to adapt to their new prosthetic devices while the crushing weight of their bodies is reduced to a more comfortable level.*

Severe burn cases, thropic ulcer sufferers, and victims of chronic hypertension will also have unusually high survival rates in the skyhook hospitals. Burn victims can be suspended without damaging skin-to-bed contact; external pressures on thropic ulcers will be largely eliminated; those who suffer from nervous disorders may be lulled into a supercalm state in the low-stress environment of outer space. Certain recreational activities such as hang-gliding may be much more soothing than their earthbound counterparts.

Leonardo da Vinci was obsessed with human-powered flight. He spent endless hours in happy contentment watching the carefree antics of sea birds curling through the early morning sky. He could feel his spirits soaring as he dreamed of joining them in their effortless journeys upward through fluid space. Someday the skyhook may make da Vinci's dream a practical reality.

Of course, he was not the first man to gaze with envy at nature's free-flying creatures. Ever since the days of the Neanderthal, men everywhere have dreamed of looping and spiraling over misty meadows. Unfortuately, bone-shattering experiences have repeatedly demonstrated that man's body is too heavy to permit self-propelled flight. However, inside an air-filled dome affixed to the skyhook 8,000 miles above the ground, a man equipped with a pair of artificial wings would actually be able to fly under his own power. At that level, gravity would amount to only one-tenth the level we experience on earth. With his body weight reduced to only 18 or 20 pounds, even a flabby stockbroker would be able to sweep around inside the dome like an oversized seagull. It would be a dynamite vacation!

At various recreation centers along the skyhook, athletes will experience other kinds of sports miracles, miracles they can only daydream about today. In regions of reduced gravity, a pole vaulter can jump 30 or 40 feet—or even higher. A duffer can drive a golf ball thousands of yards even with a bent 3-iron. And a high diver can easily execute quadruple flips off a 10-foot diving board.

The g-loads will vary in a continuous fashion as travelers move upward along the cable. Thus the gravity levels of most of the planets and their moons will be duplicated at various points along the way. Realistic museums of planetary conditions will be constructed at these locations to show visitors the general principles of space-age geology. Functioning models of various space vehicles and planetary

*Science fiction writer Ray Bradbury sees space as the ideal habitat for the handicapped. In a television special he described a race of young handicapped "swimmers" in space. He called the show *Walking on Air*.

THE SKYHOOK COMPLEX

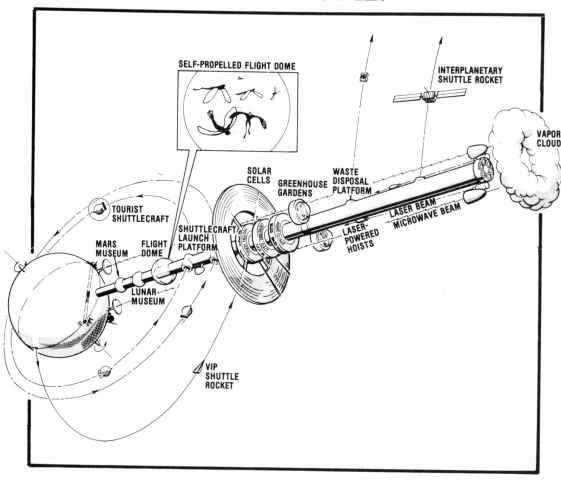

The skyhook complex, one of the most exciting spaceborne facilities of Century 21, will serve as a space-age center of culture and commerce. Its facilities, many of which are located at the geosynchronous altitude, include numerous factories, hotels, museums, greenhouse gardens, and communications links. At the flight dome 8,000 miles above earth, skyhook inhabitants and their guests will strap themselves into artificial wings and fly, under their own power, inside a transparent plastic dome.

landers may also be displayed, together with sample sports equipment so that athletes can compete under realistic planetary conditions.

If you are adventuresome enough, you may get a shot at an even more exciting diversion. You will be able to rent a small space capsule and fly into orbit on your own. If it is released from the cable 18,000 miles high, it will coast around the earth and return to the skyhook a day later to be caught in a large, soft net. Once

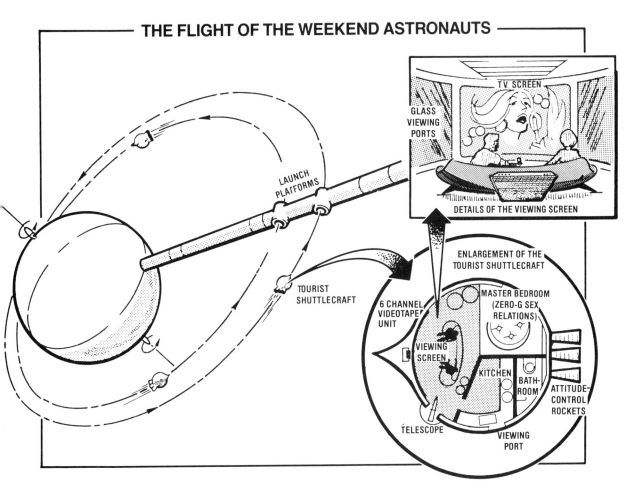

THE FLIGHT OF THE WEEKEND ASTRONAUTS

Tourists from earth who visit the skyhook complex will be able to leave the skyhook for an inspiring day curling around a lazy elliptical orbit in space. Their unpowered space capsule circles the earth and a day later returns to the skyhook, where it is caught in a large, soft net. Throughout the trip, the tourists are entertained by multichannel video tapes, plied with exotic wines, and served with tidbits and tasty snacks.

released, it will dip down toward the earth so you and your fellow travelers can get a close-up look at the ground below.

How would a typical family occupy their time during such a delightful outing? Visual observations of the earth and the stars will provide one obvious attraction. Telescopes will give them a close-up view, and videotapes will provide comments and close-up views of the major features of interest.

Weightless sports contests resembling three-dimensional billiards and handball will also be available aboard the unpowered spacecraft. Airline-style meals will be served, together with a worldwide sampling of vintage wines. But perhaps the greatest attraction of such a free-fall jaunt will be the incomparable thrill of having sexual intercourse in a weightless condition.

Misty-eyed couples in the twenty-first century may seek reservations in the space capsule as eagerly as they patronized waterbed hotels when they first became available. The fluid, balletlike motions imposed by weightless copulation will undoubtedly provide some novel sensations. Freed from their normal body weights, the couple can experiment with an endless variety of new positions as they glide through their starry canopy in space.

MANKIND'S PROMISING FUTURE in SPACE

"Given the right kind of policy direction by Congress, we can create a trillion-dollar space-based economy by the year 2010," concludes Pennsylvania Congressman Robert S. Walker. "That would be the 1984 equivalent of 35 million new jobs. If we are really serious about doing this right, we can create a $4.5 trillion economy, roughly the size of our economy today, by the year 2050."

English teacher Richard A. Methia of New Bedford, Massachusetts, has never been more than 7 miles above the planet earth, but he describes our evolving attitudes toward the cosmos in clear, vibrant terms: "The colonization of space is our fantasy," he notes, "but may be our children's livelihood."

These children of the cosmos, for whom we have high hopes, will view space with a much warmer, more rounded attitude than we do today. A few of them will actually be born there. Others, perhaps thousands, will think of it as their only home.

Someday soon you and your neighbors may be making big money in space, but even if you decide to forgo the attractive investment opportunities along the final frontier, you will still benefit from the technological marvels that will come with space industrialization.

Serious commercial development has already begun with earth observations, television distribution, accurate navigation, and the first marketplace products made in the weightlessness of space. All told, our space frontier is, today, a $22-billion-a-year business with growth rates in some sectors rapidly approaching the stratosphere. And yet today's attempts to profit from space will seem puny and insignificant to the spacefaring nations of Century 21, when colonies of astronauts will be using materials from the asteroids and the moon to construct enormous orbiting facilities, many visible from earth with the unaided eye.

These may include large "solar farms" that capture electrical power from the sun's rays and beam it down to earth, giant reflectors to supplement sun and moon, even skyhook cables that will allow us to hoist payloads into orbit for a few dollars a pound. If any of these gigantic projects do, indeed, materialize—or even if they don't—the American pioneers in space could become our fifty-first state, a state inhabited by vibrant individuals with a proud heritage, a state making important contributions to our technology, our life-style, our civilization.

APPENDIX A

LARGE COMPANIES DOING BUSINESS IN SPACE

At least 350 companies, large and small, are already involved in space-related ventures of one sort or another. The following information regarding some of the larger ones was extracted from *Commercial Space, Aviation Week,* and other industry publications. Much of it was supplied to them by the research staff at the Center for Space Policy in Cambridge, Massachusetts. Many of these companies are traded on the major stock exchanges, so their shares can be purchased through a broker by ordinary private citizens. Headquarters locations are listed, in case you may want to contact them for further information.

ALUMINUM COMPANY OF AMERICA, Alcoa Center, Pennsylvania. The goal of Alcoa is to produce a new aluminum-silicon alloy in the microgravity of space. Its research staff is also looking into the possibility of making aluminum/lithium powdered metal in orbiting factories.

BATTELLE COLUMBUS LABORATORIES, Columbus, Ohio. Battelle is looking into a zero-g product: collagen fibers, made in space, that could repair and replace human skin, tendons, and connective tissues.

BOEING AEROSPACE, Seattle, Washington. Boeing is researching the possibility of making electro-optical crystals in space-borne factories. They are also developing a large microgravity materials-processing facility to ride in the shuttle cargo bay.

CORNING GLASS WORKS, Corning, New York. This well-known company is interested in applying space-age materials-processing techniques to manufacture new types of glasses that cannot be made on earth. If this work is successful, the new glasses might be used in precision optical instruments, laser windows, and other important commercial products.

FORD AEROSPACE, Detroit, Michigan. Ford Aerospace researchers were recently awarded a contract to build two new communications satellites for Mitsubishi of Japan. They were also authorized by the FCC to construct two hybrid (combined C-band and Ku-band) satellites of their own. In the remainder of this century, Ford's 48-transponder satellites will provide domestic telecommunications, video services, and electronic teleconferencing for a broad range of users.

GENERAL DYNAMICS, San Diego, California. General Dynamics is marketing several versions of the Atlas/Centaur expendable launch vehicle to the federal government and to other private companies.

GENERAL ELECTRIC, Philadelphia, Pennsylvania. GE's researchers are working on an electromagnetic furnace to be used for materials processing in space. GE also designs and constructs satellite systems.

GENERAL MOTORS, Warren, Michigan. General Motors' scientists are planning to conduct microgravity experiments to measure the tensile strength of polymer fibers. Future investigations will include the behavior of lubricants and adhesives in the microgravity of space and studies of the fundamental qualities of combustion physics.

GRUMMAN AEROSPACE, Bethpage, New York. Researchers at Grumman are planning a series of orbital studies on the magnetization properties of manganese/bismuth alloys to see if they can make improved permanent magnets. If this work is successful, it could have important implications in the design of fractional-horsepower motors, which are used in a variety of applications, including small power tools.

HEWLETT-PACKARD, Palo Alto, California. Hewlett-Packard is exploring various possibilities for genetic engineering in space in a joint venture with Genentech Corporation.

HUGHES COMMUNICATIONS, Los Angeles, California. Hughes owns and operates the galaxy constellation of communication satellites, to which it will be adding an additional C-band and two new Ku-band satellites.

JOHN DEERE, Moline, Illinois. The spaceborne projects under study at John Deere include experiments in the formation of graphite nodules in cast iron, undesirable flotation effects of carbon in iron materials, and new approaches to control the cooling processes and the directional solidification of iron and aluminum.

MARTIN MARIETTA AEROSPACE, Denver, Colorado. Martin Marietta is one of the country's major industrial contractors for the design, assembly, and operation of launch vehicles. It is also working under contract to the Orbital Sciences Corporation to build the $30 million TOS (transfer orbit stage).

McDONNELL DOUGLAS ASTRONAUTICS, St. Louis, Missouri. McDonnell Douglas manufactures an upper stage called the payload assist module (PAM) and designs and fabricates the Delta booster, an uprated version of the early Thor. In addition, company researchers are producing pharmaceuticals in space using electrophoresis separation techniques. Recently they signed a $734 million contract with the U.S. Air Force to manufacture twenty expendable boosters for launching military payloads. Nonmilitary versions are also being marketed.

RCA, Princeton, New Jersey. RCA is a major supplier of communications satellites, and company technicians operate their own domestic satellite network. RCA is also jointly responsible for Luxembourg's Pan-European Satellite System and the Japanese BS-3 satellite.

ROCKWELL INTERNATIONAL, Pittsburgh, Pennsylvania. Rockwell International makes the shuttle orbiter and is involved in a number of other large space projects, including the competition to design and build the manned space station. On a smaller scale, Rockwell engineers are also working toward materials-processing experiments in space aboard the shuttle and the space station.

TELEDYNE BROWN ENGINEERING, Huntsville, Alabama. Teledyne Brown has proposed a commercial materials-processing support facility to be carried aboard the space station. Earlier plans for a payload support structure to house small experiments on the space shuttle will remain on hold until the shuttle flies again.

3M CORPORATION, St. Paul, Minnesota. Company officials at 3M just completed negotiations with NASA for a ten-year contract to fly at least sixty-two materials-processing experiments aboard the space shuttle. Their broad-ranging experimental program emphasizes organic chemistry, especially the growth of organic crystals in space. 3M wanted assured access to ten more shuttle flights, but NASA rejected the proposal.

UNION CARBIDE, Oak Ridge, Tennessee. The researchers at Union Carbide are examining the possibility of making high-quality optical glasses in the microgravity aboard the space shuttle.

APPENDIX B

SMALL SPACE-BASED COMPANIES SEEKING VENTURE CAPITAL

Dozens of smaller companies are already engaged in space-related enterprises or are planning to enter such a business enterprise in the near future. The Center for Space Policy (Cambridge, Massachusetts) was a major source of the information in this appendix, and *Aviation Week, Commercial Space,* and other related publications supplied some of it as well. Many of these smaller companies are soliciting outside capital from individual investors. If you are interested in making space-related investments with good growth potential, you may want to start your research with some of these contacts.

AMERICAN ROCKET COMPANY, Palo Alto, California. Low-cost space transportation is the only business of the American Rocket Company. Its engineers are designing an expendable booster to deliver 3,000-pound payloads into low-altitude orbits. It will be rigged with hybrid engines, burning liquid oxidizer sprayed onto a solid fuel.

AMERICAN SATELLITE COMPANY, Rockville, Maryland. Since 1972, American Satellite has provided the public and private sector with voice, data, facsimile, and video-conferencing services via communication satellites. In 1985, the Federal Communications Commission granted the company conditional authority to construct and launch an additional hybrid satellite incorporating both C-band and Ku-band transponders.

ANALYTIC SCIENCES CORPORATION, Reading, Massachusetts. The Analytic Sciences Corporation uses computer-processing and image-enhancement techniques to create composite images from weather satellite data. The forecasts its researchers develop in this way are shown on local and network television shows.

ASTROTECH INTERNATIONAL, Pittsburgh, Pennsylvania. Astrotech operates an efficient payload-processing facility in Titusville, Florida, in support of NASA's shuttle flights. Staff experts are also developing an upper stage to be launched out of the shuttle, based on the second stage of the Delta expendable booster. Astrotech's officials offered to raise $3 billion to finance the construction of a fifth shuttle orbiter, but NASA declined the offer.

AVIOTEX, Costa Mesa, California. Aviotex uses weather satellites to predict the weather for the pilots of small planes, who gain access to the information via computer modems in motels, offices, or their own homes. The FAA provides similar information free over the telephone, but at times the wait for a connection is unreasonably long.

BALL AEROSPACE, Boulder, Colorado. Ball Aerospace is the prime contractor for Space America's commercial remote-sensing satellite, which is currently on hold. Ball also provides satellite services and rents spaceborne hardware to commercial users.

BROADCAST INTERNATIONAL, Salt Lake City, Utah. Broadcast International uses communication satellites to distribute music and commercial announcements to Safeway grocery stores and other users nationwide.

CELANESE CORPORATION, Summit, New Jersey. Celanese is working with NASA on zero-g polymer processing and crystallization in space.

CELESTIUS CORPORATION, Houston, Texas. Space burial for cremated human remains is the business of Celestius. Company officials have contracted with Space Services, Inc., for the boosters to carry their shimmering mausoleums into 4,900-mile orbits, where they will remain in space for 63 million years.

COMMUNICATIONS SATELLITE CORPORATION (COMSAT), Washington, D.C. COMSAT was formed to take advantage of the commercial potential of space-age communications and to coordinate America's communication services with other international partners in Intelsat, a consortium of which COMSAT is the principal member. COMSAT also operates communication networks and the Comstar satellite systems. The Federal Communications Commission recently authorized COMSAT to construct and launch two more Ku-Band satellites.

EAGLE ENGINEERING, Houston, Texas. Eagle Engineering is one of the most successful consulting firms in the space business. It was formed by a group of retired engineers from NASA Houston, who do support work for the space station and market NASA's spinoff technologies. They are also involved with Space Services of America's Conestoga launch vehicle.

EARTH OBSERVATION SATELLITE (EOSAT), Lanham, Maryland. EOSAT is the umbrella name for the joint venture between Hughes and RCA that has been "privatizing" the Landsat earth-resources satellite system. EOSAT markets and distributes Landsat images to thousands of users worldwide.

EARTH SATELLITE CORPORATION, Chevy Chase, Maryland. Earth Satellite, one of the oldest and largest data-processing firms in remote sensing, provides preprocessed and annotated data from remote-sensing satellites to users worldwide.

EG&G CORPORATION, Goleta, California. EG&G is engaged in microgravity crystal-growth research. Recently, EG&G flew a payload specialist on Spacelab 3, who monitored the growth of mercuric iodide crystals for purity and perfection. Mercuric iodide is used in sensors that detect and measure radiation.

EQUATORIAL COMMUNICATION SERVICES, Atlanta, Georgia. Equatorial Communications provides small dish antennas and electronic devices capable of receiving low-data-rate communications from geosynchronous satellites. Many customers are interested in distributing or receiving fresh stock-market data.

EXTERNAL TANK CORPORATION (ETCO), Boulder, Colorado. Corporate officials at ETCO are attempting to gain title to the space shuttle's external tanks, which they would convert into manned orbiting laboratories. Negotiations with NASA are presently underway.

GENERAL SOFTWARE CORPORATION, Landorer, Maryland. General Software offers software-development services to private companies and government agencies, including those involved in value-added data processing of the images from remote-sensing satellites.

GEOSTAR CORPORATION, Princeton, New Jersey. Geostar has received permission from the FCC to launch three geosynchronous navigation satellites that can also distribute short "telegram" messages between users. Geostar's officials have signed agreements with trucking firms for at least 5,000 receivers. Eventually, they plan to develop a hand-held transmitter/receiver that will transmit messages and will be equipped with an automatically activated emergency locator beacon.

GETAWAY SPECIAL SERVICES, Belleview, Washington. Getaway Special Services will fabricate the hardware needed to fly a Getaway Special experiment into orbit. Company experts also provide documentation and paperwork as well as payload support structures, microcomputer controllers, power supplies, and tape recorders.

GLOBESAT, Logan, Utah. The engineers at Globesat are designing a low-altitude constellation of inexpensive communication satellites. It will consist of about fifty satellites in inclined circular orbits.

THE HUDSON FERTILIZER COMPANY, Murray, Kentucky. The Hudson Fertilizer Company is using data from the Landsat images to help pinpoint farmlands that could benefit from additional applications of chemical fertilizer. Company officials are hoping that this unbiased data will help them market their products more efficiently.

INSTRUMENTATION TECHNOLOGY ASSOCIATES, Exton, Pennsylvania. Instrumentation Technology Associates provides standardized equipment for Getaway Special users. Company representatives are also negotiating with NASA to perform similar services for the users of the more ambitious Hitchhikers payload program.

INTERNATIONAL SPACE CORPORATION, Melbourne, Florida. International Space is developing a freezing furnace for orbital production of infrared semiconductor crystals.

ISTAC, Pasadena, California. ISTAC markets a Bible-size navigation receiver that picks up signals from the Navstar satellites and computer-processes them in the so-called "interferometry mode" to gain extremely accurate estimates of user position. So far, ISTAC officials have sold at least twenty of their receivers for about $57,000 each. They also provide training programs and consulting services for potential users of the ISTAC system.

LOVELACE MEDICAL FOUNDATION, Albuquerque, New Mexico. Lovelace has been working with NASA to develop cell cultures in the zero-g environment and is looking into the potential for large-scale pharmaceutical production in space.

LUNAR INDUSTRIES, Houston, Texas. The long-range business plan of Lunar Industries includes the mining of lunar materials for construction purposes. Company officials are now trying to form a consortium to foster this enterprise.

MICROGRAVITY RESEARCH ASSOCIATES, Coral Gables, Florida. Officials at Microgravity Research Associates are planning to have their first commercial shuttle flight in 1989 to test their epitaxial crystal growth process for manufacturing gallium arsenide and other semiconductor materials in space. Under a Joint Endeavor Agreement already signed with NASA, the company's payloads will be carried free.

MOBILSAT CORPORATION, King of Prussia, Pennsylvania. Mobilsat submitted one of the twelve applications to the FCC for permission to construct and operate a mobile satellite-based communication system for public, industrial, and government use.

OCEANROUTES, Palo Alto, California. The scientists and technicians on the staff at Oceanroutes use the images from weather satellites to determine the optimum real-time routes for various types of oceangoing vessels. Every twelve hours they relay new instructions to each of the ships under their care. The service, which costs about $700 per voyage, is said to pay for itself thirty to forty times over in time savings, lower insurance rates, and other tangible benefits.

ODETICS, Anaheim, California. Odetics is the developer of a six-legged "walking" robot, but also builds data recorders for space vehicles and is pioneering various forms of spaceborne robotics technology.

OMNINET, Los Angeles, California. Omninet is competing with eleven other firms for FCC permission to set up satellite-based communication services for mobile users such as trucks and trains.

ORBITAL SCIENCES CORPORATION, Vienna, Virginia. Orbital Sciences is developing the transfer orbit stage to carry NASA and military payloads to altitudes beyond the reach of the space shuttle.

ORION SATELLITE CORPORATION, Washington, D.C. Orion has asked for the FCC's authorization to build and launch two satellites to handle transatlantic communications.

PACIFIC AMERICAN LAUNCH SERVICES, Redwood City, California. Pacific American is currently designing and engineering a liquid-fueled launch vehicle, the Phoenix. Fully reusable, it will take off and land vertically.

PANAR, Houston, Texas. The aeronautical engineers at Panar are planning to develop the Starfix navigation system that will operate by using leased communication channels from four commercial communication satellites.

PARTICLE TECHNOLOGY, Bethlehem, Pennsylvania. Particle Technology is selling the first commercial product made in space: tiny latex microspheres smaller than the cross section of a human hair. They are used to calibrate microscopes, in cancer research, and in the production of finely ground powders such as paint pigments, flour, and toner particles for copying machines.

SATELLITE BUSINESS SYSTEMS (SBS), McLean, Virginia. Satellite Business Systems, a joint venture between IBM, Hughes, and the Aetna Life Insurance Company, uses its own dedicated satellites to handle computer data exchange, long-distance telephone calls, and video teleconferencing. The FCC has just authorized SBS to build and launch a fifth communication satellite.

SATELLITE HYDROLOGY ASSOCIATES, Vienna, Virginia. Satellite Hydrology Associates, a consulting and advisory service for application of satellite technology, uses data from a variety of satellite systems for pollution detection, flood mapping, and civil-engineering projects.

SATELLITE MUSIC NETWORK, Dallas, Texas. The Satellite Music Network employs communication satellites to distribute classical and popular music to "networks" of FM radio stations in all fifty states. The technicians "localize" these broadcasts by using subaudible "trigger frequencies" to insert local material previously recorded by the network announcers.

SPACE INDUSTRIES, INC. Houston, Texas. Space Industries was the first firm to sign a launch service agreement with NASA. In the late 1980s it will launch an industrial space facility, a free-flying materials-processing platform that may later carry astronauts.

SPACE SERVICES, INC., Houston, Texas. Space Services is designing the privately financed Conestoga launch vehicle, whose predecessor has already flown into space along a suborbital ballistic trajectory.

SPACE STRUCTURES INTERNATIONAL, Plainview, New York. Star Net, a part of Space Structures International, is developing a hub-and-strut erectable system that can be assembled into a large rigid structure by an orbiting astronaut without tools.

SPACE VENTURES, INC., Houston, Texas. Space Ventures is marketing a commercial space-station concept.

SPACECO, Lanhan, Maryland. Spaceco is developing an environmental monitoring system to be used in the shuttle cargo bay. If NASA's shuttle repairs are successful, the system will be flown into orbit in the near future.

SPACEHAB, INC., Seattle, Washington. Spacehab is developing pressurized mid-deck augmentation modules for use in the shuttle cargo bay. These modules will be used for equipment storage, crew accommodation, space-station technology development, and research experiments.

SPOT IMAGE CORPORATION, Reston, Virginia. Spot Image is the U.S. subsidiary for the French Spot earth-resources satellite. The Spot gives its users better resolution than the Landsat and provides three-dimensional stereoscopic images for some specialized applications.

STANFORD TELECOMMUNICATIONS, Palo Alto, California. Stanford Telecommunications has been marketing time-synchronization receivers that use the signals from the Navstar satellites to synchronize distant atomic clocks. So far, several dozen of the receivers have been sold for about $20,000 each.

STARFIND, INC., Laguna Niguel, California. Starfind officials are developing a space-based navigation system using dedicated geosynchronous satellites to be launched by another privately owned company, Space Services, Inc.

THIRD MILLENNIUM, INC. (MMI), Washington, D.C. Len Cormier and his colleagues at MMI (Third Millennium) are designing a reusable single-stage spacecraft similar to a small shuttle. If its designers are right, it will be able to carry 6,600 pounds into a low-altitude orbit for a few hundred dollars per pound.

VIDEONET, Woodland Hills, California. VideoNet arranges electronic video conferences for other companies. Most of them use orbiting satellites for signal relay. VideoNet has been in this specialized business for many profitable years.

WESTECH SYSTEMS, INC., Phoenix, Arizona. Westech is researching containerless processing in space using magnetic and acoustical levitation techniques. Company officials also want to build float-zone furnaces for the production of flaw-free silicon in space.

APPENDIX C

SIX CENTERS FOR THE COMMERCIAL DEVELOPMENT OF SPACE

NASA has established six Centers for the Commercial Development of Space whose personnel are engaged in ground-based research, centering around micro-gravity-related phenomena. Most of them are interested in acquiring industrial partners. For more information you can contact any of the following:

Mr. Frank Jelinek
Battelle Center for Commercial Development of Space
505 King Ave.
Columbus, OH 43201

Mr. Charles Lundquist
Consortium for Materials Development in
  Space
University of Alabama
Huntsville, AL 35899

Dr. Paul Todd
Bioprocessing Research Center
University of City Science Center
3624 Market St.
Philadelphia, PA 19104

Mr. Charles Bugg
Center for Macromolecular Crystallization
University of Alabama
Birmingham, AL 35294

Mr. Robert Bayuzich
Engineering Materials
Vanderbilt University
Nashville, TN 37240

Dr. Milan Bier
Center for Separation Science
University of Arizona
Tucson, AZ 85721

APPENDIX D

SPACE-RELATED MAGAZINES AND PERIODICALS

Space-related magazines and periodicals will help you gain timely and accurate information on emerging technologies and promising investment opportunities in aerospace. *Business Week,* for instance, contains solid data on stock-market trends and aerospace companies, both large and small. *Technology Review* and *Aviation Week* run a variety of articles on space-related enterprises, and *Space World* is a good source of information on large space projects. These and the other periodicals in the following list will give you useful information from a variety of perspectives.

AEROSPACE, 1725 DeSales St., N.W., Washington, DC 20036; (202) 429-4600. This pictorially colorful but verbally dry publication provides its specialized readership with a business-oriented look at the aerospace industry with emphasis on broad political and financial issues such as government procurement procedures, research and development trends, Soviet defense measures, and Congressional policies toward the aerospace industry.

AIR & SPACE SMITHSONIAN, 900 Jefferson Dr., Washington, DC 20560. *Air and Space,* which is published by the Smithsonian Institution, provides its readers with a lively and informative overview of interesting events in space and aviation. A largely noncontroversial treatment, it features eye-catching graphics and readable prose.

AVIATION WEEK & SPACE TECHNOLOGY, McGraw-Hill, Inc., 1221 Avenue of the Americas, New York, NY 10020; (212) 512-2000. *Aviation Week* is often referred to as the bible of the aerospace industry. Widely quoted in more influential general-circulation magazines, it is stuffed with in-teresting facts and figures presented in a readable format. Although it is written from a sophisticated scientific perspective, it includes fast-breaking stories on important aerospace and defense-related topics such as weather satellites, the "Star Wars" defense initiative, and zero-g materials-processing techniques.

BUSINESS WEEK, 1221 Avenue of the Americas, New York, NY 10020. This popular magazine is targeted toward corporate managers and independent entrepreneurs. It does not feature aerospace coverage per se, but occasionally it does include broad-ranging information on major space-oriented corporations such as Boeing and Lockheed. It also traces technological and economic trends in the space business.

HIGH TECHNOLOGY, 38 Commercial Wharf, Boston, MA 02110; (800) 525-0643. *High Technology* focuses on business issues in such increasing technical fields as medicine, microcomputers, office automation, aerospace technology, and military contracting. It includes authoritative market projections, clear and informative descriptions of state-of-the-art technologies, and interviews with leading industry professionals.

INTERNATIONAL SPACE BUSINESS REVIEW, Media Dimensions, Inc., P.O. Box 1121, Gracie Station, New York, NY 10028; (212) 772-7068. This tightly edited publication provides potential space investors with a wealth of useful information on the aerospace industry. It covers all aspects of space industrialization, including investment opportunities, risk management, government regulations, and marketing techniques. Its articles also review emerging technologies in booster rockets, zero-g materials processing, space services, remote-sensing satellites, and the like.

POPULAR SCIENCE, 380 Madison Ave., New York, NY 10017. *Popular Science* examines science, technology, and new product developments for an audience consisting primarily of intelligent nonspecialists. Over the years it has run many interesting articles on flight hardware and space technology.

SATELLITE COMMUNICATIONS, 6530 S. Yosemite St., Inglewood, CO 80111; (303) 694-7522. *Satellite Communications* specializes in business-oriented coverage of space-based communication services with emphasis on commercial communication satellites. It covers a broad range of topics, including FCC regulations, frequency allocations, global message services, banking networks, and electronic teleconferencing. It also reviews the major technical meetings and newsworthy events throughout the world, and it spotlights key personnel changes in communications-related companies.

SCIENCE DIGEST, 888 7th Ave., New York, NY 10106; (212) 262-7990. According to its masthead, *Science Digest* is devoted to helping the interested nonspecialist "appre-

ciate the beauty of science and the adventure of technology." Most of its colorful articles are geared toward "the alert, inquisitive layman, fascinated by all facets of science." It contains informative articles on science and technology along with snappy interviews and intelligent book reviews.

SCIENCE NEWS, Science Services, Inc., 1719 N St., N.W., Washington, DC 20036; (202) 785-2255. *Science News* is a thin weekly science magazine filled with offbeat articles which on occasion provide brief coverage of space-related events and technologies.

SCIENTIFIC AMERICAN, 415 Madison Ave., New York, NY 10017. *Scientific American* is a beautifully crafted technical science magazine that gives broad coverage to a variety of scientific topics including chemistry, biology, and physics. Some of the topics—military weapons developments, medical experiments, automated telepresence, space-station design—are of special interest to aerospace professionals.

SPACE WORLD, National Space Society, West Wing, Suite 203, 600 Maryland Ave., S.W., Washington, DC 20024. *Space World* includes lively interviews with aerospace professionals together with factual descriptions of leading technologies. Potential space investors will be especially interested in its coverage of communication satellites, space-station design, zero-g manufacturing, and space-age robotics. Also included are fascinating articles on the history of space travel.

TECHNOLOGY REVIEW, RM 10-140, MIT, Cambridge, MA 02139; (617) 253-8250. *Technology Review,* which is published on the campus of MIT, emphasizes sound coverage of controversial scientific topics. Articles of interest to space enthusiasts include ones on space-station design, orbital overcrowding, emerging trends in telecommunications technology, and the like. Although the readership of this well-crafted publication is relatively small, its pithy insights appeal to many influential trendsetters, including practicing professional scientists, politicians, engineers, and social scientists.

TELESPAN BUSINESS TV, Telespan Publishing Corporation, P.O. Box 6250, Altadena, CA 91001. This specialized trade publication concentrates on the business trends and business-related applications of television technology, including cable TV, satellite networking, and satellite-based marketing techniques.

APPENDIX E

SPACE-RELATED CLUBS AND ORGANIZATIONS

Joining one or more of the many space-related clubs and organizations can be a stimulating and enjoyable way to gather additional information on how to strike it rich in space. Your participation can also help you make important business contacts. The organizations in this listing welcome members with a variety of talents and interests. Use it as a guide as you search for the perfect organization to join. The Planetary Society, the L5 Society, and the National Space Club have very different platforms, but they are all especially interesting organizations to join.

AEROSPACE EDUCATION FOUNDATION, 1501 Lee Hwy., Arlington, VA 22209; (703) 247-5839, (800) 553-2337. The purpose of the Aerospace Education Foundation is to enhance public awareness and understanding of emerging aerospace technologies and developments in the business of space. It publishes an informative newsletter, maintains an aerospace education center, and gives awards and scholarships to deserving individuals.

AMERICAN ASTRONAUTICAL SOCIETY (AAS), c/o University of Colorado, Campus Box 423, Boulder, CO 80309-0423; (703) 866-0020. The American Astronautical Society attracts mostly professional aerospace engineers. Its goal is to provide a lively forum for the discussion of past space missions, scientific developments, and government policies and also to promote the successful exploration and utilization of space. Its members support broad-ranging scientific research, hold conferences on space, and give achievement awards to deserving aerospace professionals. It publishes a bimonthly newsletter, a quarterly journal, and various technical books.

AMERICAN INSTITUTE OF AERONAUTICS AND ASTRONAUTICS (AIAA), 1633 Broadway, New York, NY 10010; (212) 581-4300. This 37,000-member professional organization is admired by practicing scientists and engineers, even those who are not members. The AIAA's efforts are devoted to the exchange of information at technical meetings and in its journals. A large technical library with computer-based abstracting services is maintained at the New York headquarters.

AMERICAN SPACE FOUNDATION, 111 Massachusetts Ave., N.W., Suite 200, Washington, DC 20002; (202) 289-2293. The American Space Foundation is a 22,000-member laymen's organization that supports the American space program and lobbies for a larger NASA budget, which its officers believe should equal 1 percent of total federal expenditures. In addition, its members bestow special awards and publish two quarterly newsletters.

HIGH FRONTIER, 1010 Vermont Ave., N.W., Suite 1000, Washington, DC 20005; (202) 737-4979. This privately funded organization supports and encourages practical governmental policies relating to the military uses of space. Its members advocate the development of a nonnuclear spaceborne defense system to protect our country against a possible nuclear attack.

L-5 SOCIETY, Promoting Space Development, 1060 East Elm St., Tucson, AZ 85719-4109; (602) 622-6351. The L-5 Society's 6,500 members are keenly interested in space industrialization and the colonization of space. Their driving goal is to create a spacefaring civilization of communities living outside the earth's biosphere. The organization takes its name from the L-5 "libration point," a specific location in space equidistant from the earth and the moon where a space colony or a facility for processing lunar materials would seem to hang "motionless" with respect to the earth and the moon. Many members of the L-5 Society are college students who provide volunteer labor for its varied activities. One member owns a poetic personalized license plate that reads "O2B N0G."

NATIONAL SPACE CLUB, 655 15th St., N.W., No. 300, Washington, DC 20005; (202) 639-4210. The National Space Club is a politically oriented organization whose members are mostly affiliated with the government, the military-industrial complex, and the public press. The purpose of this exclusive, limited-membership club is to promote the peaceful advancement of aerospace technologies and the peaceful exploitation of space. It publishes a newsletter and presents grants and awards to deserving individuals.

NATIONAL SPACE INSTITUTE, 400 Maryland Ave., S.W., Westwing Suite 203, Washington, DC 20024; (202) 483-1111. The National Space Institute promotes the space program and attempts to ensure that it is responsive to the concerns of the average private citizen. Over 11,000 members participate in the institute's activities, which include tours of launch facilities, a speakers' bureau, special media programs, and a telephone information hotline. Its publications include *Space World,* which is described in the previous appendix.

PLANETARY SOCIETY, 65 N. Cataline Ave., Pasadena, CA 91106; (818) 793-5100. This gangling 110,000-member society, founded in 1980, is "devoted to a realistic continuing program of planetary exploration and the search for extraterrestrial life." The Planetary Society attempts to enhance public awareness of space-related issues, stimulates research into the technologies needed for planetary science, and publishes a bimonthly *Planetary Report.*

SPACE EXPEDITIONS, 3131 Elliott Ave., Suite 700, Seattle, WA 98121. Space Expeditions offers a unique and exotic travel program to its members: for a $5,000 deposit held in escrow, it is offering reservations for twelve-hour tours in space beginning in October 1992.

SPACE STUDIES INSTITUTE, 285 Rosedale Rd., P.O. Box 82, Princeton, NJ 08540; (609) 921-0377. This nonprofit organization promotes the practical development and exploitation of space in ways that benefit the people living on earth. Its 5,000-plus members include companies, organizations, and individuals. The institute maintains a personnel bureau, conducts educational programs, and operates a well-stocked research library.

UNITED STATES SPACE EDUCATION ASSOCIATION, 756 Turnpike Rd., Elizabethtown, PA 17022-1161; (717) 367-6500. This international nonprofit organization serves both laymen and aerospace professionals. Its members hope to stimulate public awareness of space exploration. A bimonthly newsletter and a monthly bulletin are published by the association, which also creates excellent worldwide exhibits, runs a museum and media center, holds special workshops, and distributes audiovisual presentations.

YOUNG ASTRONAUT COUNCIL, 1211 Connecticut Ave., N.W., Suite 800, Washington, DC 20036; (202) 682-1985. The Young Astronaut Council organizes activities for budding space enthusiasts (elementary school students). Popular activities include tours of launch facilities and aerospace museums, writing contests, and simulated space adventures. The council also publishes a monthly newsletter and distributes science kits to its young members. Its organizers are hoping that someday one of the Young Astronauts will fly into space.

BIBLIOGRAPHY

The material in this book was extracted from more than 1,100 published sources: books, pamphlets, magazines, Ph.D. dissertations, technical papers, stockholders' reports. The following selection includes only the most helpful publications.

I

INTRODUCTION: THE LURE OF SPACE

Brown, David A. "Educational Expertise in Satellite R&D Opens the Way for Commercial Profit." *Commercial Space,* Fall 1985, 79–81.

Covault, Craig. "Commercialization of Space: Unique Products, New Technology." *Aviation Week & Space Technology,* June 25, 1984, 40–51.

————."NASA Formulates Policy to Spur Private Investment." *Aviation Week & Space Technology,* Nov. 26, 1984, 18.

Dyson, Freeman. "Space: Asteroid Crops." *Omni,* May 1986, 22.

Finch, Edward Ridley, Jr., and Moore, Amanda Lee. *Astrobusiness: A Guide to Commerce and Law in Outer Space.* Stanford, Conn.: Walden Book Co., 1984.

Fink, Donald E. "Crossroads for Commercialization." *Aviation Week & Space Technology,* Nov. 25, 1985, 9.

Haggarty, James J. "The Outlook for Space Commercialization." *Aerospace,* Winter 1984, 1–16.

Krogh, Lester C. "New Business in Space." *High Technology,* July 1984, 12.

Logsdon, Thomas S. "Opportunities in Space Industrialization." *Journal of Contemporary Business,* 7,3:171–184.

MacMillan, Mike. "New Job for NASA Is Marketing Management." *Commercial Space,* Spring 1986, 66–68.

Morris, Richard W., and Todd, Paul. "Developing Industrial Participation in Space: The Philadelphia Experience." *International Space Business Review,* June/July 1985, 21–30.

Pioneering the Space Frontier: An Exciting Vision of Our Next Fifty Years in Space. The Report of the National Commission on Space. New York: Bantam, 1986.

Space Industrialization Executive Summary. Final Report SP-78-AP-0055-1. Rockwell International Space Division (NASA Contract NAS8-32198) April 14, 1978, 1–39.

The Space Industry: Trade Related Issues. Organization for Economic Cooperation, Paris, France, 1985.

Wood, Peter W., and Stark, Peter M. "Made in Space: Commercializing the Last Frontier." *New York Times,* June 24, 1984.

STRIKING IT RICH IN SPACE

Bova, Ben. "Commerce on the Launch Pad." *Science Digest,* January 1985, 36–37.

Dyson, Freeman. *Disturbing the Universe.* New York: Harper & Row, 1979.

Egan, John J. "Financial Issues for Commercial Space Ventures—Paying for the Dreams." *Space Industrialization Opportunities.* Coopers & Lybrand: 1986, 39–48.

Fink, Donald E. "After Challenger: Pressing Forward." *Commercial Space,* Winter 1986, 17.

Golden, Frederic. *Colonies in Space: The Next Giant Step.* New York: Harcourt Brace Jovanovich, 1977.

Heppenheimer, T. A. *Colonies in Space.* Harrisburg, Pa.: Stackpole, 1977.

Lehr, L. W. "How to Orbit the Earth with Your Feet on the Ground." *Vital Speeches of the Day,* May 1, 1985, 443–46.

Logsdon, John M. "Status of Space Commercialization in the U.S.A." *Space Policy,* February 1986, 9–16.

Logsdon, Thomas S. *The Rush Toward The Stars: A Survey of Space Exploration.* Englewood, N.J.: Franklin, 1970.

Madwell, J. F., and Logsdon, T. S. "Space Flight Opportunities for Industry." Technical paper presented at the Space Flight Congress, Cape Kennedy, Fla., April 12, 1977.

Maugh, Thomas H. II. "First Commercial Product from Space." *Science,* 224:264–65.

Newport, John Paul, Jr. "The Mighty Molecules of Microspheres." *Fortune,* Sept. 16, 1985, 105–6.

Oderman, Mark, and Robertson, Kelly. "Watershed Year: Shuttle Accident and Budgetary Pressures Force Critical Decisions." *Commercial Space,* Winter 1986, 62–65.

O'Neill, Gerard K. *The High Frontier.* New York: Morrow, 1977.

Page, Jake. "A Special Camera Lets Viewers Fly with the Shuttle." *Smithsonian,* June 1985, 132–36.

Pioneering the Space Frontier: An Exciting Vision of Our Next Fifty Years in Space. The Report of the National Commission on Space. New York: Bantam, 1986.

Porter, Gail, and Smith, Colloer. "New Particles for Measuring Pigments, Flour, Blood Cells." *NBS Research Reports,* October 1984, 16–19.

Rockwell International. *Space Industrialization.* Final Report; 4 vols. SP-78-AP-0055-1, 2,3,4 (NASA Contract NAS8-32198), April 14, 1978.

Skoogfors, Leif. "Perfect Spheres: The First Product from Space." *Business Week,* January 30, 1984, 25.

Sobel, Robert, and Sicilia, David B. *The Entrepreneurs: An American Adventure.* Boston: Houghton Mifflin, 1986.

"Space Commerce Barriers to be Eased." *Aviation Week & Space Technology.* June 25, 1984, 18–19.

"Space Commercialization Group Includes Non-Aerospace Firms." *Aviation Week & Space Technology,* March 4, 1985, 20.

"U.S. Business Group Finds Initiatives to be Feasible." *Aviation Week & Space Technology,* June 25, 1984, 93–95.

Walsh, John. "Translating Japanese Technology into U.S. Terms." *Science,* 224:264–65.

3

SPACE-BASED MANUFACTURING

Bylinsky, Gene. "What's Sexier and Speedier Than Silicon." *Fortune,* June 24, 1985, 74–80.

Cohn, Steven M., and Cohn, Cindy A. "Financing Space Industrialization." *Space World,* November 1984, 4–9.

Covault, Craig. "NASA Promotes Commercialization of Space to Automobile Makers." *Aviation Week & Space Technology,* Oct. 29, 1984, 21–23.

DeMott, John S. "Business Heads for Zero Gravity." *Time,* Nov. 26, 1984, 30.

Dumaine, Brian. "Still A-OK: The Promise of Factories in Space." *Fortune,* March 3, 1986.

Jernigan, Camille M., and Pentecost, Elizabeth, *Space Industrialization Opportunities.* Park Ridge, N.J.: Noyes Publications, 1985.

"John Deere Plans Space Iron Research." *Aviation Week & Space Technology,* June 25, 1984, 74–77.

Koepp, Stephen. "And Now, the Age of Light." *Time,* Oct. 6, 1986, 42–43.

Kolcum, Edward H. "Company Plans to Manufacture Crystals." *Aviation Week & Space Technology,* June 25, 1984, 100–1.

Lineback, J. Robert. "NASA Eyes Crystal Processing in Space." *Electronics,* Jan. 26, 1984, 89–91.

Marsh, Peter. *The Space Business: The Exploitation of Space—How Much, How Far, How Probable?* New York: Penguin, 1985.

"Medicine Sales Forecast at $1 Billion." *Aviation Week & Space Technology,* June 25, 1984, 52–56.

Osborne, David. "Business in Space." *Atlantic Monthly,* May 1985, 45–58.

Smith, Bruce A. "McDonnell Douglas Plans to Process Large Pharmaceutical Batch in Space." *Aviation Week & Space Technology,* Nov. 18, 1985, 83–88.

"3M Seeks New Materials, Processes." *Aviation Week & Space Technology,* June 25, 1984, 65.

4

COMMUNICATION SATELLITES

Aerospace Mobile Communications: Building the Mass Market. *Aerospace America,* 1985, 49–56.

Bennett, Tamara. "Buying on Impulse." *Satellite Communications,* August 1986, 26–31.

Communications. Alexandria, Va.: Time-Life Books, 1986.

Dennis, Tom L. "On the Phone at 30,000 Feet." *Aerospace America,* June 1985, 58–60.

Feldman, Nathaniel E. "Technological Advances Are Expected to Lower Mobile Satellite Communications Hardware and Service Costs." *Aerospace America,* June 1985, 51–53.

Ghais, Ahmad F.; Branch, Paul; and Curiel, Alex da Silva. "Broadening Inmarsat Services." *Aerospace America,* June 1985, 66.

Horn, Larry Van. *Communication Satellites.* Brasstown, N.C.: Grove Enterprises, Inc., 1986.

Logsdon, Thomas S. "Orbiting Switchboards." *Technology Illustrated.* October/November 1981, 54–62.

————. "Unsnarling Signals in Space." *Technology Review.* August/September 1982, 14.

Lovell, Robert R. "Giant Step for Communication Satellite Technology." *Aerospace America,* March 1984, 54–57.

———— and Cuccia, Louis C. "A New Wave of Communication Satellites." *Aerospace America,* March 1984, 43–51.

Lowndes, Jay C. "Hughes Rates Cost of Satellites Lower than Optical Fiber Hardware." *Aviation Week & Space Technology,* Dec. 1, 1986, 73–76.

————. "Joint Venture Installs Earth Stations for Shopping Mall Teleconferencing." *Aviation Week & Space Technology,* April 21, 1986, 57–58.

————. "Pricing Strategy Is Key to Satellite Market Share." *Aviation Week & Space Technology,* Nov. 24, 1986, 45–53.

Marsh, Peter. *The Space Business.* New York: Penguin Books, 1985.

Ott, James. "Fedral Express Uses Satellites to Offer Almost Instant Delivery." *Commercial Space,* Winter 1986, 66–68.

————. "Videoconference Use Expands to Meet Rising Business Needs." *Aviation Week & Space Technology,* July 22, 1985, 157–64.

Rosenberg, Barry. "Geosynchronous Orbit." *Commercial Space,* Spring 1986, 62–68.

"Satcoms Tailor Services to Customers." *Aviation Week & Space Technology,* June 25, 1984, 181–92.

Stein, Kenneth J. "Satellites Link Mobile Communications." *Aviation Week & Space Technology,* June 25, 1984, 197–99.

Stephens, Guy M. "It's Not Just for Telegrams Anymore." *Satellite Communications,* September 1985, 18–21.

————. "Profits in Radio." *Satellite Communications,* October 1986, 45–46.

Stoddard, Rob. "Stalking the Market for Mobilestats." *Satellite Communications,* December 1986, 30–32.

Stover, Dawn. "The Satellite TV Puzzle." *Popular Science,* November 1986, 71–73.

Tracy, Eleanor Johnson. "A Watch That Gets the Message." *Fortune,* May 12, 1986, 81.

Wilbur, Amy. "From Car to Satellite." *Science Digest,* November 1985, 30.

Yenne, Bill. *The Encyclopedia of U.S. Spacecraft.* New York: Bison Books, 1985.

5

SURVEYING THE EARTH'S RESOURCES

Anderson, John W. "Remote Sensing." *Commercial Space,* Fall 1985, 70–76.

Atlas of North America: Space-Age Portrait of a Continent. Washington: National Geographic Society, 1985.

Bennett, Tamara. "Developing Remote Sensing." *Satellite Communications,* December 1986, 25–29.

Covault, Craig. "Japan: Emerging Space Power." *Commercial Space,* Summer 1986, 16–26.

David, Leonard. "Space America to Commercialize Remote Sensing." *Space World,* January 1984, 14–15.

"Easy Rider." *Aviation Week & Space Technology,* February 2, 1987, 17.

"Earth Sensors Further Japan's Efforts." *Aviation Week & Space Technology,* June 25, 1984, 151–57.

Felsher, Murray. "Satellite Remote Sensing in Oceanography: An Introduction." *MTS Journal,* 20:2, 3–4.

Greeley, Brendan M. "Commercial Marketing of Landsat Data Begins." *Commercial Space,* Fall 1985, 66–77.

———."EOSAT Develops Marketing Rules for Landsat Data." *Aviation Week & Space Technology,* Nov. 4, 1985, 48–53.

Kolcum, Edward H. "USAF Developing Training Program for Space Careers." *Aviation Week & Space Technology,* May 5, 1986, 101–3.

Lawren, Bill. "Explorations." *Omni,* January 1985, 26.

Lenorovitz, Jeffrey M. "France to Fund Two Additional Spot Remote Sensing Satellites." *Aviation Week & Space Technology,* Aug. 5, 1985, 74–75.

Loundes, Jay C. "Commerce Department Transfers Landsat Operations to Private Venture." *Aviation Week & Space Technology,* Oct. 14, 1985, 95–103.

———."Value Added to Remotely Sensed Data." *Aviation Week & Space Technology,* June 25, 1984, 125–37.

Mann, Paul. "Landsat Contract Bidders Plan Private Alternatives." *Aviation Week & Space Technology,* June 25, 1984, 61.

McElroy, John H. "Clearing the Sky." *Air and Space,* February/March 1987, 60–62.

Osborne, David. "Business in Space." *Best of Business,* 18–25.

Rothenberg, Randall. "Space Hustlers." *Esquire,* May 1984, 47–56.

Waldrop, M. Mitchell. "Washington Embraces Global Earth Sciences." *Science,* 233:1040–42 (1986).

Williams, C. P. "Space Remote Sensing." *Spaceflight,* 28:358–64 (1986).

Yenne, Bill. *The Encyclopedia of U.S. Spacecraft.* New York: Bison Books, 1985.

6

WORLDWIDE WEATHERWATCH

Bennett, Tamara. "Quality Weather Forecasting." *Satellite Communications,* October 1986, 34–36.

Covault, Craig. "Chinese Seek U.S. Assistance in Weather Satellite Program." *Aviation Week & Space Technology,* Aug. 5, 1985, 79–81.

Cromie, William J. "When Comes a El Nino?" *Science 80,* March/April 1980, 36–43.

Engle, Michael. "A New Angle on the Weather." *The Futurist,* May/June 1986, 50–51.

"Eyes in the Sky." *National Geographic World,* February 1985, 28–32.

"France Organizes Company to Promote Use of International Satellite Data System." *Aviation Week & Space Technology,* May 26, 1986, 84.

Freeman, Nelson G.S., and McNutt, Lyn. "Oceans and Ice Measurements from Canada's RADARSAT." *MTS Journal,* 20:2, 87–99.

Kerr, Richard. "Weather Satellites Coming of Age." *Science,* 229 (July 19, 1985), 255–57.

Kollinger, Dennis K., and Menyuk, Norman. "Laser Remote Sensing of the Atmosphere." *Science,* 235 (January 2, 1987), 37–44.

Lowndes, Jay C. "Value Added to Remotely Sensed Data." *Aviation Week & Space Technology,* June 25, 1984, 125–37.

Marsh, Peter. *The Space Business.* New York: Penguin Books, 1985.

Montgomery, Donald R.; Wittenberg-Fay, Ruth E.; and Austin, Roswell W. "The Applications of Satellite-Derived Ocean Color Products to Commercial Fishing Operations." *MTS Journal,* 20:2, 72–86.

Rosenberg, Barry. "TOPEX Rules the Waves." *Space World,* November 1986, 21–22.

Sherman, John W., III. "Developments in Satellite Technology for Oceanic Operations." *MTS Journal,* 20:2, 33–42.

Smith, W. L., and others. "The Meteorological Satellite: Overview of 25 Years of Operation." *Science,* 231 (January 1986), 455–62.

Walsh, John. "Famine Early Warning Closer to Reality." *News and Comment,* Sept. 12, 1986, 1145–47.

Weisburd, Stefi. "Stalking the Weather Bombs." *Science News,* Vol 129 (January 4, 1986), 314.

7

SPACE-AGE NAVIGATION

Alexander, George. "Satellites: Archeology's Newest Tool." *Times Science,* June 18, 1984, 12–13.

Cooke, Patrick. "Look Homeward, (Electronic) Angel." *Science 84,* May 1984, 75–78.

"Computer Navigation Coming to Law Enforcement." *Law and Order,* February 1985, 24–26.

"Dinosaur Hunt." *Science Digest,* June 1981, 21–22.

Elson, Benjamin M. "Transoceanic Flight Shows GPS Uses." *Aviation Week & Space Technology,* July 25, 1983, 45–48.

French, Robert L. "Automobile Navigation: Where Is It Going?" Paper prepared for IEEE position location and navigation symposium, Las Vegas, Nevada, November 4–7, 1986.

Helmes, Charles W., and Logsdon, Thomas S. "Space-Based Navigation: Past, Present, and Future." Prepared for presentation at the Annual AIAA Meeting and International Aerospace Exhibit, Washington, D.C., May 1, 1984.

Honey, S. K., and Zavoli, W. B. "A Novel Approach to Automotive Navigation and Map Display." Presented at the Land Navigation and Location for Mobile Applications Conference of the Royal Institute of Navigation, York, U.K., Sept. 9–11, 1985.

Klass, Phillip J. "Civil Use of Global Positioning System." *Aviation Week & Space Technology,* May 5, 1980, 74–75.

Large, Alen J. "Satellite Plan Seen as Boom to Navigation." *Wall Street Journal,* Oct. 25, 1983.

Logsdon, Thomas S. "Satellites Bring New Precision to Navigation." *High Technology,* July/August 1984, 61–66.

———— and Helms, Charles W. "Promising Third-World Applications of the Navstar Global Positioning System." Prepared for presentation at the Institute of Navigation Fortieth Annual Meeting, Cambridge, Mass., June 1984.

MacDoran, Peter F.; Whitcomb, James H.; and Miller, Robert B. "Codeless GPS Positioning Offers Sub-Meter Accuracy." *Sea Technology,* October 1984.

Merrifield, John T. "Fifth-Generation GPS Receiver Aims at Commercial Market." *Aviation Week & Space Technology,* Aug. 19, 1985, 123–25.

Smith, Bruce A. "Four Orbiters to Get Navstar Capability." *Aviation Week & Space Technology,* April 20, 1979, 187–88.

Stoddard, Rob. "Geostar: RDSS on the Move." *Satellite Communications,* October 1986, 22–24.

Yenne, Bill. *The Encyclopedia of U.S. Spacecraft.* New York: Bison Books, 1985.

Zygmont, Jeffrey. "Keeping Tabs on Cars and Trucks." *High Technology,* September 1986, 18–23.

8

PRIVATELY OWNED BOOSTER ROCKETS

Asimov, Isaac. "Wings for America." *Popular Mechanics,* July 1986, 193–202.

"C² Spacelines Signs for Shuttle Slots, Will Lease Cargo Space." *Aviation Week & Space Technology,* June 25, 1984, 144.

"Conestoga Booster Will Launch Human Ashes for Space Burial." *Aviation Week & Space Technology,* Jan. 21, 1985, 20–21.

"Design for Conestoga II Shaping Up." *Space World,* January 1984, 12–13.

Divis, Dee Ann. "Thinking Big by Keeping It Small: The Price and Scheduling Advantages of a Fully Reusable Mini-Shuttle." *International Space Business Review,* June/July 1985, 38–43.

Feazel, Michael. "German Spaceplane Concept Embodies Hypersonic Aircraft, Winged Orbiter." *Aviation Week & Space Technology,* Aug. 11, 1986, 70–71.

Gelman, Eric. "Blast Off for Profits." *Newsweek,* Sept. 1, 1986, 60–61.

"Getaway Specials Create New Market for Hardware." *Aviation Week & Space Technology,* June 25, 1984, 138–43.

Grey, Jerry. "The New Orient Express." *Discover,* January 1986, 73–81.

Gwynne, Peter. "Space Plane." *Air and Space,* August/September 1986, 24–33.

Heppenheimer, T. A. "Launching the Aerospace Plane." *High Technology,* July 1986, 46–51.

Kerrod, R. *Space Shuttle.* New York: Gallery Books/W. H. Smith, 1984.

Koepp, Stephen. "Scramble to the Launching Pad." *Time,* March 31, 1986, 55.

Lenorovitz, Jeffrey M. "France Selects Aerospatiale, Dassault to Develop Space-plane." *Aviation Week & Space Technology,* Oct. 28, 1985, 18.

Logsdon, Thomas S. "High Fliers." *Technology Illustrated,* December/January 1982, 24–32.

Marbach, William D. "L.A. to Tokyo in Two Hours." *Newsweek,* Dec. 16, 1985, 66.

———. "One Small Step for Free Enterprise." *Newsweek,* Aug. 10, 1981, 55.

Marsh, A. K. "Space Services Pushing Conestoga Launch Vehicle." *Aviation Week & Space Technology,* June 25, 1984, 163–65.

Meyer, Alfred. "Quatre, Trois, Deux, Un . . ." *Air and Space,* June/July 1986, 29–39.

Mordoff, Keith F. "Shuttle Hitchhiker Spurs Business Effort." *Aviation Week & Space Technology,* June 25, 1984, 102–5.

Myrabo, Leik, and Ing, Dean. *The Future of Flight.* New York: Simon & Schuster/Baen Publishing Enterprises, 1985.

Register, Bridget M. "Boosting Business into Space." *High Technology,* October 1985, 53–54.

Rothenberg, Randall. "Space Hustlers." *Esquire,* May 1984, 47–56.

Rudolph, Barbara. "Around the World in 120 Minutes." *Time,* Feb. 17, 1986, 56.

Tully, Shawn. "Europe Blasts into the Space Business." *Fortune.* May 27, 1985, 138–40.

"Two Firms Ready to Buy, Produce Shuttle Orbits." *Aviation Week & Space Technology,* June 25, 1984, 116–19.

Williams, Bob. "Space Plane: It Is Seen as 'Next Giant Step in Aerospace.'" *Orange County Register,* Dec. 26, 1986, C2.

9

TOMORROW'S MANNED SPACE STATIONS

Aaron, John W. "New Shape in the Sky." *Aerospace America,* September 1986, 30–31.

Anderson, John W. "Soviet Strides: American Launchers Are Grounded, but the USSR Program Couldn't Be Healthier." *Commercial Space,* Winter 86, 26–31.

"Are the Soviets Ahead in Space?" *National Geographic,* October 1986, 434–58.

Bekey, Ivan, and Herman, D. *Space Stations and Space Platforms—Concepts, Design, Infrastructure, and Uses.* New York: American Institute of Aeronautics and Astronautics, 1985.

Black, David C. "Telescience in Orbit." *Aerospace America,* September 1986, 44–46.

Bluth, B. J., and Helppie, M. *Soviet Space Stations as Analogs.* NASA Headquarters, Washington, D.C., August 1986.

Bova, Ben. "Power Tower: Living in Orbit." *Science Digest,* June 1985, 40–87.

Clearwater, Yvonne. "A Human Place in Outer Space." *Psychology Today,* July 1985, 34–43.

Covault, Craig. "Space Station Redesigned for Larger Structural Area." *Aviation Week & Space Technology,* Oct. 14, 1985, 16–17.

Eskow, Dennis. "Space City." *Popular Mechanics,* June 1986.

Foley, Theresa M. "NASA Weighs Private Financing of Shuttle, Space Station Projects." *Aviation Week & Space Technology,* June 2, 1986, 16–19.

Gregory, William H., "Spar Aerospace Leads the Way in Canada's Participation." *Commercial Space,* Winter 1986, 32–33.

————. "Canada Adapting Shuttle Remote Arm to Space Station Service Facility." *Aviation Week & Space Technology,* March 3, 1986, 73.

Kelly, James. "Moscow's Program Takes Off." *Time,* March 31, 1986, 58–59.

Lenorovitz, Jeffrey M. "Europeans Exploring Independent Role in Space." *Commercial Space,* Winter 1986, 25–28.

Loundes, Jay C. "Manned Workplace in Space, Started as a U.S. Concept, Now Has Global Impact." *Commercial Space,* Winter 1986, 18–21.

Marbach, William D. "NASA's Next Stop in Space." *Newsweek,* Jan. 19, 1987, 52–53.

Martin, Russell. "Space Inc." *Science Digest,* March 1985, 43–85.

"NASA Report Urges Developing Robotics, Software for Station." *Aviation Week & Space Technology,* April 22, 1985, 63.

Nichols, Robert G. "Space Station: Government and Industry Launch Joint Venture." *High Technology,* April 1985, 19–25.

Powell, Luther E.; Hager, Robert W.; and McCown, James W. "A Home Away from Home." *Aerospace America,* September 1985, 56–57.

Revkin, Andrew C. "The Space Station Takes Shape." *Science Digest,* February 1986, 61–63.

Sekigawa, Eilchiro. "Life Sciences Module for Space Station Will Be Made in Japan." *Commercial Space,* Winter 1986, 37.

Simpson, Theodore R. *The Space Station: An Idea Whose Time Has Come.* New York: IEEE Press, 1985.

"Space Industries Is Making Plans with NASA for a Space Facility." *Commercial Space,* Fall 1985, 40–44.

"Teledyne Brown Proposes Materials Processing Module for Space Station." *Aviation Week & Space Technology,* Jan. 13, 1986, 151–55.

Vallerani, Ernesto, and Piantella, Paolo. "Columbus: Europe's Piece of the Space Station." *Aerospace America,* September 1985, 72–76.

Walklet, Donn C. "Private Funds Will Bolster Tax Dollars in the Job of Financing the Station." *Commercial Space,* Winter 1986, 41–47.

10

SATELLITE SALVAGE, RETRIEVAL, AND REPAIR

Artificial Intelligence. Alexandria, Va.: Time-Life Books, 1986.

Bodanis, D. *The Secret House.* New York: Simon & Schuster, 1986.

Chacko, George K. *Robotics/Artificial Intelligence/Productivity: U.S.–Japan Concomitant Coalitions.* Princeton, N.J.: Petrocelli Books, 1986.

Cohan, Phil. "Dollars from Heaven." *Air and Space,* June/July 1986, 72–76.

Covault, Craig. "Astronauts Repair, Deploy Leasat During Two Space Shuttle EVAs." *Aviation Week & Space Technology,* Sept. 9, 1985, 21.

———."Satcom Salvage Plans Near Completion." *Aviation Week & Space Technology,* June 25, 1984, 22–24.

Ellis, Junius. "Entrepreneurs in Space." *Air and Space,* December 1986/January 1987, 98–101.

"EVA Rejuvenates Skylab Gyros, Replaces Telescope Mount Film." *Aviation Week & Space Technology,* Sept. 3, 1973, 119–20.

"The Great Big Garbage Dump in the Sky,"

Discover, January 1986, 15.

Heppenheimer, T. A. "Paving the Way for Space Tugs." *High Technology,* September 1985, 57–59.

"Junkyard in Space." *The Futurist,* February 1985, 62–64.

Logsdon, Thomas S. *The Robot Revolution.* New York: Simon & Schuster, 1984.

———.*Space Debris Retrieval.* Space Division, Rockwell International Corporation, SD73-SA-0126, Sept. 15, 1973.

———."What Goes Up into Orbit Doesn't Necessarily Come Down—at Least Not Right Away." *Technology Illustrated,* June 1983, 31–34.

Marsh, Peter. *Robots.* New York: Crescent Books, 1985.

Morris, Brian. *The World of Robots.* New York: Gallery Books/W. H. Smith, 1985.

Quinn, Hal. "Discovery's Successful Salvage Mission." *Maclean's,* Sept. 26, 1984, 68.

Robotics. Alexandria, Va.: Time-Life Books, 1986.

Thom, Evan. "Roaming the High Frontier." *Time,* Nov. 26, 1984, 16–20.

11

CENTURY 21

Beatty, J. Kelly. "Solar Satellites." *Science 80,* December 1980, 28–33.

David, Leonard. "Community into the Cosmos." *Space World,* August 1985, 9–14.

Ehricke, Krafft A. "The Power Relay Satellite: A Means of World Electrification Through Space Transmission." XXIVth IAF Congress, Baku, USSR, Oct. 7, 1973.

Evans, Bryant. "'Space Cable' a Possibility, Scientists Say." *San Diego Union,* Feb. 27, 1966.

Forward, Robert L., and Moravec, Hans P. "High Wire Act." *Omni,* 45–47.

Goldsworthy, W. B. "Mining for Composites on the Moon." *Aerospace America,* October 1985, 50.

Gouban, G. "Microwave Power Transmission from an Orbiting Solar Power Station." *Microwave Power,* 4:5 (December 1970), 223–31.

Graf, Gary R. "Space Tethers Dangle the Future on a Thread." *Space World,* October

1985, 24–27.

Grobaty, Tom. "Your Ticket to Outer Space." *Long Beach Press Telegram,* Nov. 6, 1985, B3.

Hansen, Frederick, and Lee, George. "Laser Power Stations in Orbit." *Astronautics and Aeronautics,* July 1972, 42–54.

Harris, Philip R. "Living on the Moon." *The Futurist,* April 1985, 30–35.

Heppenheimer, T. A. *Colonies in Space.* Harrisburgh, Pa.: Stackpole, 1977.

Isaacs, John D. "Satellite Elongation into a True 'Skyhook.'" *Science Magazine,* Feb. 11, 1966, 682–83.

Kantrowitz, A. "Propulsion to Orbit by Ground-Based Lasers." *Astronautics and Aeronautics,* 10:5 (May 1972), 74–76.

Kerrod, Robin. *Living in Space.* New York: Crescent Books, 1986.

"Launcher Company, Travel Agency Reach Space Tour Pact." *Aviation Week & Space Technology,* Sept. 30, 1985, 24.

Logsdon, John M. *The Decision to Go to the Moon.* Chicago: University of Chicago Press, 1970.

Logsdon, Thomas S. *Industries in Space to Benefit Mankind.* Rockwell International for the National Aeronautics and Space Administration, SP77-AP-0094, 1977.

Mueller, G. "The 21st Century in Space." *Aerospace America,* January 1984, 84–88.

"Next Fifty Years in Space." *Aerospace,* Fall 1986, 2–7.

O'Leary, Brian. "Lunar Base." *Science Digest,* January 1985, 59–63.

O'Neill, Gerard; Driggers, Gerald; and O'Leary, Brian. "New Routes to Manufacturing in Space." *Astronautics and Aeronautics,* October 1980, 46–51.

Pearson, J. "Using the Orbital Tower to Launch Earth-Escape Spacecraft Daily." Presented at the 27th IAF Congress, Anaheim, Calif., AIAA Paper IAF-76-123, 1976.

———. "Anchored Lunar Satellites for Cis-Lunar Transportation and Communication." Presented at the European Conference on Space Settlements and Space Industries, London, Sept. 20, 1977.

Waldrop, Mitchell. "Space Commission Sets Goals for 21st Century." *Science,* June 1986, 1339–40.

INDEX